W9-CKD-320

Innovating in
Higher Education

SRHE and Open University Press Imprint
General Editor: Heather Eggins

Current titles include:

Catherine Bargh *et al.*: *University Leadership*
Ronald Barnett: *The Idea of Higher Education*
Ronald Barnett: *The Limits of Competence*
Ronald Barnett: *Higher Education*
Ronald Barnett: *Realizing the University in an age of supercomplexity*
Neville Bennett *et al.*: *Skills Development in Higher Education and Employment*
John Biggs: *Teaching for Quality Learning at University*
David Boud *et al.* (eds): *Using Experience for Learning*
David Boud and Nicky Solomon (eds): *Work-based Learning*
Etienne Bourgeois *et al.*: *The Adult University*
Tom Bourner *et al.* (eds): *New Directions in Professional Higher Education*
John Brennan *et al.* (eds): *What Kind of University?*
Anne Brockbank and Ian McGill: *Facilitating Reflective Learning in Higher Education*
Stephen Brookfield and Stephen Preskill: *Discussion as a Way of Teaching*
Ann Brooks: *Academic Women*
Sally Brown and Angela Glasner (eds): *Assessment Matters in Higher Education*
John Cowan: *On Becoming an Innovative University Teacher*
Gerard Delanty: *Challenging Knowledge*
Heather Eggins (ed.): *Women as Leaders and Managers in Higher Education*
Gillian Evans: *Calling Academia to Account*
Sinclair Goodlad: *The Quest for Quality*
Harry Gray (ed.): *Universities and the Creation of Wealth*
Andrew Hannan and Harold Silver: *Innovating in Higher Education*
Norman Jackson and Helen Lund (eds): *Benchmarking for Higher Education*
Merle Jacob and Tomas Hellström (eds): *The Future of Knowledge Production in the Academy*
Peter Knight and Paul Trowler: *Departmental Leadership in Higher Education*
Mary Lea and Barry Stierer (eds): *Student Writing in Higher Education*
Ian McNay (ed.): *Higher Education and its Communities*
Elaine Martin: *Changing Academic Work*
David Palfreyman and David Warner (eds): *Higher Education and the Law*
Craig Prichard: *Making Managers in Universities and Colleges*
Michael Prosser and Keith Trigwell: *Understanding Learning and Teaching*
John Richardson: *Researching Student Learning*
Stephen Rowland: *The Enquiring University Teacher*
Yoni Ryan and Ortrun Zuber-Skerritt (eds): *Supervising Postgraduates from Non-English Speaking Backgrounds*
Maggi Savin-Baden: *Problem-based Learning in Higher Education*
Peter Scott (ed.): *The Globalization of Higher Education*
Peter Scott: *The Meanings of Mass Higher Education*
Anthony Smith and Frank Webster (eds): *The Postmodern University?*
Colin Symes and John McIntyre (eds): *Working Knowledge*
Peter G. Taylor: *Making Sense of Academic Life*
Susan Toohey: *Designing Courses for Higher Education*
Paul R. Trowler: *Academics Responding to Change*
David Warner and David Palfreyman (eds): *Higher Education Management*
Diana Woodward and Karen Ross: *Managing Equal Opportunities in Higher Education*

Innovating in Higher Education

Teaching, Learning and Institutional Cultures

Andrew Hannan and Harold Silver

The Society for Research into Higher Education
& Open University Press

017563

Published by SRHE and
Open University Press
Celtic Court
22 Ballmoor
Buckingham
MK18 1XW

email: enquiries@openup.co.uk
world wide web: www.openup.co.uk

and
325 Chestnut Street
Philadelphia, PA 19106, USA

First published 2000

Copyright © Andrew Hannan and Harold Silver, 2000

All rights reserved. Except for the quotation of short passages for the purposes
of criticism and review, no part of this publication may be reproduced, stored
in a retrieval system, or transmitted, in any form or by any means, electronic,
mechanical, photocopying, recording or otherwise, without prior permission
of the publisher or a licence from the Copyright Licensing Agency Limited.
Details of such licences (for reprographic reproduction) may be obtained
from the Copyright Licensing Agency Ltd of 90 Tottenham Court Road,
London, W1P 0LP.

A catalogue record of this book is available from the British Library

ISBN 0 335 20537 2 (pb)   0 335 20538 0 (hb)

Library of Congress Cataloging-in-Publication Data
Hannan, Andrew, 1951–
    Innovating in higher education : teaching, learning, and institutional
cultures / Andrew Hannan and Harold Silver.
        p.   cm.
    Includes bibliographical references and index.
    ISBN 0-335-20538-0 – ISBN 0-335-20537-2 (pbk.)
    1. Education, Higher–United States.   2. Educational innovations–United
States.   I. Silver, Harold, 1928–   II. Title.

LA227.4 H36 2000
378.73–dc21   00-035992

Typeset by Graphicraft Limited, Hong Kong
Printed in Great Britain by St Edmundsbury Press, Bury St Edmunds, Suffolk

Contents

017563

Preface

The origins of this work lay in a wish of the Partnership Trust to survey the impact of the innovations in teaching and learning that it and its associated companies and organizations had rewarded during the period 1988–95. After discussions with the ESRC and the invitation to the Plymouth-based team to undertake the research, the purpose was widened and the new set of funding bodies was put in place. The two-phase strategy of exploring the experience of innovators and then the institutions related to the different funding arrangements for each year-long phase. The context of the study was also changing, and one outcome of the Dearing report on higher education in 1997 was a growing commitment to a vocabulary of learning and teaching, indicating a priority for the former. This vocabulary was visible in the literature and the national policy making. On the ground, however, in discussions with teaching staff, as well as in the titles of units and personnel and existing institutional policy and strategy statements, teaching and learning remained dominant during the life of the research. We have therefore retained here what is best conceived as a compound noun of 'teaching-and-learning' in this form.

We have in this study talked to innovators identified by various means, as well as to randomly selected other teaching staff. We have talked to people whose roles include the encouragement of and support for innovation. We have talked to innovators who welcome such support, and others who do not recognize its existence or its adequacy. We have talked to innovators who pursue their initiatives or their vision in institutions or units that welcome the initiatives or the vision, and we have talked to others who continue their pursuit in situations where they are ignored, resisted or mistrusted. We have explored institutions, departments and other units that give priority to innovation in or enhancement of teaching and learning, and others that define the higher priority of research. We have met some that aimed, to a large degree successfully, to balance the two, before national pressures began to mount to do so.

We have heard strong assumptions about who the innovators are, but also weak assumptions about what an innovation is and why it is attempted. We have heard firm views equating innovation with technology, and weak understanding of how technology can be or result in innovation. We have heard strong defences of excellence in teaching and learning, together with weak applause for innovation. We have met widely different perceptions of the purpose and nature of innovation, and widely different contexts in which people innovate, in which policies advocate and promote innovation, and in which strategies encourage innovation – and in which strategies or the lack of them inhibit it.

Such are the complexities of research that asks, or that is asked, apparently simple questions: about what innovation means, how to identify it and the reasons for it; what it means to be an innovator, and the consequences; whether innovation is necessarily a good idea, and how its success can be judged; and whether, in teaching and learning, it is innovation or excellence that matters. We began with some assumptions about such questions, and then reformulated our answers, and in some cases the kinds of questions we asked. Some of these issues are raised in Chapter 1, and our procedures for examining them in Chapter 2. From then on we enter the description, analysis and discussion. In some places we mainly allow the voices of the interviewees to tell the story, while in others we attempt our own depiction of the institutions, their procedures and inhabitants – the innovators and others. What is not present, because the scale and definition of the research did not permit it, is the direct voice of students. It is there by inference and report, but student views of teaching and learning, innovative procedures and institutional behaviours have had to be left to other studies.

A small amount of material used in the book was also used in Hannan, A., English, S. and Silver, H. (1999) Why innovate? Some preliminary findings from a research project on 'Innovations in teaching and learning in higher education', *Studies in Higher Education* 24(3): 279–89, and Silver, H. (1999) Managing to innovate in higher education, *British Journal of Educational Studies* 47(2): 145–56 (copyright Blackwell Publishers Ltd/Standing Conference on Studies in Education). All the working papers, conference papers and other documents resulting from the project can be accessed on its website (http://www.fae.plym.ac.uk/itlhe.html).

Acknowledgements

The study on which this book is based has been concerned with innovators and innovations, and with their institutional contexts. The study was conducted in two separate but interrelated phases, conducted under the aegis of the Learning Society Programme of the Economic and Social Research Council (ESRC) (award reference numbers L123251071 and L123251074). Funding for the first phase was also provided by the Higher Education Quality Council (before it was replaced by the Quality Assurance Agency), and for the second phase by the Department for Education and Employment and the Higher Education Funding Council for England. The outcome is an attempt to present and analyse a range of issues relating to innovation in teaching and learning, and to locate these in a number of case studies of universities.

We would like warmly to thank the ESRC and its co-funders, not only for their financial support but also for assistance in other ways. Ros Rouse and Alex Monckton at the ESRC helped considerably to pilot us through some difficult waters relating to a complex funding arrangement. The Advisory Group that brought together representatives from all the funding organizations made an extremely valuable contribution to the progress of the study and we are indebted to the members for their encouragement and help. The University of Plymouth and its Faculty of Arts and Education not only hosted the study but also gave much appreciated support of many kinds.

As a belated member of the stable of projects under the Learning Society Programme we benefited from our contact with the extremely creative group of researchers working on the other 13 projects. The Director of the Programme, Professor Frank Coffield of the University of Newcastle, made an incalculable contribution to the progress of the study, and we are particularly grateful for his interest, advice and critical judgements, though there were sometimes difficulties associated with allegiance to different football teams.

We have worked in the study in 16 institutions, 15 in the first phase, four of which, with one additional university, became case studies for the second phase. We have had invaluable collaboration from everyone concerned – the vice-chancellors and others who gave their permissions, other senior managers and the heads of educational development units, learning support services and similar units – who helped in the process of identifying innovators and in making arrangements of many kinds. In total we had interviews or group discussions with 360 people, all of whom agreed without demur to take part. 'Gatekeepers' at institutional and departmental or school level commented on our substantial draft reports on each university in the second phase. Staff who took part in our pilot project at one university responded to a return visit, which we made to discuss findings at the end of our first phase, and others, from all 15 first-phase institutions, accepted an invitation to discuss the findings at a 'mini-conference' also at the end of the first phase. During the second phase we distributed copies of the case study reports to all those we had interviewed at each institution, along with an invitation to comment, to which many responded. Combining these various features, therefore, the study proved to be extremely interactive.

It has been an intensive and rewarding experience, shared by one other member of the research team. Susan English has worked with us all the way through, formally as research assistant, but in fact as a colleague taking part in all aspects of the research, its planning, interviews, data analysis and the confrontation of the problems associated with complex research. Only her involvement in a related study towards a PhD has distanced her from any direct part in producing the book of the study.

We owe special thanks to Kate Hannan and Pam Silver for their invaluable support.

1
Introduction: 'Innovation'

People and policy

Understandings of 'innovation' depend on where and why it occurs in institutions, organizations and systems. In higher education the 'innovator' may be a person, a team or a committee, or a government department or funding agency. When the Dearing report on higher education recommended 'to stimulate innovation' as one function of its proposed Institute for Learning and Teaching (National Committee of Inquiry 1997a: 128) it thereby added further policy clothes to an already extensive wardrobe of policy-driven innovation. The history of innovation in teaching and student learning since the Second World War has in fact involved individual experimentation; curriculum innovation; the increasingly diverse application of new technologies for educational purposes; responses to changing student numbers, structures and funding; problem based, resource based, open and other strategies of learning. It has involved broad change in curricula, institutional structures and the working of institutions and their sub-units – alongside long established and familiar processes. The story of innovation is one of significantly changing meanings.

People innovate, institutions innovate and manage innovation. National funding agencies sponsor innovation, but the intentions and meanings differ. At system and institution levels innovation is defined explicitly, if often ambiguously, within frameworks, priorities and directions. It is less and less possible in higher education to innovate outside these frameworks, since funding, reputation and even professional survival may depend on working within them. For an individual to pursue innovation outside strategic planning and responses to internal and external review and judgement may be seen as eccentric, at worst as dangerous. Nevertheless, people do innovate, for all sorts of reasons, sometimes even with encouragement, recognition or reward. We are not directly concerned in this discussion with all kinds of innovation, although they may be contextually or contingently important to teaching and learning, and they emerge as such in the discussion. Curriculum innovation within departmental, faculty and institutional frameworks, for example, is often (unlike individual innovation in teaching and learning) the product of formal, policy-related decision making, or dependent on it. Institutional innovation has included such areas as management and governance as well as curricular and learning strategies. In the United States, the considerable literature of innovation has most frequently been concerned with institutional policies and strategies. In relation to teaching and learning there are often reservations about the value of a vocabulary of 'innovation' rather than, say, 'development', which has less of a connotation of novelty and more one of serious and safe planning. 'Innovation' does, however, have currency in higher education, though a more established one in industrial production and related processes.

The 1990s have in fact been alive with the sound of innovation. Amidst, and often because of, unwelcome or unfamiliar pressures in higher education, inducements to innovate in teaching and learning have often, paradoxically, been strong and the response widespread. Throughout the 1990s innovation was encouraged in the UK from such different directions as Enterprise in Higher Education (EHE), the Open Learning Foundation (OLF) and Higher Education for Capability (HEC), and in more targeted disciplinary or technological terms by the Higher Education Funding Council for England (HEFCE) through the Teaching and Learning Technology Programme (TLTP), the Computers in Teaching Initiative (CTI) and the Fund for the Development of Teaching and Learning (FDTL). Some of these covered the UK, others were specific to England, and were sometimes matched by parallel initiatives elsewhere. From 1989 to 1995 innovative developments in teaching and learning (mainly by individuals or course teams) were rewarded by the Partnership Trust and its associated industrial and commercial companies and organizations. Innovation has been publicized by a range of journals, yearbooks, manuals and compendia with 'technology', 'media' and 'innovation' in their titles. Innovation has been the focus of conferences and websites. There have been echoes in nationally conducted audits and assessments, in institutional staff development activities and in dissemination by the Staff and Educational Development Association (SEDA). Innovations in assessment, as set out for example in a directory by the Assessment Strategies in Scottish Higher Education project (Hounsell *et al.* 1996) have indicated or implied new ways of teaching and learning. Changes in curricula at subject or knowledge boundaries or in modular or other structures have also frequently implied changes not just in what but also in how teachers teach and students learn. Round every new technological corner there have been possible shifts in teaching behaviours. Innovation and cognate vocabularies have entered the mainstream of institutional organization, national commission and publishers' catalogues.

Pre-history

All of this has deep roots in a lively 1950–1980s 'pre-history'. The modern profile of innovation in teaching and learning began to take shape during the Second World War, when the US in particular was adapting and developing a range of equipment and materials (including films and film strips) for military training, and then in surveys of existing provision during and after the war (see, for example, Dale *et al.* 1950: 84–95). The most significant thrust, however, came with B.F. Skinner's sequence of papers in the 1950s on such topics as 'The science of learning and the art of teaching' and 'Teaching machines' (see Skinner 1959). It was here that the language of 'reinforcement' and 'small steps' entered the common parlance of educational strategic thinking: 'The whole process of becoming competent in any field must be divided into a very large number of very small steps, and reinforcement must be contingent upon the accomplishment of each step' (Skinner 1961: 153). Teaching machines were 'an example of the technological application of basic science' (ibid.: 182, 1–22 appendix) and the most influential aspect of Skinner's work. This, in the 1950s and early 1960s, was the beginning of a continuing tension at all levels of education in Britain and many other countries – a tension between an emphasis on a more structured approach to learning and more 'student-centred' or 'independent learning' approaches.

In higher education the early debate focused on lecturing versus group discussion methods, a debate associated particularly with Jane Abercrombie (much of her early work on medical and science education was published as M.L. Johnson). *Universities Quarterly* published a symposium in which lecturing was dismissed by a former Canadian and Scottish vice-chancellor as having survived Caxton because it 'is cheap and easy ... The reasons for preferring the class to the lecture seem to me overwhelming' (Fyfe 1950: 241–2). 'Other devices' were preferred by an academic from Yale – 'the tutorial, the seminar, the discussion class – are much better at giving that all-essential intellectual exercise and self-discipline' (Mendenhall 1950: 262–3). Defences of the lecture method emphasized, for example, that it taught students to listen and concentrate. The debate around lectures and small group or free group discussion continued in the 1960s in the University Grants Committee annual reports, in the Robbins report on *Higher Education* (Committee on Higher Education 1963) and notably in the Hale report on *University Teaching Methods* (Committee on University Teaching Methods 1964). The implications of the debate became wider as the emergence of computers was beginning to be seen as a way of 'permitting the learner to ask questions of the machine' (Hilgard 1964: 56). Sir Eric (later Lord) Ashby told an American audience that Skinner's programmed instruction only rewarded rote learning and responses that are in agreement with the programme. Even though he was ambivalent about the effect of computers on education, what he hoped for was the development of 'really

sophisticated machines, which could conduct a dialogue with the student'
(Ashby 1967: 363–5).

Into the 1970s

The use in higher education of 'innovations' (in the plural) as a description of outcomes, 'innovation' as a description of a process, and the 'innovator' as a category of actor became salient vocabularies in higher education
during the 1970s. The earlier debates about teaching strategies and experiments with programmed learning, the use of 'audio-visual aids' (ava) and
'educational technology' (ed tech) had had little impact on higher education.
Until the mid-1970s innovation in British higher education was embodied
in three main forms. First, from the beginning of the 1960s, the new 'green
fields' universities were exploring new curricular structures, including interdisciplinary programmes, and The Open University emerged as a major
innovation and force for innovation in higher education, beginning its
broadcasts in the early 1970s. Second, the post-war momentum of 'ava' and
'ed tech' moved from programmed learning to tape-slide formats, overhead
projectors, video, closed circuit television and other exploitations of technologies that were becoming available on the market. Some of these forms
of innovation related primarily to schools and teacher education, others
to a small number of enthusiasts in higher education. Third, the interest
in small group teaching and other ways of undermining the centrality of
lecturing spread very slowly from the 1950s. The Hale committee on *University Teaching Methods* found a very patchy use of audio-visual aids, 'a small
minority' of staff using sound-recorded material, and 'a few' references to
closed-circuit television. At 'most' universities in 'most' subjects the lecture
remained 'the main vehicle for instruction' (Committee on University Teaching Methods 1964: 52, 98–102).

The emergent interest of the 1970s was not just in the scatter of curricular, media and teaching 'innovations', but also in constructing cumulative
or strategic approaches to 'innovation', especially in teaching and learning.
The Nuffield Foundation established a Group for Research and Innovation
in Higher Education in 1972 and it reported over a four-year period on a
modest range of course developments and teaching activities in the universities and in two-thirds of the recently created polytechnics. The teaching
developments reported by the Group were from the universities, and although the polytechnics and the Council for National Academic Awards
(CNAA) were taking various kinds of initiatives the Group found few that
were of direct interest in teaching and learning. The polytechnics were
preoccupied with institutional restructuring, but also with such new curricula as business studies and the possibilities of modular structures. There
were, of course, pedagogical implications of such processes as the conduct
of sandwich courses, which had been established by the CNAA's predeces-
sor, the National Council for Technological Awards. The Nuffield Group

found that it was in some disciplinary areas of the universities (a significant proportion of its examples were in engineering and science) that teaching innovation was mainly to be found.

The Nuffield Group was operating at a time of deteriorating national economics in the early 1970s, and innovation ceased to be identified with the initiatives of newly created institutions, except for The Open University. The Group's first newsletter in 1973 reported on 'numerous' changes in curricula and 'the development of new teaching/learning situations', some of the latter involving 'more active student participation in the learning process' (Nuffield Foundation Group for Research and Innovation in Higher Education 1973a: 3, 9). Not for the last time innovative change had to contend with, and in some cases result from, unfavourable economic conditions. Other examples of investigation and debate were emerging, sometimes involving researchers or developers who were connected with the Nuffield Group in various ways. The Society for Research into Higher Education had come into existence in 1965–6, and from then on it became a vehicle for discussion of particular innovations and innovation strategies. For example, in 1966 it brought together a group of members with an interest in studying methods of teaching in higher education (Abercrombie 1970: Foreword). In 1969 it set up a Study-group on Innovation in Higher Education, convened by K.G. Collier, Principal of Bede College, Durham, and including: Jane Abercrombie, then head of an Architectural Education Research Unit at University College London; Ruth Beard, at the time Professor in a Postgraduate School of Studies in Research in Education at the University of Bradford; and Tony Becher, Assistant Director of the Nuffield Foundation and Director of the Nuffield Group (Collier 1974: appendix).

These all helped to shape the new interest in teaching and learning. In 1974 Collier edited *Innovation in Higher Education*, which contained a chapter by Abercrombie on 'improving the education of architects' and one by Beard on 'promoting innovation in university teaching', together with other case studies of teaching projects and innovations (ibid. 1974). In 1970 Beard's *Teaching and Learning in Higher Education* was published, which covered theories of learning and accounts of programmed learning, computers, independent study and a range of new techniques, backed up by a bibliography in which medical and science education featured prominently (Beard 1970). Her *Research into Teaching Methods in Higher Education* went through four editions (with the addition of co-authors) between 1967 and 1978, responding increasingly to research associated with 'the efficiency and productivity of university education' (Beard *et al.* 1978: 14). Abercrombie was active in the Society for Research into Higher Education (SRHE) and was continuing her pioneering work in group teaching. For SRHE she wrote *Aims and Techniques of Group Teaching*, going through four editions between 1970 and 1979. By the fourth edition, and also in Abercrombie and Terry *Talking to Learn: Improving Teaching and Learning in Small Groups* (1978), she was reporting on projects funded by the University Grants Committee from 1972. From the third edition of *Aims and Techniques* she was suggesting that 'the struggle for recognition of the claims of teaching in small groups had already succeeded, at least in many places' (1979: Preface).

In 1971 SRHE devoted its annual conference to the theme of 'Innovation in higher education' (Flood Page and Greenaway 1971), and in 1973 held a European symposium, the proceedings of which were published as *Individualising Student Learning: the role of the new media* (SRHE 1973). The first session was chaired by Ruth Beard, and a key contribution was made by Professor Lewis Elton of Surrey University. Elton was a key player in the field, not only taking part in developments at Surrey and in science education in higher education generally, but also chairing a CNAA committee on teaching methods from 1975 (CNAA 1981: 84). He was to write extensively on innovations in the field. In this 1973 symposium Elton outlined and analysed the 'upsurge' from the early 1960s of an interest in new teaching methods, including individualized self-paced work, and he emphasized higher education's debt to the Nuffield Foundation for funding and investigating innovations (SRHE 1973: 2–6). The Nuffield Group reviewed Elton's work to introduce the Keller Plan on independent learning at Surrey and he took part in the Group's conference on 'independence in learning' (Nuffield Foundation Group for Research and Innovation in Higher Education 1973b: 20; 1974: 20).

Individual, guided and directed

Innovation was now more firmly on the higher education agenda. Description and discussion appeared in *Universities Quarterly* and the SRHE's *Studies in Higher Education*. Journals of educational media development had begun to proliferate in the US and Britain during the 1960s, under the particular impetus of programmed learning. An International Council for Educational Film changed its name in 1966 to the International Council for Educational Media (with a secretariat in Paris). The first issue of its *Educational Media International* appeared in 1976, published in London, and it reported on discussion in an 'Innovation and Information Working Group' (*Educational Media International* 1978). The literature of independent, flexible, open and other forms of learning reflected the interests of psychologists, the exigencies of the classroom and the pressures of policy, economics and new priorities, including a focus on teacher–student interaction, competing directions within a diversifying higher education system, and the availability of new technologies and media. Confidence in conventional lecturing was being undermined (Bligh 1971).

Into the late 1970s the innovator was still largely the individual enthusiast, perhaps tuning in to opportunities opened up elsewhere, adapting new media, occasionally responding to international outputs in the psychology of learning, or simply experimenting with something different. From the late 1970s the contents, practice and understanding of innovation changed.

The most directly influential impact was that of changes in institutions and the higher education system. The context had become one of accountability, the thrust of which was determined by Labour policies and made preeminent by the Thatcher administration from 1979. The increased public visibility of higher education practices in the late 1970s and 1980s turned powerful searchlights on all aspects of higher education operations in the university and polytechnic sectors, which became a single sector in 1992. Sectors and institutions responded differently, but existing structures for staff and educational development were strengthened, or new ones created. Efforts at innovation did not diminish across the period, but its functions were increasingly institutionalized. A period of 'guided innovation' had begun.

An increasing policy and funding emphasis on improvements in teaching coincided with political attacks on 'incompetent teachers' in higher education. The Government's 1985 Green Paper expressed as one of its 'main concerns' the issue of 'quality of teaching', and focused the question of quality 'first and foremost on the quality, competence and attitudes of academic staff' (Secretaries of State 1985: 4, 28). Staff appraisal entered the agenda. An additional pressure from the 1970s was that of expansion: 'Hitherto, universities had given little thought to the way teaching is carried on or to ways of measuring its effectiveness. It has required the duress of growth to make them do so' (Mackenzie *et al.* 1976: 18). Underpinning policy shifts towards greater accountability, however, was also the increasing realization that institutions also needed more coherent approaches to the use of computers and other new technologies as aids to learning. In the mid-1960s when the Brynmor Jones committee reported on *Audio-Visual Aids in Higher Scientific Education* (Jones Report 1965) educational computing was only just beginning its journey into higher education, but by the end of the 1970s it was one of the driving forces of policy making on teaching and learning nationally and institutionally. One educational technology activist reflected in 1985 on the changes of the previous two decades:

> We no longer worship at the altar of 16mm films, or linear teaching machines, or multi-media approaches, or feedback classrooms: now it is the computer and its flamboyant half-brother, interactive video. There is one notable difference: computers are glamorous, up-market and, best of all, superb generators of money. (Unwin 1985: 65)

They also meant investment, frequently at the expense of other things.

'Guided innovation' in teaching and learning was destined to be increasingly subordinated to 'guided new technology development' and what Americans called 'improvement of instruction'. Innovation had become strategic, and governments were involved in promoting innovation for a cluster of national purposes. The lead was set by the United States with considerable federal and other funds being invested in the promotion of improved learning. From the mid-1960s the US Office of Education and other agencies used a variety of strategies to promote improvement, and invested strongly in doing so (Hawkridge 1978: 61–4). Between 1966 and 1969 the American government alone invested more than $2.5 billion in experimentation and research with 'instructional technology' (Carnegie Commission on Higher Education 1972: 45). A stream of directories and analyses emanated from government and private sources, listing and explaining resources and methods concerning 'technologies for learning' (for example, Weisgerber 1968; Meisler 1971). A typical directory of *New Media and College Teaching* in 1968 covered everything from television, films and telephone to programmed instruction, computer-aided instruction, overhead projectors and simulation. It concluded with messianic confidence that all these 'breakthroughs toward improved instruction are opened by the waves of experimentation that are inundating campuses of all sorts in all parts of the nation', and resistance based on 'inertia and poverty' was being eroded by 'the increasing force of successful examples'. The future 'for anyone who believes that new media can encourage better teaching is bright' (Thornton and Brown 1968: 46). In Britain the same trend was apparent, including under the stimulus of the Hale committee in 1964 (Committee on University Teaching Methods 1964; Unwin 1969). The process accelerated in the 1970s and 1980s as the economic imperatives grew stronger and higher education faced increasingly difficult problems.

In Britain the 'waves of experimentation' became more and more centrally generated, with schemes that involved encouragement, funding, evaluation and dissemination. Given the diversity of institutional cultures and structures, however, lessons were also being rapidly learned at national level. Centrally *generated* schemes did not mean central *control* or institutional *uniformity* in implementation. Enterprise in Higher Education (EHE) was initially directed at raising consciousness amongst students and staff of a narrow version of 'enterprise'. Though much of the implementation had implications for skills acquisition and understanding of the needs of the workplace, in practice a central cascading model encountered strong counter-reactions. EHE meant, for example, student profiling and employer involvement, but it also came to mean a range of initiatives and developments – often 'innovations' – originating with individuals or the teaching-oriented units of institutions. These included curricular developments such as materials production and assessment experiments, but they also addressed equal opportunities issues and promoted student-centred teaching initiatives. In many institutions new teaching-focused structures and staff development activities were outcomes of EHE policies. EHE funding enabled ideas for change to be put into practice, with available finance, staff time, encouragement, networking with like-minded colleagues, and expert support.

Centralized policy on innovation could (like all policy making) be transformed in the implementation process, and although 'directed innovation' was a defined framework, within it initiatives could still remain possible.

The framework was more or less rigid and matched to varied extents the purposes of innovators at different levels in institutions. National programmes to promote the use of communication and information technologies (including the Teaching and Learning Technology Programme) were more prescriptive as to projects and outcomes. The Fund for the Development of Teaching and Learning, although largely subject-specific and with defined aims, opened up extensive possibilities for initiatives by teaching staff. Bidding processes, such as those regularly undertaken by the Department for Education and Employment for its projects, were policy-driven and largely related to specified policy-related areas, such as work-based learning or key skills (for example, DfEE 1998). These nevertheless also offered scope for some individuals, groups or units to pursue aims relating to their curricular and teaching experience. All such centrally promoted schemes provided important incentives to approach teaching and learning issues on a collaborative basis within and across institutions. Despite its initial narrow motivation EHE profoundly influenced the trend towards these forms of directed, policy-driven frameworks for innovation. In one sense the trend closed off or discouraged individually determined directions, but it also offered opportunities for interpretation and flexible initiatives within firmly defined boundaries. Outside those boundaries other kinds of innovation did not die, but they became more sporadic and difficult to sustain.

'Guided innovation' was being not so much transformed as merged into forms of 'directed innovation'. Incentives to innovate came from national government and its agencies and from institutional management, but remained a possibility for individuals facing, in most institutions, profound changes in the teaching/learning dialogue. This was influenced by increased student numbers, more diverse student constituencies and moves in such directions as skills-oriented curricula and learning outcomes, and increasing competition from the mounting emphasis on research. There was often strong resistance among teachers and students to an abandonment of traditional teaching methods and to using 'instructional media' (Moore and Hunt 1980) and student-centred approaches. For example, many British and other students in what the Americans had begun to call 'the me generation', or under mounting financial pressures, preferred what they saw as examination-preparation methods (Silver and Silver 1997: Ch. 7).

In the new conditions, however, it was clear to many staff that the old forms of lecture and seminar were not working. Student constituencies were becoming greatly more diverse, expectations were different, the burden of assessment was becoming alarming, the new and pervasive shapes of modular and semesterized courses were changing teaching and learning styles and rhythms, and the outcomes of higher education were being questioned by employers and the professions. The results at institutional or professional levels included a wide variety of strategies, such as the adoption of problem-based learning for the professions relating to medicine, and the adoption of new staff development programmes for new and existing teachers.

Meanings

'Innovation' and 'change', often used interchangeably, had become key vocabularies in educational practice and policy by the 1980s. They were used as headings in national reports, were fundamental to government department and agency initiatives in information technology and in teaching and learning. They appeared in institutional contexts sometimes as keys to solving urgent financial and other problems, or in relation to student recruitment and diversification. They were the focus of increasing educational and economic literatures internationally, for example those emanating from the activities of European community organizations. This kind of discussion of the meanings of innovation centred particularly on strategies for successful industrial and commercial performance in an increasingly competitive market-place. In education 'innovation' often seemed coterminous with 'new technology'. In addition to universities' own funding of developments directed towards enhanced learning, significant external funding was secured, an increasing proportion of which was directed towards computer-assisted learning. In higher education, as in other sectors of public life, 'innovation' had an increasing range of meanings.

Innovation in higher education has generally been taken to mean a planned or deliberate process of introducing change, directed towards (but not necessarily achieving) improvements or solving or alleviating some perceived problem. Such changes may be new to a person, course, department, institution or higher education as a whole. An innovation in one situation may be something already established elsewhere, but its importance for this discussion is that initiative takers and participants see it as an innovation *in their circumstances*. A difficulty at the heart of the definition is the association of different kinds of innovation with different motivations. Achieving change or the solution of a problem may result, in one instance, in the improvement of the learning outcomes for particular students, or in another instance in financial savings or staff redundancies. It may raise the profile of a teacher or a department in relation to one set of criteria (notably teaching quality assessment) and lower it in another (notably preparation for a research assessment exercise).

There are other ambiguities. It is not always obvious whether an innovation is an act of creation or of adaptation (or imitation), and innovation may not in fact be 'new', just as in some other area an invention may not be without precedent. The distinction between an invention (which may or may not ever be used) and an innovation (which may be the later exploitation of an invention) has been crucial to discussion by economists (Schumpeter 1976: 132; Freeman 1982; Stoneman 1983: Chs 2 and 3). There are social, situational factors involved in determining both invention and innovation. In industry the 'systematic' search for innovation has similarities to some aspects of higher education:

It is change that always provides the opportunity for the new and the different. *Systematic innovation therefore consists in the purposeful and organ-*

ized search for changes, and in the systematic analysis of the opportunities such changes might offer for economic or social innovation. (Drucker 1985: 31. Author's italics)

Innovation may be a short-term strategy for maximizing profit or overcoming an immediate crisis, or it may be a long-term market strategy. It may or may not be coherent or consensual, depending on the resolution of tension between common interest and unequal power. Some of these aspects apply in higher education, though with considerable differences arising from higher education as a 'system', with different kinds of aims, pressures, regulation and funding. One important feature of innovation in higher education is that it often stems in a sustained and interactive way from ideas and the use of materials already introduced into the market-place.

Some of the analysis of the trends suggested by these concepts and distinctions raises a number of difficult questions for a discussion of higher education. A new way forward in one place may already have been abandoned in another place for a more promising alternative (or may even be a feature in some dissemination of 'good practice'). In higher education parallel 'innovations' have often taken place under 'guided' funding arrangements, supported by 'change agents'. Neither the latter nor the initiative takers necessarily see themselves as 'innovators'.

'Innovation in teaching and learning', and then increasingly from the Dearing report in 1997, the changed emphasis on 'learning and teaching', has become a regular feature of discussions of higher education, but it is also a difficult vocabulary. Although used as a single concept, this kind of innovation may not have similar implications for teacher and for learner. There is no necessary relationship between the two. An innovation in students' learning procedures may be independent of any 'teaching' in its traditional sense. A change in what teachers do may have little or no effect on what or how students learn. Introducing new technology is not necessarily innovative for learning, if it simply means delivering lectures by video to larger groups of students. Putting lecture notes on the Internet may not be different from photocopying them (itself once seen as an innovation). Some uses of computer-assisted learning may actually make learning less student-centred. American 'instructional technology' was once seen as 'a step forward because the *improvement* of learning should be the main objective . . . whereas much of its effort . . . has hitherto been concentrated on doing better what perhaps should not be done at all' (Mackenzie 1970: 175).

Some clarifications are important at this point. First, innovation may aim to bring about improvement, but does not necessarily produce it. Innovation involves intention, planning, effort, but may either fail to produce outcomes, or may produce dubious or 'wrong' outcomes. Second, 'improvement' is itself controversial, as much social theory and social history has suggested in recent decades: improvement has often been interpreted to mean a more effective form of control. Third, 'whose innovation?' and 'for what purpose?' are crucial questions. It is easier, at departmental or institutional levels of decision making, to change the structures, environment, resources, opportunities, for student learning, than to change the culture of teaching. Individual teachers may be suspicious of the motives. Technological, organizational and other changes can, at these levels, be the outcome of decision, arrived at by fiat or negotiation. Although curricular change may sometimes imply changes in both teaching and learning processes, it is immensely more difficult to achieve any basic change in attitudes towards teaching than in the organization of the curriculum. Since the establishment of the Council for National Academic Awards and new sectors of higher education from the 1960s, and then monitoring procedures covering the whole of higher education in the 1990s, curriculum change has become increasingly enshrined in committee decision, policy document, validation record, module handbook, assessment detail. Despite curricular differences, features of change may be common. One study of influences that affect course development suggested that the sources of change were similar across the disciplines. In physics, for example, the influences were categorized as system-led, institution-led, resource-led, discipline-led, academically-led, educationally-led, profession-led and consumer-led (Boys *et al.* 1988: 66–8) – applicable, of course, well beyond physics and the natural sciences. In spite of overlap of contexts and responses between curriculum and teaching and learning, there remains an important boundary.

The long history of technical or technological intervention in higher education has, until recently, shown little fundamental change in the teaching and learning encounter that has its roots in the ancient Chinese, Arabic and medieval European spread of higher learning. Printing or the early twentieth-century educational technologies such as various forms of visual presentation or programmed learning did not supersede the lecture and tutorial relationship. The difference between earlier twentieth-century educational innovations and the present and potential innovative impact of communication and information technologies lies not just in the nature of the technologies but also in the driving forces of change with major, immediate implications for higher education.

Our understanding of innovation generally is therefore contextual at all stages of the trajectories it may follow. The investigation reported and analysed here is inevitably concerned with individual innovators and innovations, but also with institutional and national policy-driven innovation and contexts for innovation, and with institutions as environments that encourage and inhibit innovation. The discussion in the following chapters therefore ranges from understandings and perceptions of innovation by individuals to interpretations of institutional culture and change. Addressing innovation in teaching and learning means addressing the system of higher education in microcosm. Innovation 'in their circumstances' is a product of people interacting with people, in contexts that include institutional structures and disciplinary as well as institutional cultures. It is concerned with student numbers and constituencies, the quality of learning and the higher education experience, and the influence of resources and recognition. It relates to support for and opposition to change, to the negotiation or the imposition of priorities at all levels of higher education, and to the directions in which government and national agencies see and help to determine the forms of change. At the centre of the investigation and the discussion are people taking a variety of initiatives in a variety of institutional contexts.

2

Researching Innovation

Since teaching and learning, their processes and outcomes, have become more prominent in the national agenda of higher education, innovation has also captured greater attention, as it has internationally in industry and commerce as well as in education. If individuals, institutions and governmental and other policy-making bodies are engaged in a search for improvements and new ways, then addressing innovation means understanding not only individual initiatives, but also the institutional and other environments to which they relate. Increasingly these environments have included the sweep of technological change and the changing directions of institutional policy and behaviours.

It is not an easy task, therefore, to investigate the operational and conceptual ramifications of innovation in a system as complex as higher education in the United Kingdom. The history has been long and the institutional and systemic variations many. In response to this complexity this study was undertaken on the basis of a two-phase model, which combined elements of both survey and case study. From the outset, it should be emphasized, the investigation was designed to be concerned with innovations at the level of undergraduate teaching and learning. The first phase (1997–8) focused on the experience of innovators, that is, those who had been involved in the introduction of methods of teaching and learning new to their situations, at universities where there was clear indication of such innovations having taken place. The terminology throughout this discussion is that of 'universities' as the available sources for an initial trawl to identify innovators did not produce sufficient information relating to other institutions of higher education. The second phase of the study (1998–9) involved in-depth case studies of particular universities in order to assess the impacts of the institutional structures, processes and culture generally as a context of innovation.

The first phase

The purpose of the study, therefore, was to see how innovation happened, where, when, by whom and for what reasons. It was to encompass the kinds of innovation taking place and their life histories and status within their institutions and beyond. The aims were formulated for the ESRC and its co-funders in September 1996 in such broad terms, with different emphases in the two phases (which strictly speaking, given the funding arrangements, constituted two separate but related investigations). For the first phase the key elements in the statement of aims involved identifying:

- the motives, sources of ideas, successes and failures of innovators in a range of subjects in a variety of institutions, and implications for staff satisfaction and rewards;
- the characteristics of innovations generated by individuals, institutions, internally and externally available funding, external scrutiny, national policies and programmes, international models and research;
- the factors (inter-personal, institutional and structural) that do or do not stimulate and support innovation;
- the contribution of new developments in information and communication technologies to innovations in teaching and learning;
- innovation as creation, adaptation, transfer, development, dissemination;
- the contexts of innovation, including those of finance and institutions' scale and structure.

It was clear at this introductory stage that curriculum change, modularization and access, for example, also related to teaching and learning but would be contingent rather than central features of the study. The focus was to be on innovations that were intended to shape the learning interface of students with teachers, one another, the technologies and materials. On the wider canvas it was clear that this included such developments as problem-based learning, open and distance learning, computer-based or supported learning, work-based learning and various forms of independent learning.

For the first phase the selection of institutions to visit was based on the frequency of their appearance in various indices of innovation (c.f. Appendix D for full details). These included directories of innovations (by such bodies as the Staff and Education Development Association and some subject-based associations); subject specific and generic journals of higher education (such as *University Chemistry Education* and *Studies in Higher Education*); directories and other reports on the EHE experience of the late 1980s and early 1990s, as well as reports on successor activities; publications relating to the Teaching and Learning Technology Programme (TLTP) and other national initiatives to promote computer-based and other developments in teaching and learning; lists of Partnership Trust award winners; conference proceedings; books (particularly edited collections of reports), theses and other material. Some other organizationally held records were consulted, notably those of the Higher Education for Capability (HEC) organization, at the time being transferred from the University of Leeds to Middlesex University. In the final selection of universities to visit it was possible to include a wide geographic spread as well as a rough balance of representation from old and new universities. As a result of this process interviews were conducted at 15 institutions (c.f. Appendix B for a full list). Six of these were 'new' universities (former polytechnics, which achieved university status in 1992) and nine were 'old' universities. Two of the latter were a former College of Advanced Technology and a former Scottish Central Institution, which became universities in the 1960s, and one a 1960s 'green fields university'. Two of the 'old' institutions belonged to the University of Wales, two were in Scotland and one in Northern Ireland.

Universities to be visited were asked not only to help to arrange interviews with people who had been identified as innovators, but also to suggest others who were involved in significant innovation and those in the institution who had particular or general responsibility relevant to the enquiry. Most commonly these suggestions came from an educational development unit or similar unit, or from a pro-vice-chancellor or chair of a teaching and learning committee. A pilot visit was conducted to one university, involving interviews and a number of formal and informal discussions. On the basis of all these preliminary procedures a total of 221 interviews were conducted in the 15 chosen institutions. Information was also collected from individuals in the form of supporting documentation relating to their initiatives, or from central sources relating to institutional policies on teaching and learning (in some cases these included such material as committee minutes and draft policy statements). At the end of the first phase an initial analysis of the information collected was discussed on a return visit to the institution where the pilot study had been conducted, and a preliminary report on the findings was also discussed at a 'mini-conference' with representatives from each of the universities visited (Silver *et al.* 1998). The general content of the findings was confirmed by these meetings, which also provided guidance for the second phase of the project. This process of report writing, dissemination to participants and feedback, which constituted a kind of 'triangulation', proved to be a valuable aspect of the study, and was again applied (with necessary modifications) to the institutional case studies that then followed.

The second phase

For the second phase a highly focused, intensive study was conducted of a relatively small number of institutions. Five universities were selected, with one exception, from the first-phase list. The exception was The Open University, which it had not been possible to include in the type of investigation conducted in the first phase, but which was very important for the second phase, partly because of its particular style of operation and partly because it is UK-wide. Of the remaining four institutions, three were in England and one was in Scotland. The English universities included one of the 'older' universities (Nottingham), one '1960s' university (Salford), and one 'new' university (Middlesex). The Scottish university was Glasgow.

In August 1998 the purposes of the second phase of the study were set out as follows:

- To explore the higher education institutional climates/frameworks that support or inhibit innovation in teaching and learning.
- To continue the exploration of 'new patterns of teaching and learning' begun in the first phase and needing further understanding in the context of institutional climates/frameworks.
- To consider how higher education institutions embed, or fail to embed, innovations in teaching and learning.
- To investigate the impact of national policies on institutional approaches to the funding and support of innovations in teaching and learning.
- To explore the operation of institutional sub-structures that are intended to affect, or that impinge on, institutional or individual efforts to innovate in teaching and learning (including educational development units or their equivalent, staff development units, teaching and learning committees, and the work of senior management responsible for teaching and learning).

The focus for the second phase was therefore clearly on the institutions, their structures and processes affecting teaching and learning, and the position of innovation in these contexts – these institutional cultures. The strategy adopted was to approach these processes, and perceptions of them, from 'top down' and 'bottom up' directions – the latter of which involved the random sampling of teaching staff who were not necessarily themselves innovators. The former covered the roles and views of senior administrators, heads of selected units (mainly faculties and departments), and key players in the policy- and decision-making committee structures of the university. For the 'bottom up' approach it was decided to talk mainly to teaching staff from two subject areas in each institution. The idea was to choose one discipline found in all five institutions, thus controlling to some extent for differences determined by subject-specific factors. 'English' (which had a somewhat different configuration in different universities) was chosen for investigation in every case, as it was one of the few mainstream subjects present in each institution. The other subject area chosen was intended to be in some way unique or prominent in the university visited. At Glasgow this was Medicine; at Nottingham, Biological Sciences; at Middlesex, Business Studies; at Salford, Electrical and Electronic Engineering; and at The Open University, Technology.

The thrust of the interviews in the first phase had been towards the innovators, the nature of the innovations, the reasons for innovating, sources of support, the continuity or otherwise of the innovations, perceptions of colleagues, countervailing research and other pressures, recognition and rewards (c.f. Appendix E for the phase one interview schedule). In the second phase the 'top down' questioning included a focus on the place of teaching and learning and innovation in mission and policy, the roles of senior staff, the financial and any other support system, the institution's response to external pressures and opportunities, and the operation of the reward system. 'Bottom up' interviewing in the second phase also looked for staff perceptions of the relevant institutional structures and processes, including those directly concerning teaching and learning, staff attitudes towards policy and its implementation at different levels, the importance of the subject and the department (or other basic unit such as the 'school'), and perceptions of the importance attached to teaching and learning, including innovative approaches. In both cases in the second phase the questioning pointed towards the nature of institutional culture or sub-cultures, and with a particular interest in the ways in which disciplinary, departmental or other contexts helped to shape institutional, sub-institutional and individual attitudes towards maintaining or changing teaching practices and student learning (c.f. Appendix E for phase two interview schedule).

In the second phase a total of 117 individual interviews took place (34 at Glasgow, 17 at Nottingham, 21 at Middlesex, 22 at Salford and 23 at The Open University), with a rough balance of 'top down' and 'bottom up' in each institution. This strategy of collecting data from staff at different levels of the institutional hierarchy proved successful as a means of exploring the perceptions of a range of participants. Attempts were also made to hold focus group discussions in each university. Only at Glasgow did this not prove possible, as the group that attended (in this case at the invitation of the University) proved to be too large and too diverse in terms of both subjects and positions in the institutional hierarchy). At Nottingham two such group discussions took place (one group of four staff from English, the other of four from Biological Sciences), at Middlesex two (five staff from English and seven from Business Studies), at Salford one (three staff from Electrical and Electronic Engineering) and in The Open University one (four staff tutors and student counsellors from the Southern Region). The total number of staff involved in the second phase was therefore 144, making a total of 356 across the two phases (nine of these appearing in both phases). The focus group discussions proved particularly rich as a source of data concerning the views of those whose jobs were principally concerned with teaching (and sometimes research), who were in closest contact with the students and often saw themselves as charged with carrying out rather than instigating institutional policies. As indicated above, it was not possible to attempt any systematic, direct investigation of student views (as distinct from the frequent staff comments on student reactions), largely because the scale of any such study, particularly in reaching recent cohorts of students, was outside the scope and resources of the research team.

The first stage of analysis was to put together the data collected from interviews and discussion groups with that derived from documents and observation after each visit. It is important to note that although a majority of interviews were tape recorded, the tapes were used purely as a back-up for the analysis. Because of the sensitivity of a good deal of the discussion the recording process was not complete, and transcribing the tapes that did exist was not appropriate. Interviews were conducted either by a single interviewer or in some cases by two or even three interviewers together. All interviewers had a facility for making detailed notes during the interview, including of direct quotations, and the notes were typed up and shared amongst the interviewers immediately after each visit. In this second phase a case study report was then written on each institution. In the case of Glasgow, Nottingham and Middlesex, those parts of the reports that referred to specific subject areas were then presented to departmental 'gate-keepers'. At Salford the numbers interviewed in each of the chosen subjects proved too few to make it possible to write separate reports on those departments, whilst the structures and focus at The Open University made a different approach necessary, especially in relation to the work of course teams rather than departments. Once any departmental reports had been cleared the full report was sent to the institutional 'gatekeeper' (the vice-chancellor or a nominee such as a pro-vice-chancellor or other senior manager). Any necessary corrections or other revisions were then made and the institutional report was sent to every member of staff who had been interviewed or who had taken part in a discussion group, inviting further comment on the accuracy of the description and on the issues raised. A return visit was made to Middlesex University, where a meeting was held with senior staff to discuss a draft of the report, which was then finalized and made available, at the University's request, for wide internal circulation. In general, the feedback received from all levels of these second-phase universities was overwhelmingly positive, broadly confirming the description and analysis, with minor corrections suggested and additional points raised.

In both phases of the study interviewing was directed towards multi-level activities and perceptions and the interviews were therefore both semi-structured and open-ended, in order to take account of the wide diversity of experiences and views being explored. The aims of the study were set out for all interviewees and focus group participants in an ethics protocol (c.f. Appendix F) sent to everyone in advance. Further explanations of the purposes, procedures and outcomes of the study were given in interviews as required, and complete anonymity of individuals was assured in both phases of the study. Only in the second phase, with the permission of the vice-chancellor in each case, was it agreed to name institutions, while still safeguarding the anonymity of individuals within them – hence a coding system (explained in Chapter 3) for quotations from individuals. In the event, the procedures adopted, including those for feedback to individuals and to institutions, made possible a study involving a high level of interaction.

3

The Experience of Innovators

The innovations

From the first-phase interviews emerged a picture of what sort of innovations were taking place by individuals in teaching and learning in UK universities, together with a glimpse of one of the focal questions for the second phase – the relationship between these individual initiatives and the wider interests of the institutions. The first phase made it possible to go beyond the clues garnered in the initial trawl of sources of information regarding innovations, to identify detailed examples of some of the principal forms of what innovators saw as innovations in their situations, and to categorize the examples (c.f. Appendix A for a more detailed typology than is outlined in the examples below). The focus here, therefore, is on innovations by individuals or in some cases small groups or teams of staff.

Group or team work

An anthropology tutor in one university divided students into groups with a brief for each of them to choose a particular society and prepare a presentation on it. In the same university media students worked on group exercises reflecting the pressures of a newspaper office or television studio. Tutorials in social work in the university were conducted on the basis of group activity. Group work in law in the university included the production of 'group essays'. In a different university, group work directed towards acquiring team skills included peer assessment. Media students worked in groups on community projects under the auspices of a media organization. At a third university, biology and biochemistry students were divided into teams, each of which picked a topic at random, and explored a variety of sources (using the library and Internet) to acquire and share information about it, and then give a poster presentation. Here and in other universities some groups reported back to a panel of staff or outsiders, some reported from one group to another, others reported back to the whole class. Group work (for example, design teams) is sometimes interdisciplinary. It either partially replaces lectures, or as in the final year of a physics or building construction course, can replace lecturing altogether and focus on group projects. In one engineering course groups work in a kind of pyramid fashion, with students noting questions raised by the tutor, then working in pairs, then pairs coming together and finally reporting. This last case operates on the basis of the tutor's commitment to 'co-operative learning' (akin to work in the primary classroom).

Although some interviewees thought that group work was more difficult, or impossible, with the increased numbers of students, others thought that group activities were a solution to increased numbers. Pressure on staff time was not necessarily reduced by this strategy, and in some cases it increased – though in different forms – as a result of the demand for tutorial guidance or more interactive forms of assessment. Group work was one of the central types of innovation encountered, across subject areas and in different years of degree programmes. It was justified, for example, as developing students' responsibility for their learning when working in teams, the acquisition of employable skills, particularly communication skills, and the research techniques involved in some forms of group project work.

'Real world projects'

A related innovation in many universities and subject areas was one that involved students in work on real problems in a variety of firms, services and occupations, involving employers in some way and providing students with experience relevant to possible future employment. Law students at one university worked with charities or other organizations on legal advice and the preparation of advisory leaflets, and local employers were involved with chemistry students at the same university working on real environmental problems. At another university drama students have worked in conjunction with a local theatre, watched rehearsals, sold tickets, planned their own performance in relation to the one being staged at the theatre. Students taking a unit on agricultural management have worked with a local farm and bank on real problems associated with the running of the farm. At a third university students working in pairs for environmental agencies conducted projects on real issues and are accountable to the agencies for their findings, and economics students working in teams conducted case studies in industrial settings and the employers were involved in the briefing of students and hearing them report. Student motivation, improved learning and understanding of the relationship of knowledge to work and social experience, are frequent threads in explaining the reasons for such 'live' or 'real world' projects.

Simulation

An activity for students on one course involved role-playing participants in a coastal management scheme for a tropical country, with occasional tutor inputs to alter the parameters (for example a coup or withdrawal of an American oil company). Marine studies students at another university sat at computers 'steering' ships into port. Pharmacy students simulated dissection (A level students with no experience of dissection, poor laboratory equipment, preference not to use real animals). Archaeology students cannot take strategic decisions on real digs about where to make a trench, but they can when using computer software. Spectrometers are expensive and larger numbers of students cannot have access for demonstrations – instead, simulation is possible using computer and video. Groups of students on a business course cannot start up a new business, but they can simulate doing so. These kinds of innovations are not quite as frequent, but there is a significant scatter of them across the institutions.

Presentations

Inseparable from many of the above are student individual, but more frequently group, presentations. Oral presentations of findings from projects or other group activities take many forms, with group assessments of various kinds linked to coherent group performance and individual participation within it. Tutorials may involve students splitting into groups to discuss and report orally. Group-conducted scientific experiments may result in formal presentations to the class. Presentations, particularly of 'real world' projects, are often made to an assessment panel of staff and invited outsiders (including employers). Oral presentations also involve explaining findings to accompany a poster presentation. Group work in philosophy, English, biology or chemistry, resulting in the requirement to communicate outcomes to an audience can for some students prove taxing, but the educational and employment benefits are seen by the innovators concerned to be important. There is widespread reference, not only from those staff with industrial or other experience, to employers' comments on graduates' inability to communicate, as well as their difficulty in sharing in team work. Employers were therefore seen as supportive of student group work and presentations in the kinds of examples given here.

Skills development

The elevation of transferable, core or key skills to major components of national and institutional policies seems to make it difficult to include such skills in a discussion of innovations. For many individuals and in a variety of institutional contexts, however, skills have indeed for a long time been a target of innovative activity. Under the EHE programme many of the initiatives were expressed in terms of generic or subject-specific skills, in subjects as diverse as law and geography, ancient history and music. As early as the 1970s some innovators were experimenting with means of introducing students to communication skills in particular. Support from EHE or other sources has often been emphasized as important. BP, for example, following on from EHE, established a programme for 'team development' in partnership with universities, using work in teams or 'learning groups' to develop 'core transferable skills'. Teaching staff in science and engineering could develop their own development skills and link the experience with their own teaching initiatives.

For individuals intending to innovate in their teaching practices, this has in general meant attempts to adapt the teaching situation to forms of interaction with students in order to combine skills and knowledge purposes. Skills development through history, in one instance, was designed 'to tackle learning skills through a critical engagement with the nature of the subject', embedding skills learning in the search for truth and evidence in historical study. Study skills have been the target of a variety of discrete modules. One course whose students have problems in locating suitable employment has introduced a series of 'skills weeks' associated with profiling. Elsewhere a special core skills module has been incorporated into the subject and, as in many institutions, the module has been oriented towards career education. One engineering course introduced a learning unit on transferable skills at the beginning of the 1970s, the focus of which turned to 'qualities' rather than 'skills' (qualities having to do with attitudes, approaches, creativity, values).

What is clear from these and other cases is that the introduction of skills or 'competency' objectives is not simply a curriculum change, but part of an attempt to restructure the teaching–learning relationship for the benefit of more effective or differently accentuated student learning. The staff interviewed talked not only about skills but also about changes in teaching approach and student response. One such description was of a skills-oriented course in humanities that aimed to involve the students in problem solving, dealing with situations, 'driving the active and oral presentation side', getting students actively engaged, 'valuing the fact that they will make mistakes, getting them to work with others, using language effectively'.

Seminars and lectures

Lectures, as some interviewees emphasized, are indeed medieval, preceding the invention of printing. Tutorial and seminar encounters of staff and students are a long tradition of British higher education, but innovations in recent years concern how they are run. In many subjects staff have opted to turn seminars from staff-dominated or staff-controlled to student-led events. It became the rule in these cases for staff, perhaps after an initial briefing in

017563

the first week or at intervals, to hand over the preparation, chairing and other functions of the seminar to the students: 'the presence of staff stifles discussion' (geography), 'they don't need me' (philosophy), 'students decide what material they need and ask me to bring it' (rural management), 'we reversed the assumption that seminars are under the staff and that they provide the agenda' (history). Concern about the efficacy of lectures has been debated in British academic journals, higher education commissions, research and common rooms since the 1950s in particular, and innovations relating to this concern were widely represented in this study. This was especially the case in subject areas and institutions where student numbers had risen considerably. In law one tutor described lectures as a means of 'throwing out ideas and challenging received wisdom', but as 'an inefficient mechanism for analysing and knowing what anything is about'. Having drastically reduced the amount of lecturing, he used student-led seminars to tackle legal problems, focusing on controversial issues and documentation. Students chose the issues and the sequence, and learned how 'to talk to each other as well as to me'.

Attempts to make lecturing more interactive have also been made. In maritime studies one lecturer split the sessions into an introductory formal lecture followed by workshops, brain-storming sessions, role play, discussion in groups that appoint a spokesperson and share views with other groups. In the case of a very large group in English, pre-reading is required, and the lecture is interrupted at intervals for students alone or in pairs to conduct little tasks and respond in various ways: 'I coax them, cajole them, and it's fun'. In engineering, a lecturer uses an introductory lecture to provide information and ask questions, following which the students work in pairs or groups: 'In a traditional lecture it's only the lecturer who understands. I am not a "teacher", I am a "provider of student learning"'.

Assessment

A change in assessment procedures was an extension of many of these innovations, but could also be an independent innovation. Pressures to simplify assessment came from increased student numbers, from modular and semesterized structures, and from staff unwilling that new teaching strategies should be constrained by traditional forms of assessment. A diversification of first-year laboratory practicals and reports in pharmacology was accompanied by self- and peer-assessment. In law or accountancy in one university students were given choices of mode and timing of assessment. In a work-based learning (WBL) scheme, under learning contracts negotiated between student, tutor and employer/workplace mentor, assessment of learning outcomes is part of the agreement, including 'the type of evidence that will be presented to assess the learning outcomes achieved'. Varied combinations of self-assessment, group peer assessment and tutor assessment exist in courses in different subject areas. Within faculty and institutional regulations these new types of assessment represent negotiated percentages of the over-all marks or classification of the students (other marks generally being contributed by more conventional assessment methods, possibly an exam-ination, long essay or other assignment). On one practical theatre course the 'final product' amounted to 40 per cent and the 'course contribution' 60 per cent, the latter being based on 'log-book, report, group self-assessment, individual self-assessment, peer assessment and tutor assessment' (in com-bination with outside experts and external examiner). For each element in this process explicit criteria are laid down, as they are for the assessment of the various kinds of presentation discussed above. Innovative forms of assessment may respond to the pressures to reduce tutor effort under the impact of student numbers and demands on time, but this may not in fact be the outcome. The gain is generally held to be a more coherent innovation.

Other

There are too many prominent types of innovation to be able to illustrate them separately. Experiments with proctoring, peer counselling or 'supple-mental instruction', for example, were discussed in three universities visited. WBL was a major development in three of the universities visited. Resource-based learning (RBL) or open learning (the vocabulary in this as in some other cases is used interchangeably) was significant in one univer-sity. Problem-based learning (PBL) was widely used in medical-related and nursing education (until very recently PBL was used internationally only or predominantly in these areas). WBL, RBL and PBL can all result from an individual or group initiative within the institution, but are more likely to be closely related to or part of institutional policy relating to access, more effective use of resources, or responsiveness to external policy or pressure. The same is true of some uses of Information and Communications Tech-nology (ICT). Such initiatives require institutional endorsement, which is not necessarily the case with innovations promoted by individual innov-ators. This does not deny them their inclusion in a discussion of innovation, but they illustrate the importance of extending the discussion of innovation to levels of decision making beyond the level of individual initiative that was the target of the first phase of our study.

General

There are important points to make about all of the above:

1. Such examples are generally of staff who are in a small minority (some-times of one) in teaching in this way on the course or in the department or school.

2. Although the intention of the staff concerned is always to improve student learning in the particular circumstances, it cannot be assumed that this is always successful. Staff were often willing to comment on difficulties, including the fact that some students might not welcome the strategy, resistance by colleagues (of what they may see as an 'oddball' or 'maverick' way of doing things), and in a small number of cases why the innovation had failed (for example, when EHE or other funding ended).
3. Staff involved in taking these initiatives were sometimes aware, sometimes not, of similar developments in their subject or in other subjects, but were always clear that what they were doing was new and sometimes radical in their circumstances.
4. Issues of quality were seen as involved in many of these initiatives, but it was not possible to pursue in depth how they related to institutional or other quality assurance procedures. Nor was it possible to evaluate learning outcomes of innovation, or to assess the value of the infrequent systematic evaluations conducted by those involved. In some cases the responses of external examiners were mentioned, and in some there was evidence that students performed no worse, and often performed better, academically as a result of the innovation. What was clear was that innovations were expected to be justified within the monitoring procedures of the university, or those of the faculty or other delegated authority.

The innovators

The above description of the kinds of innovation taking place does not, however, provide us with all the information needed to answer one crucial question. Why do people in higher education become involved in innovation? As MacDonald (1974: 6–8) wrote with reference to schools, 'Innovation is often described as a bandwagon. Its potentialities as a hearse have been neglected'. Yet, he argued, innovations can have 'punitive effects' as they may 'severely increase work loads', 'initially undermine confidence and competence', and, 'often make teachers unpopular with colleagues, who may suspect their motivations, resent their usually favourable allocation of resources, and feel threatened by their ideas'. MacDonald also emphasized that such involvement can be a 'career risk' for teachers, particularly when the innovation:

1. departs from the specialized subject structure on which promotion is based;
2. embodies values that are sufficiently innovatory to threaten the establishment;
3. involves the teacher extensively with pupils of limited ability.

The question he posed was, 'What makes innovation functional for the individual, and what kind of rewards do or would compensate for such effects?'

In the first phase of this study 103 people responded to a question about what had motivated them to introduce new methods of teaching and learning (for an analysis of the subject identity of first-phase interviewees c.f. Appendix C). Their responses were then analysed in terms of the reasons given, the categories being generated inductively. Many of those interviewed referred to more than one motivation or described their reasons in terms that could be classified under several headings. Any indications of frequency, therefore, must be taken as indicative rather than definitive. Nonetheless, responses to this open-ended question do give an interesting indication of the relative scale of impact of different factors. Thus, 34 of these 103 interviewees explained that their involvement in innovation was motivated by what they saw as the need to improve student learning, 31 by the need to respond to changes in student intake, 21 by the need to address the demands of external agencies and 11 by the need to adapt their methods of teaching and learning to cope with curriculum change or internal reorganization.

Each of these categories is illustrated below by quotations taken from our interview notes (those in quotation marks are verbatim from interviewees, the remainder are from the immediate notes). Here and in later chapters first-phase interviewees are identified by category of university (N for 'new university', O for 'old university') followed by their institutional and individual number, making it possible to detect where the institution and the interviewee are the same or different.

The need to improve student learning

This category includes reference to reasons such as to 'motivate students' (10 mentions), a 'better way of doing it' (9), the 'previous method did not work' (8), 'prepare the students better for when they leave' (4), needing to help 'students having difficulty' (3), the desire to 'give students more responsibility for their own learning' (3). For example:

Intrinsic – through pedagogy itself, urge to get them to see. (O4.8)

Difficult to teach programming, lecturing is not effective. Need more efficient ways of teaching – very high student:staff ratios. (N6.10)

Primary motivation is not to cope with extra numbers but because this method is more productive and gets better results and student feedback is very positive: 'they get a lot out of it'. (N6.13)

(He) reckoned that one of the driving forces behind innovations of this kind was that students showed a great deal of interest, he thought that a higher proportion of students have a fascination with computers and that that is something that could be exploited for learning purposes. (O12.1)

Worked with colleague . . . in team of 8–9, disillusioned with standard textbooks, looked at different methods. Felt that students were not turned on by standard managerial textbooks, so got them to read novels instead. Novels are about complexity of relationships, which is what management is about. This succeeded in turning students on . . . (N5.11)

'Students have been short-changed by being denied the creativity of maths and being fettered by the drudgery of slavish repetition of standard questions – they deserve better and we as a society and as academics need better'. (O2.10)

Changes in student intake

The reasons given included 'student numbers large or increasing' (19 references), increasing 'diversity of student intake' (9), 'students lacking skills' (4), the need to be 'more efficient' to cope with larger numbers (4), and even, a 'fall in student numbers' (3). For example:

Student numbers have more than doubled. From 25–26 she now has 61, and this has 'major impacts on the way I teach'. (O13.11)

You can't do small group teaching with 150 students, so she had to confront the question – how? (O13.4)

Innovations started before [a national system of Teaching Quality Assessment was introduced] with change around in staff and huge increase in student numbers. Was intake of 45, now over 100. Difficult to cope with numbers in practical classes . . . the real driving force was increase in student numbers. (O4.7)

Got wider variety of students, different backgrounds, some not ideal but entitled to do the course. Had to be more aware of background and be able to respond . . . Crisis in that students turning away to other courses and lack of their prior preparation with two sciences at GCSE, poor A level results, etc. Was inspired by . . . notion of 'the one minute lecture' (given by students). (N6.4)

Demands of external agencies

In this connection mentions were particularly made of the 'demands of employers' (9 references) and the Teaching Quality Assessment (TQA) process (5), formulated by the Secretaries of State responsible for education in the four regions of the UK in 1991, and designed for implementation by the Funding Councils (Secretaries of State 1991: 28–31). With somewhat different procedures around the UK, TQA involved external assessment of the quality of teaching, with major implications for the institutions themselves. Responses to TQA and other external procedures, including those of professional accreditation bodies, expressed in this study were mixed. For example:

The oral presentation idea came out of a TQA visit, which 'shook people up'. (O13.1)

There has been radical change in health care. There is a faster turn-over on the wards and there are problems regarding the length of time the assessor can spend with the student. This is one reason why the student has been given more control and responsibility. (O4.14)

Industrial pressures – future employers want graduates with wider range of subject knowledge, broader education and transferable skills. Have had good feedback from employers. Students said to be articulate, capable of expressing themselves – seen as outcome of project work. (O3.11)

Curriculum change or internal reorganization

Six of these respondents mentioned the effects of 'modularization' and three the need to change teaching and learning methods to deliver a new curriculum. For example:

Entirely pragmatic ... performance director saw problems following modularization, 'modularization is the big driver'. Needed to formalize performance as modules for credit – needed help. (O4.9)

Tried to teach in the old way, but found couldn't do so because of increased numbers and modularization. Huge numbers – 1200 in a year on one module, 300 in a final year option. More than a 40 per cent fail rate. (N6.11)

Much of what they were involved with was curriculum change and student learning was affected indirectly. For example, one of the main features was project-based team work with a knock-on effect of students helping each other. (O12.22)

Motivation in general

Underlying all of these reasons for innovation was a sense that 'the water was getting hotter' and something had to be done. Employers were com-plaining that graduates did not have a broad enough education or did not have the communication and other skills they needed. The traditional meth-ods were not working. Students were said to be too passive. Some means of involving them more had for a variety of reasons become necessary. All staff interviewed could adduce such reasons for making changes in teaching and learning procedures, without necessarily accepting the label of 'innovator' for themselves.

An important feature of the situation faced by these innovators is their understanding of their difficult position at the point where internal and external pressures meet. This meant that they were aware, first, of factors beyond their control, 'externalities', which included institutional budgets, staffing, resources; policy regarding student numbers; structural changes – semesterization, modularization and other curricular changes; and technological change. Second, they were aware of 'internalities' that included not only such features as teacher–learner interaction, personal satisfaction and dissatisfaction, but all those external factors that have become translated with increasing intensity into the teaching situation. Innovators were often caught between, on the one hand, their own established teaching style and understanding of the purposes of higher education, and on the other hand the changes associated particularly with greater student access. They saw themselves as the point at which traditional notions of 'lecturing' and student learning were in tension with the need to satisfy new student needs in the dramatically changing conditions of higher education and the employment market. Interviewees emphasized that innovation was also increasingly seen to be in sharp competition with research, with policy definitions of 'teaching excellence', and with departmental and institutional needs for accountability in their ever widening frameworks.

Sources of inspiration and encouragement

Whilst explaining their involvement in innovation and in answer to the 'why innovate?' question, 73 of the 103 interviewees referred to various sources of inspiration and encouragement (many identifying more than one). Of these, 20 mentioned previous experience (having taught in a previous institution using the 'new' method, having experienced something similar in industrial employment or through school teaching), 19 cited support from within the institution (an innovative department, the influence of colleagues, a supportive institution), 16 referred to various forms of staff development (conferences, staff development and staff training), 13 explained that their involvement in innovation was driven by their own strongly held beliefs, 12 referred to being inspired by examples from other institutions, 8 said they were motivated by a concern to make their own job more interesting and 7 claimed that their attempts to improve their teaching derived from aspects of their own research. One category of staff includes those whose innovation, and perhaps whose motivation, was in some way bound up with support. This could have consisted, for instance, of the moral support of a head of department or dean, funding, or the imprimatur of a national disciplinary network. A parallel category includes those whose innovations may or may not have had financial or other support but who were committed to their innovations regardless of whether support was forthcoming and in spite of negative or hostile attitudes. Many of those interviewed fitted into the latter category and they were often very grateful to talk to people who were seen in some way to be recognizing their achievements by discussing their experiences as innovators.

Becoming an innovator

Very few of the staff interviewed saw themselves as inherently 'innovative people', though some did describe themselves in such terms as being 'at home with change' or willing to take risks. All those selected for interview as identified innovators were, however, comfortable with being interviewed on that basis. More important than *being* that kind of person was a common awareness of how and when they *became* involved in a process of innovation. Factors such as gender, status and age may, of course, affect involvement in innovation. On the basis of the interviews, however, there is little evidence that gender is a significant factor in the likelihood of staff to innovate. Obtaining promotion or seniority may make it easier for staff to introduce new methods. At one institution becoming head of department did make it more possible for one male member of staff to innovate, as it did for a female member of staff at another university when she became module leader. In terms of *when* lecturers were most likely to begin to innovate, a complex picture emerges of the relationship of their innovation baptism to all the motives for innovating discussed above. It relates, for example, to previous involvement in school-based or industrial innovation, the opportunities offered by EHE in those universities that received government funding for the programme, other institutional or nationally available funding, the rate of increase of student numbers, and their roles and status on and after appointment. A possible typology is as follows:

- Young academic staff who 'settle in', and wait to become established and 'secure' before considering taking innovative initiatives. This is the case notably for staff entering their first appointment in some of the old universities, where teaching remission is often given in the first years to enable young staff to establish their career (and assist the university's research rating) by focusing on research as much as possible.
- Staff of all ages and backgrounds who, on appointment, inherit teaching situations which are 'not working' for various possible reasons, and who feel (and in some cases are encouraged to feel) that immediate change is necessary for recruitment, student satisfaction or performance.
- Staff appointed with important skills that they (and others) might consider need to be applied rapidly to the teaching of a particular course or range of modules. This applies to staff with computer and other technological skills at a time of staff shortages and a search for new solutions.
- Staff who are impatient to innovate when appointed because of their previous experience and commitment.

Conclusion

From these findings it is apparent how important tutors' personal commitment to teaching and to their students was to their individual efforts to innovate. The most popular reason given for involvement in innovation was to improve student learning (34 of the 103 interviewees citing this motivation). However, there were many who were obliged to change their methods due to circumstances beyond their control, particularly an increase in student numbers or a shift in student intake (31 interviewees referring to this as a reason for innovation). The answer to the dilemma posed by MacDonald above is a complex one, but it seems that innovators will take on extra work, learn new skills, court unpopularity with other staff and take risks with their own careers so long as they feel that by doing so they can improve the quality of their teaching, and/or, if they feel that circumstances are such that they have no choice but to depart from their old methods to cope with new demands.

It is interesting to note the limited role that financial incentives played in all this. The possibility of funding was mentioned very rarely, its availability being more of a facilitating than a motivating factor. Perhaps surprisingly, the prospect of promotion or other conspicuous rewards was not mentioned in this context (although it was raised in answer to other questions that were included in the interviews). This is partly a product of the fact that only a minority of the institutions visited gave special prominence to involvement in innovations or excellence in teaching in the promotion process, and even in those that did there was a great deal of scepticism about its impact. The reality was that the great majority of the innovators interviewed believed that involvement in innovation was unlikely to result in promotion and thus they had not been motivated by that aim when first setting out to introduce new methods into their teaching. It is important to emphasize (and c.f. also Chapter 8) that focusing on initiatives in teaching and learning, rather than giving priority to research, was widely, almost universally, perceived as a career hazard by staff interviewed in all types of university – in spite of policy moves to give greater recognition to teaching.

However, having chosen to innovate it was important for the innovator to obtain support, to have the space and facilities to introduce new methods, to receive encouragement and even reward, particularly if the innovation is to go beyond the narrow confines of the initiator, or if involvement in innovation is to become more general. One of the most significant findings of the first phase of the study was that the nature of the institution and its sub-units (faculties, schools, departments, etc.) were very important factors in the innovation process, influencing the incidence of innovation, its success and the likelihood of its becoming embedded. Discussion with innovators therefore pointed to the question important for the case studies in the second phase – what factors have affected the success and failure of attempts to innovate in the different kinds of institution?

4

The Institutions: Structures, Roles and Change

The case studies

The four first-phase universities chosen for the case studies represented different histories, structures, research backgrounds and often policy directions. The Open University was added not only because it is by far Britain's largest university and operates on the basis of distance learning, but also because it has very different approaches from many. The focus for the second-phase case study visits was to be the institutions, their structures and processes affecting teaching and learning, and the position of innovation in these contexts and cultures. The remit for this study included: 'What institutional climates/frameworks support or inhibit innovation in teaching and learning?' Operationally, this was then extended to include the concept of organizational or institutional culture, since activities and outcomes are influenced both by the structures ('frameworks') and cultures (which imply something more pervasive and interactive than 'climates').

The strategy adopted was to approach these processes, and perceptions of them, from 'top down' and 'bottom up' directions. The former was intended to explore the roles and views of senior administrators, including heads of faculties and departments or schools, and key players in policy- and decision-making committee structures. For the 'bottom up' approach the focus was on two subject areas – English and one other. In this second phase the emphasis was strongly on the nature of institutional culture or sub-cultures, with a particular interest in the ways in which disciplinary, departmental or other contexts helped to shape attitudes towards maintaining or changing teaching practices and student learning. The first-phase interviews with innovators, and also with some senior staff responsible for relevant committees or units, had already provided evidence of their perceptions of the institutions in which they worked. The university's 'image', 'mission' or 'culture' emerged as important, positively or negatively, to many of the innovators. Its research orientation could be seen as helpful in providing a challenging context for teaching development, or unhelpful as a competitor, making it difficult to obtain recognition or support. Staff with extensive contacts in other universities sometimes commented about their own institution as a context for innovation: 'this university is more supportive than other institutions seem to be', 'this university is more political than others', 'this university has an alienating atmosphere'. In one research-oriented university a physics lecturer commented: 'This university wants people to perform well in whatever interests them. It is therefore a hard university to work for' (given the high expectations). A colleague in biological sciences also commented that 'the university has an innovation ethos'. A change of vice-chancellor or deputy or pro-vice-chancellor, or an appointment of a pro-vice-chancellor to be responsible for teaching and learning or to chair a teaching and learning committee or similar body, was mentioned, frequently in some institutions, as having had a major influence on movement towards a greater profile for teaching and learning.

In some universities, however, strong criticism was levelled at what were seen as excessively centralized decision-making processes: 'modularization was forced on us under duress' (law lecturer in an old university); 'my own school is supportive . . . this is a university where things are dictated from the centre, it is centrally driven . . . there was internal resistance to modularization and semesterization, but people were simply told it was coming, at a stroke' (engineer in a 'new' university). In addition, perceptions of the operation and value of committees and policy making were conditioned to some extent by differences in the historical strengths and roles of departments, schools and faculties in different universities. For certain kinds of innovation institutional policy was not only of direct importance, but also in some cases the genesis of the innovation. This was notably the case with the advent of such institutional policies as those on information and communications technology or involvement in and partnerships with the community and the region. Reference was often made to the distance between university policy and its implementation.

The policy process has involved the production of institutional policies or strategies for teaching and learning, with titles such as 'A Policy for Student Learning' or 'Strategy for Teaching and Learning'. The aims might include to be 'an innovative university' and the emphasis might be on 'the critical importance of teaching and learning', specifying qualities that the university sees as important for its students, for example: 'The university wants to encourage students to take a more active responsibility for their own learning experience . . . to encourage self-reliance and self-regulation' (Middlesex University 1997: 8). Staff interviewed in all the universities did not always know of the existence of such policy statements, and when they did there were mixed opinions about their seriousness. Mixed views were also voiced about 'educational development units' or their equivalent, though attitudes were generally positive. Under titles such as Teaching and Learning Support Unit or Centre for Learning Development almost all of the universities visited in both phases had a unit of this kind, though often with different remits. These generally included promoting, supporting and in many cases helping to finance initiatives in teaching and learning. Their activities were matched in some universities by departmental or faculty committees or 'officers' or other agents appointed to help to enhance teaching and learning, in some cases seconded to work with the central unit.

It was from such starting points and questions about the factors that encouraged or inhibited innovation that the study of the five universities in the second phase was approached. A snapshot of each of them will assist in discussing the focal issues of teaching and learning and of innovation. It is crucial to note, however, that the pace of change has been so swift in recent years that even while the study was being conducted significant developments were being planned or taking place. The snapshots below nevertheless suggest features of similarity and difference within which teaching and learning and innovation can be addressed.

The University of Glasgow

At the time of the visit the University had approaching 17,000 students (including research students), compared with 9683 in 1992–3. Its average student:staff ratio was nearly 20:1 in 1998, compared with 15.26:1 in 1992–3. The University's income had grown from £156 million in 1992–3 to some £200 million in 1997–8. By 1996 the University was forecasting an accumulated deficit of £4 million by 1998–9, and action to overcome this position included the predicted loss of 90 full-time posts. This figure was in fact to prove much greater. A new Principal, Professor Sir Graeme Davies, was appointed in 1995.

In 1998 the University had eight faculties, most of them coterminous with 'planning units', and where this was the case the dean of the faculty was also appointed as head of the planning unit by the Court. As dean, the role was essentially one of academic leadership, and as head of the planning unit the role was also one of budget manager. Senate (with over 300 members) was the supreme academic body, chaired by the principal and with an elected member of the senior academic staff serving as clerk. Court, with representation from within and outwith the University, was chaired by the rector, elected by the student body of the University (a medieval tradition in Scotland, reaffirmed at Glasgow in the early eighteenth century). Court was the governing body and financial authority of the University, from which the budgets of the planning units derived.

The University committee of most relevance to this study was the Committee for Educational Development and Innovation (CEDI), which was being replaced at the time of the project visit by a Committee for Education Strategy and Resources (CESAR). CEDI was a sub-committee of the Education Committee, one of the main committees of Senate (alongside the Committee for Research). Although the Education Committee's brief covered everything to do with academic matters, its principal concern was with the approval of new courses and course changes, not the details of teaching and learning. Prior to the November visit a new Vice-Principal (Learning and Teaching) had been appointed and CESAR was to have dual account-ability, through this Vice-Principal to the Principal, and less directly to the Education Committee, of which the Vice-Principal was a member. A dis-cussion paper entitled 'Towards a learning and teaching strategy' for the University was also issued in November 1998.

With some 17,000 students Glasgow is a large, urban university, recruiting some 45 per cent of its full-time undergraduates from homes within 30 miles of the city (and some 30 per cent of its full-time students are resident in their 'parental/guardian's' home during term-time). Some 16 per cent of its students are recruited from the UK outside Scotland. The University's government funding and external quality assessment come through the Scottish Higher Education Funding Council (SHEFC), whose procedures are in various ways different from those in other parts of the UK (but the details of these differences are not central to this investigation). The University is a major player in the research field, with research grants and contracts of some £70 million per annum. As in most other universities pressures to perform well in the research assessment exercise, for financial and reputation reasons, resonate within the University (the RAE is discussed in Chapter 8).

Like other 'old' (and many 'new') universities in the UK, Glasgow has a strong structure of departments, schools and faculties, and the balance between central control or policy making and devolved autonomy was also an important context for this study. These sub-units have committee structures that vary but include teaching and learning, undergraduate teach-ing or similar committees, quality assurance committees and boards of studies. Glasgow is heavily dependent on its devolved management struc-ture, including its deans (one described himself as a 'middle manager'), associate deans, heads of departments and schools. The deans' combined role, in most cases, of academic leadership and financial management has given them and their immediate colleagues a pivotal position in the faculties and the University. The University's structures, notably the Edu-cation Committee, provide a strong, formal, University route for the approval of new courses and course changes, but changes of approach to teaching and student learning are a matter largely for negotiation within departments. Where a whole subject area plans to change curricular and teaching direction, as when the Medical School moved towards problem-based learning (PBL), the University's central machinery becomes involved in considering not only the curriculum but also the viability of its proposed 'delivery'.

As a result of the EHE initiative of the late 1980s and early 1990s, the national development of teaching quality assessment, and other factors affecting institutions' attention to teaching and learning, all four of the universities re-visited in the second phase had developed learning support, educational development services or similar units (The Open University's structures, serving the same purposes, are necessarily different). Glasgow's

Teaching and Learning Service is one such unit (with proposed changes, including of title, when joining the new Faculty of Education then being formed from the amalgamation with St Andrew's College). Its remit has included academic staff development, courses for new staff, courses for hourly paid teaching staff and the dissemination of good (including innovative) teaching practices. The University is proud of having achieved the largest number of 'excellent' ratings for teaching of any Scottish university, and sees this as part of its tradition of and commitment to good teaching. Departments obtaining these high ratings have included top research departments. The University's response to quality assurance requirements is articulated through its Quality Assurance Office, whose work to advise the University on the quality of educational provision has been directed at encouraging 'the continual improvement of the quality of teaching, learning and assessment'.

Funding to support innovation (in teaching and in teaching-related curriculum development) has been available through a number of channels. External funding, from EHE, the (Scottish) Fund for Innovation in Teaching and Learning (FITL), Teaching and Learning Technology Programme (TLTP) and other sources, has been prominent in recent years, and in this Glasgow's profile is similar to many (but not all) other universities. Internal funding for these purposes is of two kinds: through the budgets allocated to faculties and departments, and from Strategic Development Funds disbursed by the Principal.

The University has undergone a period of recent change, financial stringency, staff cuts, responsiveness to the new climate of quality assurance and to the Dearing and Garrick report recommendations. 'In the mid-1980s', said one senior manager, 'Glasgow was not responsive to outside initiatives . . . it was a centralist university which was inward looking. Now it is responsive . . . The centralism and inwardness have abated'. The same respondent described the individual faculties as also being more active and responsive. A second senior manager commented that: 'Glasgow is very much a bottom up organization. We don't have a culture of principals or vice-principals saying: "this will happen, do it now". It's not that kind of organization.' Not all interviewees, of course, agreed with such formulations, but there is no doubt that wider responsiveness to changes beyond the University has been a recent feature of the University.

From heads of departments, schools and faculties, and senior managers there was a unanimous sense that these changes have been important. There had been a 'paradigm shift' and the University was seen as changing or having changed at all levels, including a changed attitude on the part of many staff ('they have changed hugely over the past three or four years', even though some still prefer 'keeping things as they are'). One description, by a faculty associate dean, of change in relation to innovation emphasized:

The 'culture' of the institution is changing. Teaching and learning innovation would hitherto have been at department level. Now there is 'larger commonality' – as seen by the Principal's appointment of a new post of Vice-Principal (Learning and Teaching), pointing towards a degree of co-ordination not yet there . . . Innovation has been largely bottom up, and new issues are top down.

The discussion document 'Towards a learning and teaching strategy' and the new Committee for Education Strategy and Resources were also elements in this judgement. Such comments point towards a degree of certainty that something basic was happening, alongside uncertainty about the implications for the relationships between the University policy-making machinery and the basic units. Within the faculties there was widely seen to be a 'fair pace' of change, and though change could come from the centre there was no doubt that 'the department is still the key locus of the teaching effort', even when in some cases this entailed 'embracing the new and keeping the old'. The University machinery was not generally perceived as erecting barriers.

Most of the 'managers' interviewed operate at an intersection, where they are accountable to their own internal constituency and an external framework (including SHEFC or other national bodies). An Israeli study of heads of department identified conflict arising from 'dual loyalty to external groups – various officers in the larger community of the institution – and to internal groups – students and instructors' (Kremer-Hayon and Avi-Itzhak 1986: 106). A Scottish study defined the position of academics as one with conflicting prime loyalties: 'To her or his students? To the institution? To the "academic community"? To a sponsor? Or to him – or herself?' (Schuller 1992: 33). Such conflicts apply to the 'manager', whether or not engaged in teaching students. A popular American description of the structure of educational institutions in the 1970s as 'loosely coupled systems' (Weick 1976) remains a feature of Glasgow and other British universities, though the strength of the coupling has increased considerably in succeeding decades as a result of increased need for central university accountability and responses to national procedures.

The power of faculties is viewed, even by their leadership, with a certain ambivalence. Faculties' roles in response to the 'move to managerialism' are not always clear. Proposals for major course changes come to the faculty and minor ones are dealt with in the departments. Where departments are clustered into 'schools' (here and in some other universities) within a faculty this intermediate level may act in a relatively informal way for purposes of communication and coordination or it may have a fuller managing function. Important developments in ICT have been promoted at school and faculty level, as with a 'computer classroom' and in teaching programmes of the School of English and Scottish Language and Literature, and also the appointment of a Director of Humanities Computing. Serious policy and practical concerns may be addressed at faculty level. The social sciences faculty, for example, became aware that even well qualified students found it difficult to 'engage effectively in the learning process', with adverse effects on essay writing, reading and arranging their work. The faculty therefore found resources to appoint what it called an 'effective learning adviser', a role mirrored to some extent in the University's Teaching and Learning Service and elsewhere in the University. The faculty of engineering was described as having 'to some extent . . . a "culture of innovation"', with proposals for change generated at department level and major ones coming through to the faculty.

The interviews conducted with deans, associate deans and heads of departments produced a unanimous emphasis on the role of the department in matters pertaining to teaching and learning. Changes within some departments were highlighted as concerned with moves towards a research culture or discussion of more diverse ways of handling a changing curriculum or increased student numbers. Not unexpectedly, the emphasis in some departments was on collegiality and discussion; in others (as had emerged also in the first year of the project) on the difficulty of change when opposition came, for example, from older or more senior colleagues. Within departments, schools and faculties individuals who acquire diffused authority have diverse but important roles. An early technological development in one department was possible because the enthusiast spent a period as dean. Associate deans with a particular brief for teaching and learning are able to exert pressure and influence – and they described their intersecting role between institutional policy making and faculty or departmental needs or opportunities. One associate dean described how he 'brought together the view from below and from the University, as well as from off campus'. The crucial roles of 'middle managers' emerge very clearly from this picture, as does the continuing strength of the department as the environment for the discussion of teaching and learning, and for attempts at innovation by individuals or small groups. Both of these features are present, though not necessarily with the same prominence, in the other campus-based universities discussed later.

Middlesex University

At the time of the visit Middlesex University had over 23,000 students. In 1997–8 more than 51 per cent of the full-time students were mature students (21 years old or over on admission), as were 95 per cent of the part-time students. Fifty-one per cent of full-time students came from homes in the London area, and 20 per cent were from Europe and elsewhere overseas. The University at the time consisted of seven major and two smaller sites spread across some 140 square miles of North London in five boroughs. The University also has a widespread network of regional and international partnerships of various kinds. At the beginning of the 1990s, when it had nine 'associate colleges' in the region, the University started to develop a new pattern of relationships. It now has 13 such colleges, four of which were keen to develop their higher education provision in conjunction with the University. Middlesex and these four colleges have formed a Higher Education and Training Partnership, the purpose of which is described in a brief mission statement as being 'to provide high-quality, accessible, innovative, relevant and cost-effective lifelong educational and training opportunities and, thereby, to contribute significantly to the economic, social and cultural well-being and success of the communities it serves'. At the time of the visit the five institutions were finalizing an agreement and considering such matters as a common Credit Accumulation and Transfer Scheme and staff development.

The University's annual income is close to £95.7 million, £5.8 million of which derives from research grants and contracts. In the 1996 RAE the University had moderate success in the middle assessment ratings but none in the top (5 and 5*) ratings. Less than half of the staff were submitted as 'research active' and of these 48 per cent were in areas rated on the lowest grades (1 and 2). The present Vice-Chancellor, Professor Michael Driscoll, came to the University as Dean of the Business School in 1989, and became Vice-Chancellor in 1995. From the academic year 1997–8 the University's six faculties and 26 schools were restructured into eight schools. Each new school has a dean and three directors, one of whom is designated 'director of curriculum, learning and quality' (CLQ), including responsibility for promoting initiatives for teaching and learning. Within the schools each 'academic group' elects its own chair, and courses in a given subject area are the responsibility of a 'curriculum leader'. As part of the University's commitment to interdisciplinary studies the schools, even where they have a main campus base, operate on more than one site. Each site has a Campus Dean of Students.

The key committees of the Academic Board include those for Academic Planning, Academic Standards and Quality, and Research. The directors of CLQ play a vital role in relation to teaching and learning, both within their school and as a coordinating group with senior management across the University. Two key roles of responsibility and liaison in this respect are those of the Deputy Vice-Chancellor and the Pro-Vice-Chancellor (Quality and Standards). The Vice-Chancellor chairs the Academic Standards and Quality committee. The directors of CLQ are responsible to their deans, who report in turn to the Deputy Vice-Chancellor and thence to the Vice-Chancellor.

At the time of the first visit, in November 1997, the University's *Mission Statement* and *Corporate Plan* (originally agreed in 1992, revised in 1997), emphasized both quality teaching and its encouragement of students 'to take a more active responsibility for their own learning experience', and also research as 'part of the core activity of the university'. This was part of a move away from a firmer ambition at an earlier stage to become a university with a strong research component. This process was further confirmed in 1998 by a revised *Mission Statement, Vision* and *Corporate Plan*. The *Mission Statement*, for example, proposes that 'Middlesex will be a student-centred university that will provide opportunities for lifelong learning to a diverse range of students within a culture of scholarship and development of knowledge'. The *Vision* and the *Corporate Plan* heighten the emphasis on teaching and learning. The former mentions research only as necessary to 'support learning'. The strategic objectives in the latter place 'high-class research' sixth in a list of seven, after 'innovative methods of learning' and promoting 'a culture of lifelong learning' – and then as a support for postgraduate programmes and the needs of the regional economy and local communities. These emphases were to colour some of the discussion during the visit.

In defining itself as a 'modern regional university', student-centred, and with an international reputation and partnerships, the University's object-ives emphasize access for a wide range of students and preparation for lifelong learning. Its size, spread of campuses and diversity of intake reflect its objectives. Its undergraduate population includes large contingents of, for example, business, nursing and health-related students, and it has a substantial proportion of mature students. The School of Health, Biological and Environmental Sciences is allocated £5 million from HEFCE funding but receives double that amount from its nursing contract. From 1992, at the time of its first *Mission Statement*, the University recognized that it would not be able to go down the route taken by some research-driven modern universities, and its struggle to define and re-define itself underlay many of the perceptions of the University discussed in the interviews.

The restructuring of the University had a number of purposes, including accommodating a continuing decrease in funding, too great an involve-ment in 'basic administration' by academic staff, and a wish to protect 'the point of academic delivery and support for students' from the full force of resource constraints. In 1991 the then six separate institutions had tended to operate without common practices and procedures. They required to be forged into a coherent, single university and the revised structure was based on 'a more rigorous academic planning model', which would enable such objectives as involvement in regional initiatives to be achieved '**across** the University' (Middlesex University, Management Team 1997: 1–2, emphasis in original). The University was anxious that the plans of its sub-units should reflect the mission and other University strategic documents. From 1993 the University had a common academic framework (for example, standard-izing examination arrangements and length of modules and introducing a single credit-based scheme, with what one senior manager described as 'a lot of commonality but significant differences'). The validation process was also described as meaning 'huge centralization, it helped to create an institution, a corporate identity'. Unlike the older universities visited and in ways familiar to other expanding former polytechnics, Middlesex had there-fore spent more than half a decade restructuring itself in order to create the conditions for achieving a 'corporate identity'. Some staff in the new, large schools of the University found it difficult to recognize the 'direction' it was taking, could not 'get a handle' on it, or did not feel that the object-ives had been translated into experience at their teaching and administrative levels. Many of the staff were still coming to terms with the growth in student numbers over the past six years (although they were told they were now entering a more stable period), alongside the fact that there had been 60 voluntary redundancies between 1997 and 1999.

Questions of balance or conflict between teaching and research have a common resonance but different formats and outcomes amongst (and within) universities. At Middlesex the redefinition of objectives led to interpreting the role of high-class research as supporting teaching, and particularly postgraduate programmes, an interpretation not always approved or understood by teaching staff. Although it was not going to be a research-led university, senior managers emphasized that it had pockets of valuable research. Staff sometimes saw research versus teaching and learning in terms of a hierarchy or sometimes as co-existing in parallel. This was a particular version at Middlesex of the common tensions between research and teaching discussed later in Chapter 8. At a policy level the University is anxious to establish not just that they co-exist, but that research supports learning. This also explains discussion in some interviews of the possibilities and uncertainties of research into teaching and learning alongside or versus 'mainstream' subject research. Since Middlesex has a modest, scattered amount of research on which to build, part of the continuing problem is how the University or school decides on selective support for research development. One important policy direction is clear from the documentation – a commitment to redesigning assessment methods and reducing lecturer contact so as to ensure an increase in students' 'autonomous learning'. Internal University funds to support new developments in teaching and learning have been available in various forms since the end of the EHE programme, which had been a source of encouragement and support for many of the innovators interviewed. There had, for example, recently been a £350,000 'academic initiatives fund', most of which had been used to develop resource-based learning. Some of the staff interviewed had received support from these University sources for curriculum development and related teaching and learning purposes.

Middlesex has been and remains driven by change and the expectation of change. The principal contexts of teaching and learning have been subject to rapid changes of many kinds, some of them (for example, increased numbers) familiar to other British universities, and some (form of merger and multi-site operation) more distinctive of Middlesex. The University-level changes have included a strategy of raising the status of teaching and its policy of developing resource-based learning – both widely perceived as difficult to achieve with the present level of resourcing and staff workloads that inhibit materials development. A survey of staff opinion in 1997 showed that much of the restructuring and many of the objectives were seen as controversial and based on what was often described as too little consultation. The new deans and directors of CLQ had a difficult responsibility in interpreting policy and guiding their schools, with all the differences of scale and tradition.

The senior management were aware that change encounters delay and resistance: the new policy playing down research 'will take a long time to work through', 'it is unlikely that all staff are committed' to the student-centred policy. A lot of hard work remained to be done at all levels of responsibility to implement fully the policy directions identified by the University. At school level the tension between research and teaching and learning was generally seen as serious. Changing things, in the words of one senior lecturer, tended to involve 'lots of meetings', working for consensus, 'networking, getting them on your side', and introducing change 'without alienating staff and students . . . getting across the message that lectures aren't best . . . giving more choice of alternatives'. Working to achieve change required persistence ('put my head down and drive it through'). Much had, indeed, changed, and one member of staff attributed this in part to the Dearing report, which 'had an amazing impact, it made people stop and think'.

There was regular comment on the obstacles and resistances encountered in attempts to introduce change. The most common included 'bureaucratic procedures', which are 'the main stumbling block'. Some staff commented on difficulties of access to support funds, while others commended the sources of funds that were available. The bureaucracy was sometimes associated with quality assurance, 'which is frustrating, bureaucratic and slows everything down', an issue that was being addressed by the University at the time. One principal lecturer offered a picture that included: greater centralization and monitoring; a lack of uniformity between schools – something that dissuades people from innovative approaches; mixed messages from the centre, and more difficulty in changing things from the bottom up. An obstacle to change that was regularly underlined was staff 'workload', or 'the burden of administration', emphases that recurred across universities of all kinds in both phases of this study. The problem was experienced in different ways at different levels of responsibility, but the message from many staff was clear: the intention of the restructuring had been to reduce the burden but it had not yet happened in practice. One member of the teaching staff thought that the workload was greater than in 1992 because students required more input – given increased numbers and lower standards of school attainment, and another pointed to 'too many students, not enough resources, a split-site campus causing great difficulty, a wide range of students, and restructuring'. At a time of strategic change, staff expectations, experiences and perceptions vary immensely.

Perceptions of the meaning of change focus particularly on structures. The new schools are intended to permit academic planning to 'come upwards . . . with differences of content and emphasis', though the plans are required to meet the University's corporate objectives, including explicit targets for teaching and learning. A dean of school shares responsibilities in relation to the curriculum and teaching and learning, primarily with the director of CLQ. For practical purposes, however, it is the 'academic groups' and their chairs, together with the 'curriculum leaders', who are most involved in the courses and their presentation. The roles of chairs of academic groups include the development of curriculum research and the initiation of new academic developments. Curriculum leaders are appointed to 'lead the development and delivery of subjects and programmes'. Interviews with five directors of CLQ suggested that their work on quality issues and curriculum development involved both content and learning strategies, and that 'learning development' was well placed on their agendas. One talked of the role as addressing 'delivery, alternative teaching methods and assessment strategies', as well as 'bringing the school together with a whole school strategy'. The structural context for teaching and learning and related activities at Middlesex is therefore a multiple and interrelated one. It involves institutional policy and decisions, the operation of new structures and responsibilities, and in immediate terms the work of a number of people occupying newly defined and intricately related roles.

A number of characteristic features emerge particularly clearly from this picture. All the changes can, as elsewhere, be placed in the context of interaction with wider social and economic processes, including the University's commitment to partnership at the local and regional level (but also internationally). This commitment can be seen as a continuation and enhancement of that which was basic to the former polytechnics when, before 1992, they were part of locally controlled advanced education provision. In the case of Salford, as we shall see, an equivalent commitment arose in quite different circumstances. The fundamental feature that Middlesex shares with other universities has been the requirement in the recent past to shape internal responses and adaptations to frequent and accelerating external pressures. The situation has not been entirely new, as most such adaptations in higher education – in Britain as in other countries – have been in response to external circumstances, including wars and political upheavals, or pressures resulting from social, financial, policy or other exigencies. 'The truly major changes in university life', commented Clark Kerr in the United States, 'have been initiated from outside', and he cites such forces as:

> Napoleon in France, ministers of education in Germany, royal commissions and the University Grants Committee in Great Britain, the Communist Party in Russia, the emperor at the time of the Restoration in Japan, the lay university governing boards and the federal Congress in the United States . . . (Kerr 1964: 105)

The modern American system, he also emphasizes, was moulded by two great impacts from outside the universities – the nineteenth-century Land Grant movement and federal support of scientific research during the Second World War (ibid.: 47–8).

Nineteenth-century Oxford and Cambridge were reformed from outside, and the shape of the new universities was determined by local and national movements. At the level not of system change but of understandings of what is meant by a university Sir Walter Moberly suggested after the Second World War that 'within the last century there has been more than one revolution in the conception commonly held of its fundamental aim and methods' (Moberly 1949: 30).

More recent writers internationally have extensively discussed what is meant not just by change but also by its management in higher education and more widely (for example, de Woot 1996; King and Anderson 1995) and its impact on 'institutional culture' (discussed in Chapter 6). Parallels with business or other public organizations are discussed in terms of 'flexible responses', 'unfreezing' beliefs, knowledge and attitudes, and 'absorbing new or alternative attitudes and behavior', and moving organizations from 'a result-oriented mode to a learning mode' (Beckhard and Pritchard 1992: 14). The Dearing report set its discussion in a picture of 'the changing context for higher education' – 11 kinds of change (economic, technological, social, cultural, demographic, educational . . .) that help to explain changes in higher education itself since the Robbins report on higher education in 1963 (National Committee of Inquiry into Higher Education 1997a: 51–69). What was new in the 1980s and 1990s was the rapidity of the changes and their impacts at many levels, including in the responses of universities and the ways in which they were made. The nature of the choices made by management and teachers in this situation, however, are not explained by the situation alone.

The University of Nottingham

At the time of the visit the University had nearly 17,000 students, plus 5400 students registered with the School of Continuing Education (the total has a full-time equivalent of 15,259 students, some 2000 of these having come from the merger with the Mid-Trent School of Nursing and Midwifery in 1995). The total had roughly doubled since 1992/3. Some 10,700 students were studying for undergraduate degrees, almost all of them full time. The percentage of mature students on the undergraduate programme (aged 21 years and over at the date of entry) was 6.7 (lowest in science), and 56 per cent of undergraduates were female. There were more than 1000 international (non-EU) undergraduate students.

Measured on any scale – the research and contract income of over £50 million a year or the number of the highest grades (5 or 5*) in the Research Assessment Exercise – Nottingham is a major research university. In the 1996 RAE 89 per cent of the staff were submitted as 'research active', and of these 69 per cent were in units given the ratings of 4, 5 or 5*. The University has an international reputation as such, and was one of the founder members of Universitas 21, an international grouping of universities with distinguished reputations in research and teaching, though with a major emphasis on its being an international grouping of 'research-intensive universities'. A common view expressed during the visit was that the University's philosophy was to try to place teaching in a research context. Nottingham was widely described as a 'research-led university'.

The University's committee structure reflects its sense of mission during the past decade, evident from the way it formulated its 1995–9 'University Plan':

> The primary aim of the University is to sustain the high quality of its provision as one of the leading research Universities in the United Kingdom. The commitment to all activities being research-led is complemented by an undertaking that the learning environment and teaching provided to all students should be of the highest quality.
> (University of Nottingham 1995: 1)

At the end of the 1980s the University had replaced a complex committee structure with one that includes two strong advisory committees to Senate – a Research Committee and a Teaching Committee. The terms of reference of the latter, chaired by the Pro-Vice-Chancellor for Staffing, Quality and Standards, is to advise the Senate on 'teaching, learning and assessment strategies and policies'. It monitors their implementation, as well as 'developments and trends' externally and within the University. A Teaching Enhancement Committee was created in 1995 as one of the Teaching Commitee's sub-committees, alongside the creation of a Teaching Enhancement Office and the allocation of support funding of two kinds for 'the integration of new approaches to teaching': a Rapid Response Fund, to support smaller projects, including Computer Assisted Learning, and a Strategic Development Fund for larger projects. Faculty Teaching Committees, the secondment of staff part-time within faculties as Teaching Enhancement Advisers to work with the Teaching Enhancement Office, the role of the Training and Staff Development Unit and associated teaching staff, complement this central provision in support of what the University describes as a dynamic process of 'perpetual enhancement'. The University had recently adopted a schools structure within faculties, and the schools were seen as more powerful than departments used to be. Conversely faculties were seen as having been weakened (and disappeared in one case, and relegated to an annual meeting in another). This affected, for example, the distribution of finance (now direct to schools) and the future shape of internal quality audit, which had hitherto been organized on a faculty basis. Senate itself had also become more streamlined ('more like a board meeting' as one member commented).

Several aspects of the above brief description underpinned much of the discussion about teaching and learning and the University as a context. First is the sense of a strong central steer for the University as a whole, reflecting both changes in higher education nationally and the appointment in 1988 of Sir Colin Campbell as the new Vice-Chancellor. Second is the powerful sense of the University as being 'exceptional' (in a description by one senior lecturer) or 'unique' (a senior manager) in its combined emphasis on research and teaching. Third is the recent history of the University's commitment to the 'perpetual enhancement' of teaching, beginning with its involvement in EHE and continuing through its more recent successes in attracting, by the time of the visit, external funding of £450,000 for various aspects of implementing this commitment.

The targeting by the University's policy, structure and monitoring procedures of both high quality research and teaching is not unlike some other 'old' universities in this respect, but Nottingham arguably maintains the balance better than others, as a result of a strong policy and practical investment in the improvement of teaching and learning. This was not seen as adversely affecting research, and conversely some respondents described the honours degree itself as being 'research based'. A pro-vice-chancellor chairs the Teaching Committee, a senior professor chairs the Teaching Enhancement Committee and another chairs the Teaching Quality Assurance Committee, and some internationally eminent research professors spend time on these and other committees at school and university level concerned with issues relevant to teaching, as well as themselves teaching undergraduates. Even those staff strongly committed to teaching enhancement, however, felt driven at the present time by the requirements of the RAE ('a vicious diversion', said one senior professor). Although many staff saw teaching and learning as secondary to research, the University's aim to achieve a balance, and its widely recognized successes in developing one, were one element that differentiated the University from some of its peer institutions.

Nottingham has one of the highest student per place application rates in the country, tending to attract students straight from secondary school, with only a small percentage of mature students. It has in the recent past made a concerted effort to recruit a higher proportion of students from its region. Many of the developments relevant to this study have in the past decade had strong support from, or were driven by, the University's central management. This applies, for instance, to the University's participation in EHE, the development of the Teaching Enhancement Office and a centralized system of Student Evaluation of Teaching. The University was at the time of the visit in the final stages of developing a new campus close to its present one, and one feature of it was to be a resources centre that would further enhance the University's provision of support facilities for students and staff.

As an old university there is resistance in the University to going down the route of what one person described as the 'central diktat' associated with the new universities, but recognition on the other hand that a devolved system has many difficulties ('We cannot change how we run the University, but we also cannot allow everyone to "do their own thing"', was one comment made at a meeting on quality assurance). In this respect Nottingham reflects the dilemma of old universities confronted in recent years by the need for more transparent procedures.

Change as explored at Nottingham in the second phase of the study had more to do with the contexts and nature of incentives than with initiatives by individual teaching staff. One senior member of the University, echoing the kind of historical point made above, commented: 'Significant change never takes place without external pressure. The push has to be on institutions . . . on departments via the institutions'.

Others reflected on the experience of teaching quality assessment (TQA) visits or the research assessment exercise. At Nottingham as elsewhere there were mixed messages about the value of TQA, but given the University's emphasis on excellence in teaching, discussion produced more positive responses about TQA than in other universities visited (given the known identity of these universities it is not possible to code or otherwise identify respondents as was possible for those in the first phase):

TQA has had a huge impact. It made us more aware of what was needed and made us get organized and systematic. (Lecturer)

TQA took over our lives for 18 months and we will never be the same again. (Head of department)

Everyone sees the importance of the Teaching Enhancement Office now, especially because of TQA. (Professor, board and committee chair)

TQA had some impact. Mostly things were happening already, but it forced a tidying up process. (Lecturer)

The main lever for change has been TQA. Modularization made a big impact too. (Senior lecturer)

TQA was most appreciated where it confirmed the direction in which the unit was already moving either of its own accord, or as a result of other pressures or encouragement within the University. It was probably least appreciated where it simply meant a priority zigzag every few years between the assessment of teaching or research.

The University's recent history following the experience of EHE is important, since those who were involved or witnessed the developments gave it credit for providing a crucial impetus. Many of the innovations discussed in the project's first visit had been launched in the context of EHE. Nottingham was one of the old universities that realized the potential of the EHE initiative, and it helped towards a climate of opinion in which the University could produce an imaginative continuation policy, including the creation of the Teaching Enhancement Office. As in other universities the importance of EHE lay in understanding that it was possible to mould the kinds of activities to which the government funding was directed. An evaluation report on the five years of EHE in 1995 underlined the impact on teaching and learning:

The focus on the development of skills/competences as a major aim of EHE has inevitably led to many teaching and learning practices moving away from a didactic style to a more learner-centred one where students are engaged in project work, CAL packages and experiential learning. In all the projects visited, students were encouraged to take more responsibility for their learning and monitor their own progress . . . (University of Nottingham 1995: 21)

In the process of change there is no divorce between external and internal pressures, given that the latter are in direct or indirect ways often a response to the former. 'This is a changing place, forever changing' commented one experienced member of staff, and 'excessive' commented another. Although some developments within the University drew on other external funding after EHE ended, change was associated by many people with individual innovators or change agents at various levels of the University. Externally funded projects often arise from interests already being pursued or germinating within an institution, and in turn influence further activity within the institution. At Nottingham it is perceived to be important that the University has welcomed such external support. In January 1998 the University announced the award of three grants that totalled £450,000, two for work in the key skills area and one (shared with the University of Newcastle) for the development of personal and academic records for students in higher education. The latter originated in a realization in the School of English Studies that modularization had adversely affected the student/ tutor relationship, and a £200,000 grant from the Fund for the Development of Teaching and Learning enabled a system to be developed whereby students recorded their own progress. Another £200,000 grant, from the Department for Education and Employment was specifically targeted at the development of key skills 'within a traditional university'. Senior people in the University were aware that such skills were already beginning to be incorporated into parts of the University curriculum, and staff involved in such projects explained that they did so as a result of experience in addressing the difficulties or needs of their own students. Not all research-oriented universities have been or would be as welcoming for projects in this kind of area, and the views and roles of the vice-chancellor and other senior staff and committees are clearly important in this respect.

Nottingham is in some respects both a centralized and a devolved university. It has strong leadership with what some interviewees described in terms of vision, others in terms of increased hierarchy and a drive for efficiency. There is a small Management Group (of which faculty deans, for example, are not members). There are no 'deputy VCs' as in many, particularly 'new', universities, and the pro-vice-chancellors are senior professors who serve on a rolling basis. Considerable responsibility is transmitted from Senate to the key committees, where relevant debates take place, informed by the work of sub-committees such as that concerned with teaching enhancement. The pro-vice-chancellors also represent an important additional conduit for information and intelligence (as well as power), since each of the four PVCs has specific responsibility for particular faculties and presents their case to the Management Group.

Each school has a Teaching Committee and a Teaching Quality Review Committee, the latter of which is responsible for preparing for teaching quality assessment. The most common view, however, was that as far as teaching and learning and much that related to them were concerned the agenda was driven from 'the top'. This was part of the change in the

University's management and the operation of the structure. One senior lecturer commented:

> The faculty used to be a thriving entity with a strong sense of academic community. Now the University is much more business oriented, there is a change in management style, promoting the image, looking for growth opportunities and supporting initiatives in teaching.

The change in approach to management also carried through to the operation of faculty and school committees and their leadership. The process was sometimes criticized and resisted, but there was also approval for some implications of the changes – a greater sense of drive, what a professor with long experience of Nottingham described as 'a feeling of elan, confidence and success', though varying across the University. The new structure and traditional higher education values of community and collegiality were often seen as in conflict. The disappearance of departments and the weakening of faculties, within the total University management context had for many people created a different kind of university environment.

As a high profile, highly research conscious university, Nottingham at the same time strongly encourages developments relating to teaching and learning, and also sees itself as 'a traditional university'. From the first-phase visit emerged the question of whether this represented a sustainable tension or balance. There are literatures in this connection that seem out-of-date, and in one case non-existent. The importance of leadership, specifically in relation to vice-chancellors, was a significant thread at Nottingham, but the existing literature does not address the relationship of leadership to the research/teaching tensions that have become salient in recent years. Schein, for example, gave considerable, even excessive, weight to the role of leadership in creating and changing organizational culture:

> The further I got into the topic of organizational culture, the more I realized that culture was the result of entrepreneurial activities by company founders, leaders of movements, institution builders, and social architects. As I began to think through the issues of how culture changes, I again realized the centrality of leadership – the ability to see a need for change and the ability to make it happen. (Schein 1985: x–xi)

More elusive, distributive or negotiated forms of leadership were the focus of other contributions to the literature (for example, Cohen and March 1974; Middlehurst 1993), but the focus has increasingly turned to the centralizing tendencies of higher education institutions in the late twentieth century. Elements of all of the interpretations of leadership may be found in the contemporary university, but the nature of leadership and authority in relation to the issues under discussion here have yet to be explored and explained.

The same applies to the much discussed but under-researched experience of academic staff faced with the choices and dilemmas associated with higher education at the end of the twentieth century. What is involved is the very meaning of an 'academic' or 'teacher in higher education' or 'lecturer'. The rise of research as a dominant focus in the university is well documented (for example, Veysey 1965: Ch. 3; Geiger 1986) but such, mainly American, literature does not reach as far as the academic faced with research and teaching as immediate career choices in the new conditions, which Nottingham in the UK has navigated better than most. Nor does the most recent literature of 'professionalism' reach into this experience in higher education (for example, Clark 1987; Perkin 1987). Aspects of where academics stand in relation to issues such as equity or academic freedom can be gleaned from some recent literature, including a published colloquium on 'What does it mean to be an academic?' (Nixon *et al.* 1998). The experience of the academic, like the nature of leadership, emerges from the picture of Nottingham as it does with important differences elsewhere, but has not yet given rise to a serious, analytical literature.

The University of Salford

At the time of the visit the University had some 20,000 students, 12,000 of whom were full-time undergraduates and nearly 4000 part-time undergraduates. Of the total 13.5 per cent were international (including EU). The University's annual income was over £110 million. Research grants and contracts accounted for just over £6 million. For the 1996 RAE 43 per cent of staff were submitted as research active, with a small scatter of gradings at the higher levels and 62 per cent in units graded as 1, 2 or 3A/B. The new Vice-Chancellor, Professor Michael Harloe, who took office in 1997, initiated consultation that led to the publishing of a *Strategic Framework* document (University of Salford 1998), within which 'Teaching and Learning' was a prominent section. He also initiated a programme of restructuring that reduced eight faculties and 38 departments to four faculties and 17 schools, and this was being implemented at the time of the visit. The faculty deans had been appointed, as had three associate deans in each faculty (covering teaching, research and enterprise respectively). The intention was to produce a less unwieldy management team, more cognate schools that could mean new discipline combinations and more innovation, and more effective budgeting and administration. The larger faculties and the new associate deans would also end the existing division between departments and the separate 'institutes' that were the bases for research.

As with other universities visited, student numbers had substantially increased, with a staff:student ratio of 1:30 being not uncommon, and tutorial group sizes having at least doubled in the recent past (often taking place at fortnightly rather than weekly intervals). An important feature of the University's planning was its intention to strengthen its already major commitment to widening participation and its relationships with the region. Recommendations for implementation had been drawn up in October 1998, and an audit of the University's current practices had been carried out. Also in 1998 a policy document on Academic Information Services had been produced, alongside the report of a task group on 'the impact of new technology on teaching and learning'. The University was already engaged in a partnership research project with the cities of Salford and Manchester, Cable and Wireless Communications and the Manchester Training and Enterprise Council, aiming at the development of a Metropolitan Area Network that would provide a telecommunications infrastructure for application to business, education, health and the region generally.

These examples of University development signal an institution also going through a period of major change, defining or redefining its strengths and purposes. More than with many other institutions visited, the issues at Salford have to be set in the context of a rapidly changing recent history, different from that discussed above in the case of Middlesex. The Royal Technical Institute (later College) was founded in 1896, and it became a College of Advanced Technology in 1956 and the University of Salford in 1966. In 1996 it merged with a large higher education college, the University College Salford, and a College of Nursing and Midwifery. Many such mergers nationally have brought together different traditions, but in many cases from the 1960s the merging institutions covered complementary subject areas. At Salford, however, the merger was more recent and involved significant overlap in subject areas, and the University and the College were more equal in size than had been the case in other mergers. Especially since a severe financial cutback in 1981 the University had developed very substantial areas of collaboration with industry, and both the financial crisis and the merger had meant changes that raised important questions of institutional direction and image. The transition from 'the old' to 'the new' university in 1996 was welcome to many, resisted by some, painful in many respects. The new Vice-Chancellor arrived little more than a year after the merger, and reflected in interview on some of its implications:

> The merger with a large HE college was different from anywhere else. It meant a serious issue of identity. It was the closest thing to a technological university, in need of decent research. It had strong links with industry. At first, when the merger took place, people said: 'We don't know what sort of university this is'. Was Salford's past identity out of date? Was it a millstone? No. This was in fact the strongest card to play, it needed to be reinterpreted. Salford needed to be a technological university like others in Europe, and like them to have strong social sciences and research . . . Some British universities had adapted in that way and if it had not been for the events of 1981 Salford could have been like them.

During visits in late 1997 and again in the spring of 1999, explanations of the present were frequently offered in interviews in terms of this recent past, a struggle not only for institutional identity, but for faculty, departmental and individual identities and statuses within the new institution. Perceptions of policies and decisions, as well as restructuring, therefore often carried discernible messages from people's experience of the recent past.

The merger led to important differences across the new institution, depending on whether similar departments were amalgamating ('being shoved together' in one description), or whether a unique college department was being transferred. Some departments in the University felt repercussions of the merger without being directly involved. In some of the newly merged departments the two different traditions remained distinct ('the old College department still seems quite separate'). The difference was often described in terms of research versus teaching, the former being predominantly associated with the old University. The result could be a continued heavier teaching load, and therefore poorer promotion prospects, for former College staff. Broadly speaking, however, there was a sense that the merger had been rushed through, and the old structures had just 'carried on'. Hence the new round of restructuring, and the pervasive sense of this recent history.

Both traditions in the new university had placed emphasis on the strength of the departments, and they became 'paramount in the new University'. The University was 'traditional in organization, decentralized – departments were autonomous'. Resistance to the restructuring into larger schools reflected both that autonomy and the loyalty to subjects – as well as opposition to particular combinations ('in some cases a bit awkward', according to one senior manager, but 'they might spark some interesting innovation'). Although there was no plan for sub-structures within the new schools, there was evidence of some 'divisions' already beginning to take shape.

It was not only in the structures, however, that change was perceived, often as endemic. Policy formulation and implementation (more or less completely or successfully) could produce ripples of various kinds. For example, as at other universities, there was a range of responses to ICT policy and practice, including criticisms of its design or efficiency, and the anxiety reported from one department that the new electronic databases would be taken as 'gospel' by students, who may not explore alternative sources of data. The 'research institute' structure, for example, had originally been created separate from departments 'for tactical reasons', had intended to be interdisciplinary and to help at the time of the merger when there were many small departments. At the time of the restructuring, however, this division was seen as a weakness, with research not supporting teaching. The short time-scale between changes of policy direction obviously played an important part in views of the University expressed by many teaching staff.

Changing policies and strategies relating to teaching and learning have to be seen in these changing contexts. An ambitious EHE programme (1990–5) was another context, placing emphasis on 'learning rather than teaching, with students accepting more responsibility for their own learning', as well as on the importance of staff development 'to help them apply rigour to the analysis and development of the skills and competencies their students need' (University of Salford 1995a: 5). The final EHE evaluation considered that 'Enterprise has allowed Salford to establish a culture of educational development' (University of Salford 1995b: 18). The presence of an active Pro-Vice-Chancellor with a specific remit for teaching and learning meant that policy development was accompanied by an implementation strategy, during and after the end of the EHE programme. One dean commented that 'EHE had a big impact, because part of the scheme had to do with embedding – it didn't go away at the end'.

The 'culture of educational development' was not uniform across the University, before or after the merger, but relevant machineries were in place, particularly with the establishment of the Educational Development Unit (EDU). This brought together existing staff development and other units important to activities for the enhancement of teaching. As a key support mechanism the EDU continues the impetus given by EHE to staff and curriculum development, and also continues the support previously given to such activities at University College Salford. The University had a Capability Enhancement Programme in the 1980s, and a feature of the interest in teaching and learning before, during and after EHE was 'innovation in teaching and learning encouraged by internal funding' (Carboni *et al.* 1996: 4). Such strands in the University's support policies and processes were essential contexts for the ways in which teachers in particular situated their roles and activities in their understanding of the University. Commitment to teaching and learning was clearly affected by how interviewees interpreted institutional change, its causes and outcomes.

Given the prominent tension in the university system between research and teaching, resolved in various ways or left unresolved, it is important to remember from the Salford experience that the history of institutional mergers, particularly from the 1970s, has left a clear mark across many institutions, or in particular parts of them, on how staff interpret their priorities in general and in relation to teaching and learning in particular. In many European countries, Australia and elsewhere, including the UK, mergers took place between universities or other higher education institutions and teacher education colleges, or amongst the colleges, or with nursing and other health-related institutions, and in other ways. Much of the analysis of these mergers relates to the creation of new sectors of higher education, or larger institutions intended to encompass a range of activities with intended financial or other implications. There is little literature of the experience of participants in the combination of traditions, exemplified so vividly by Salford (but c.f. Venables 1978; Arbuthnott and Bone 1993).

Salford also exemplifies the trend seen above in the case of Middlesex of building strong community and regional links, a trend in the Salford case associated with survival decisions from 1981, and resulting in a considerable range of partnerships with industry, commerce and public services in the region. The 'university–community interface' has been the subject of extensive debate and analysis (Goddard *et al.* 1994), the target of policy by government, employers and other bodies such as the Council for Industry and Higher Education (CIHE). 'The local and regional role of higher education' was one of the strongest messages of the Dearing report on higher education (National Committee of Inquiry 1997a: Ch. 12). What Salford illustrates, however, is the need to go beyond discussion of a university's 'roles' and 'relationships' in this connection, and to consider the experience of close partnerships, the impact on the culture of the institution, and implications for teaching and learning. This, in some institutions, is part of the context for the discussion of innovation, and in both phases of this study there have been substantial examples of a direct connection between such partnerships and innovations in teaching and learning.

The Open University

The Open University is different in a number of crucial respects from all other UK universities. It does, of course, have staff and students, provide courses and award degrees and conduct research. It receives funding and is subject to quality assessment from the same national bodies as other universities, but operationally the OU is different. The 1000 or so salaried academic staff are involved with teaching and learning and innovation differently from their colleagues in other universities – notably they do not 'teach' in the same sense, and their involvement in the creation and development of courses and course materials is different. They belong to departments and faculties that have profoundly different relationships to courses, teaching and learning than their counterparts elsewhere. They belong to the OU at Milton Keynes (which is not a 'campus' in the same sense as other universities), or to one of the OU's 13 regions, which have the function of recruiting, registering and supporting students, as well as appointing, training and supervising 'associate lecturers' (ALs). At the OU 'teaching and learning' are not the concern of teachers in classrooms, laboratories or lecture theatres (except sometimes for summer schools), but of academics and other staff in course teams, or staff tutors in the regions (who may also be members of course teams at Milton Keynes), and of some 7000 part-time ALs. Of the full-time academic staff 54 per cent were submitted for the 1996 RAE, and none of the resultant gradings were at the lowest (1 and 2) levels, and none at the highest (5*) level, but 44 per cent were at the middle range (3A/B) and 56 per cent at the higher levels (4 and 5).

The relationship between over 160,000 students and the OU is unlike that of students and other universities, except where the latter have developed distance programmes (on a comparatively small scale). Many other universities (particularly the urban 'new' universities) have large intakes of mature students, but the OU's profile is unique. Its students are part-time, and constitute roughly a quarter of all part-time students in the UK. Only 4 per cent of its undergraduates are under the age of 25, with 86 per cent in the age range 25–54 and 10 per cent being over 55.

The OU is structured around what Costello describes as 'the creative area', 'the operations and administrative divisions' and 'the regions' (Costello

1993: 6–9), though the interactions amongst these are basic to the way the OU functions. Essential interaction is between academic staff at the centre and in the regions, and the variety of staff engaged with planning, designing, preparing, publishing (in various forms, on paper and as part of broadcast and computer-based communication), sustaining and monitoring courses and student performance. Academic staff and others do conduct research (including in specialized units), and they have subject and professional allegiances as do staff elsewhere. The University has policies on such things as research, study and research leave and promotion as do other universities. The core operations of the OU in relation to teaching and learning, however, have different configurations from those of other universities. Three important concepts underpin an analysis.

Supported open learning
This is in fact a more appropriate description at the OU than that of 'teaching'. From the outset the OU's approach to distance or open learning involved a strong element of student support and guidance, providing students with both an opportunity for independent learning and support of various kinds, given that many of them have little or no recent experience of structured learning. A recent OU strategy document addressing its roles in lifelong learning emphasized:

> Supported open learning has been, and will continue to be, the OU's principal teaching mode. Supported open learning is student centred. It is the provision of specially designed, high quality, multiple media teaching materials, together with personalised tuition, learning feedback and support. We have successfully developed a system of tutor support, assessment and counselling which allows for interaction between students and tutors in a variety of ways, including written correspondence, computer communications, telephone contacts, face-to-face meetings, and residential schools. This . . . provides an integrated learning package . . . (The Open University 1997: 7)

A proposal for a 'learning and teaching strategy' in 1999 involved outlining the key features of the OU experience for students: 'learner-oriented, active learning, resource based, self-paced, modular, course-based, supported open learning, course team approach, scale and quality, production and presentation, central and local (The Open University 1999: 2). Students encounter this 'integrated learning package' and its underlying philosophy through the OU's total strategy as embodied in its regional recruitment structure, and through the particular features of supported open learning chosen by course teams to present the content of particular courses. The OU began by taking what one senior lecturer described as 'a discredited text approach and made it work', producing courses collaboratively in teams, 'with heavy duty external assessment and intensive peer review'. It also incorporated 'the fruits of educational research' and embedded them in the support system. At the time of the visit the process was being adapted to a range of new technologies.

Course teams

Course teams are the crux of the OU's approach to teaching and learning. A team is created for every course and it is responsible for the course from its initial planning and throughout its life. The teams provide 'the normal working method for all the central teaching staff' (but also for many regional staff tutors). They were described in 1974 as 'the most important of all The Open University innovations . . . The course team is the powerhouse of the University' (quoted in Riley 1975: 1). The extended and intensive team working 'makes the role of lecturer at The Open University rather different from the conventional higher education post' (ibid.: 6). The fact that course teams are very frequently inter-disciplinary, and may originate with individuals and informal groups as well as within the formal structure, places them in many respects outside that structure. They may involve people, for example, from the Institute for Educational Technology, the Academic Computing Service, the design and publication units of the OU and the regions (staff tutors who are also members of the central faculties), as well as external experts and consultants. The elected chair of a course team may be a lecturer, and the team may include one or more heads of department, a faculty dean or other senior staff, as well as a course manager. The team chair is outside the formal management structure but given the dependence of the OU on the successful production of new and revised courses, the chair and the team have a position of relative influence and power within the University. However narrow a course content, the team is not coterminous with a department, and though a course has to be approved by the University before being placed on offer, in the process of producing courses there is considerable scope for innovation. With regard to the interests of this study, it is the course teams that form the creative core of the University.

Innovation

Innovation has a different presence at the OU from elsewhere. The first Vice-Chancellor of the OU recalled writing in his application for the post that 'the OU would revolutionize higher education by its teaching methods because of the appalling quality of teaching materials then being used in British universities. That turned out to be a fair prediction' (Perry 1994: 14). If the OU began by inventing innovative materials and the processes within which they were used, innovation continued to raise possibilities at all stages of its development. The roles of the regions, the appointment and training of ALs, tutorials by telephone and on-line, the investment by the University in new directions and initiatives by individuals, experimental units to explore new software or the roles of 'knowledge media', point towards a kind of generic or institutionalized approach to innovation in the OU. An innovation may, of course, become traditional, and systems inevitably contain tendencies to inertia. The old way, however innovative its origins, may not be amenable to change. The very nature of the OU, however, means that innovation in teaching and learning and their contexts cannot be discussed in the same terms as in higher education where students are on campus, and are 'taught' differently – even if their learning is mediated by materials and technologies. One senior manager talked of innovation happening often 'in spite of the existing frameworks'. A workshop in the mid-1980s came to the view that successful innovation in the OU was 'very much dependent on the creativity and self-motivation of individuals', but individual creativity and self-motivation needed to be 'directed towards the realisation of institutional goals' (Melton 1986: 3). More perhaps than in other institutions, innovation relates to tensions that are less observable in formal structures.

From December 1998 a process of reorganizing the Academic Board committee sub-structure was taking place. A final review report to the Academic Board that month proposed the organization of six boards, including a Learning Technologies and Teaching Board (LTTB), and across the period covered by this study the reorganization was taking place. The previous structures and details of the new ones are not important here, except to note that under the LTTB a Teaching and Learning Innovation Committee (TLIC) was coming into existence. The aims of the LTTB included: 'to develop and maintain the University's Teaching and Learning Strategy' and 'to establish University guidelines which ensure an appropriate balance of teaching and learning methods for all courses and qualification routes'. The TLIC aims included to provide an overview of 'effective use of new teaching methods, new learning materials and new ways of combining existing teaching elements in the context of other methods of teaching and supporting students'. It also aimed to assess whether 'new teaching and learning methods would deliver an appropriate experience for students', to develop and maintain a strategy for the support of course teams and ALs in 'the effective use of new teaching methods', to disseminate good practice in new teaching methods, to coordinate development projects 'in support of new learning materials, media and tuition methods', and to advise on new teaching and assessment strategies (OU 1998: 4–5, 23–6).

The pro-vice-chancellors chairing these various boards relate to one another across their particular remits, for the curriculum, students (including access) and learning technologies and teaching. These responsibilities and structures reflect the continuous requirement of the OU that its widespread and complex activities be sustained, and a potential for change be supported. Not everyone, of course, interprets these structures in this way. One faculty dean thought the degree of central planning was 'quite alarming' and increasing. The strong, universal commitment to the OU and its mission that we encountered in the interviews was sometimes accompanied by an undercurrent of scepticism about the amount of bureaucracy. Costello found this in the early 1990s, with many staff who had not had management roles seeing the University as 'obstructive and impenetrable':

'The University' is used as a general term to encompass a feeling of frustration or inertia . . . It is an impersonal and non-specific term which comes closest to the negative interpretations which are conventionally associated with the term 'bureaucracy'. Interestingly when referring to the University in a positive light the term which tends to be used is 'the OU'. (Costello 1992: 29)

Perceptions of planning differed as much as perceptions of structure. Planning at the OU is directed towards the implementation of its strategic aims, and it reaches down into the operational units of the University. The units produce annual rolling plans which, while formulating objectives and reviewing implementation, reflect assumptions about courses and their presentation. The 1999 five-year plans include, for example:

The Faculty will pioneer innovative uses of technology in teaching, course production and delivery . . . (The Open University, *Faculty of Technology* 1998: 28)

Members of Faculty instinctively put what in abstract terms is called innovation at the heart of their work. (The Open University, *Faculty of Arts* 1998: 13)

Although departments as such do not directly produce courses and determine their presentation, they perform contingent roles – including staff development, scholarship, research and the maintenance of what one sub-dean described as 'the traditional "community of scholars" atmosphere'. Course proposals do go through faculty (or in some cases school) and then University committee procedures.

Services are provided to students by a partnership between the full-time Regional Centre staff and the ALs. At the time of the visit, the Southern Region, for example, had 80 members of staff, held 8500 annual tutorials at 35 centres as well as one-to-one support when needed. 'Introductory' meetings were held at 29 venues and 2600 telephone calls were made by ALs to introduce those who did not make the meetings. A total of 1300 students attended study skills workshops. In addition to the faculty-based staff tutors there are also student counsellors. The senior counsellor is an inter-faculty post, with the role of supporting students in their learning in a generic way. The director of the region is involved in implementing University policy, coordinating student support and AL staff training, as well as using student feedback to influence policy on boards and committees.

Maintaining the system and promoting change are therefore functions of a wide variety of individuals in key positions. The Pro-Vice-Chancellor responsible for learning technologies and teaching is particularly involved in helping to promote and support new initiatives. The deans, in association with their sub-deans, conduct what one dean described as the 'trick of getting the balance of the role right, presenting the faculty views to the University and the University's view to the faculty'. One sub-dean described receiving proposals for inclusion in the faculty five-year plan – department heads, he commented, 'do not have a huge role' in this process; they solve staff problems and planning issues, and help with course teams once they are established. One head of department focused a description of the roles involved on the planning of courses within the faculty process, helping to plan course teams and meeting their needs, departmental cooperation in connection with teams developing courses that cross departments, staff training, promotion and research. Course chairs, managers and teams operate both within and outwith these structures. Course chairs were described as 'not in the power structure, but powerful'. They report either to the head of department or to a sub-dean.

An important question concerned the reasons for recent emphases on planning for major change (the theme of its 1997 *Plans for Change: Lifelong Learning for a New Era*). One Pro-Vice-Chancellor, aware of being generally viewed as 'impatient for change', discussed changes in the pipeline and identified a series of incentives and pressures. 'Eternal vigilance' was necessary to remain a healthy institution – given the rapidity of technological change'. 'The global competitive market' was growing, as was the UK higher education system, with more universities 'heading towards distance learning and becoming more flexible for student learning'. Most OU students were over 30 and this was a depleting market'. Another Pro-Vice-Chancellor thought there were now more reasons for change than before:

> The OU constantly wishes to do better what it is already doing. There is academic motivation and environmental change and a need to improve the quality of the student learning experience and the effectiveness of the OU. These are permanent reasons for change. The OU is good at collecting student data . . . tutorials do well but many students cannot attend . . . The OU is not as flexible as it could be – if it were it would be more complex and more expensive.

The Vice-Chancellor's view was that:

> It is not a seller's market any more (the queue for places at the OU has disappeared). There are nationally more and a greater variety of students, and there is more competition. There are more students with undergraduate degrees, and market needs are changing. The University for Industry has come on stream (described by one politician as 'doing for the future what the OU did for the past', which has made the University take notice!). The delivery vehicles of teaching and the format of the courses have evolved. The OU has evolved with the technologies at just the right rate – one cannot go too fast or too slow.

In all such discussions change could be mentioned in the same breath as inertia in the system, some of it resulting from tension between academics and the support services. The 1986 workshop on 'Innovation in The Open University' concluded that the implementation of new ideas depended to a large extent on overcoming opposition from vested interests. For example, staff not directly involved in developing an idea may find themselves being asked to take on extra workloads or to change their modes of operation in order to help implement the innovation, and unless they are committed to the new ideas they are quite likely to object to the proposed changes. (Melton 1986: 6)

'Vested interests' was not a phrase that surfaced during this study. Some of these reasons for resistance remain, as they do in other universities, but there were staff who emphasized the possibility of successfully 'kicking against normal practices', and innovating 'in spite of the existing frameworks'. It was acknowledged at senior levels that it was not easy to deal with inertia in the University system and inflexibilities of various kinds. The issue was particularly clear in discussion about whether and how the University might introduce short courses, and these were being actively planned at the time of the visits. They had hitherto been resisted as too complex for the existing structures to administer, and therefore as expensive. One interviewee thought this illustrated 'a very constraining and fixed system at the OU – a tension between providing for existing students (who like long courses) and encouraging in new ones by offering something different in the form of short courses'. The April 1999 'Learning and teaching strategy' proposal looked forward to 'a more adaptive model of our course development-production-presentation system enabling the University to be more rapidly responsive to changes in demands' (The Open University 1999: 2).

Inertia in the system, the strength of 'normal practices' and difficulties in relationships between the 'creative' and 'operations and administrative' areas, are understood and made explicit. At the level of course planning, however, awareness of them does not generally seem to be inhibiting. As one sub-dean put it: 'courses are about innovation all the time'. Others, especially course chairs, thought there were opportunities simply to 'get on with it'. 'Dedication', commented one participant about colleagues in course planning and production, 'is beyond anything in other universities, people will go to any lengths . . . motivated by their very keen and demanding students'.

General

What we have in these five universities is a picture of rapid change, not only more sustained than in the past, but also profoundly affecting the collective and individual portraits. Comparisons and contrasts become difficult when changes very similar in their justifications and vocabularies nevertheless disguise important continuities. Characteristics of the nineteenth-century universities included their relative stability, their clear and unswerving purposes, their relatively predictable student population and teaching force, their curriculum that changed slowly and then mainly in response to changes in the development of knowledge. In the late nineteenth and twentieth centuries the pattern of British and other universities diversified, but the characteristics of each type of institution remained roughly constant. The policy- and economy-driven changes imposed from the 1970s accelerated the pace of change within the system and within individual institutions. Staff perceptions of their immediate and institutional environments were coloured by the ways in which these could be seen to respond, unpredictable shifts in the distribution of power and influence within the institution and in seismic changes in the teaching situation. This involved, in various configurations, increased student numbers and diversity, the pattern of terms and semesters, assessment requirements, the assessment of teaching quality and research output and associated pressures, the constant redefinition of the traditional.

Each of the five universities reflected these changes, but each retained strong individual characteristics. While all were perceived by many of their teaching staff as 'increasingly managerial', 'more centralized', 'less collegial' – or a variety of similar judgements – they offered contexts for teaching and learning and their development that were different in important respects. However constraining they might be, innovative teaching staff working in these contexts undoubtedly found different ways of bypassing or exploiting their own institutional structures, or found interstices where they could follow their predilections. However, when universities plan for the strategic direction of developments or the 'delivery' of courses, they do not necessarily intend to allow space for forms of innovation not defined in their strategies. Significant variations in these contexts therefore include recent and sometimes longer term historical legacies, different expectations and aspirations regarding research outcomes, funding and reputation, the responsibilities of committees and individuals, policy and operational procedures of all kinds – and in general the nature of the response process to the difficulties – and sometimes the opportunities – of change. These institutional outlines therefore suggest the basic similarities and differences within which it is possible to consider teaching and learning and the contexts of innovation. The details given are largely those of structure, and to some extent process and procedure, but these do not equate culture, which is the focus of later discussion.

5

Teaching and Learning

Pedagogy and innovation

Innovation implies premeditation and some level of private or public explanation and justification. It is deliberate and involves a conscious or intuitive intention to make purposive and possibly abrupt or radical change. The enhancement of teaching and learning does not *necessarily* entail any of these. Improving practice may also engage critically with it, but it may also be a technical adaptation, a form of massage. Politically, however, the importance of an institutional or departmental commitment to the improvement of teaching and learning allows and can even cause innovation. Such a commitment, translated into a strategy, shares the purpose of improving student learning, but may, for example, improve communication without changing anything else. The Dearing report suggests that 'the consensus among many educators is that depth of understanding is fostered by an active approach to learning' (National Committee of Inquiry 1997a: 114) but there are three difficulties: 'educators' may or may not mean 'teachers'; large numbers of teachers do not engage in 'an active approach'; how is the transition to using an active approach best achieved? A policy or a strategy for enhanced teaching and learning can raise questions that it may not answer or address, about what and how students learn in a particular kind of encounter with the teacher, curriculum content, aim and process. The innovator of necessity goes further and creates situations in which the processes become explicit and are reconstructed. Innovators may not be clearly aware that this is what they are doing, and may deny any radical stance, but they *are* aware of going where their teaching and learning assumptions and practices have not gone before. It is possible for a generic teaching and learning strategy to benefit from and recommend the innovator's travel plan, and in some circumstances the innovator may be grateful for the change of environment that an emphasis on teaching and learning brings about.

Curriculum change has been institutionalized as long as universities have existed, but pedagogy – in either an old version of how teachers 'deliver' what they teach, or a more recent version with more interactive connotations – is a recent entrant into higher education discourse. 'Pedagogy' was a focus of research and debate in relation to schools in the United States and the UK in the 1970s particularly. There are a number of assumptions about schooling that make it possible to analyse pedagogy in terms of the 'situation' – the teacher's responsibilities, power and control, the continuity, stability and parameters of the teaching–learning relationship, the legal and social requirements placed on teacher and student. The school's 'pedagogical situation' is recognizable, and its elements were theorized in the 1970s especially in a large variety of ways, but in the UK with particular attention to issues of power and control in traditional or progressive settings and with defined student constituencies. Bernstein's influential approach to 'Class and pedagogies' (1975) and a number of authors' contributions on teaching, learning and the organization of knowledge in Young's *Knowledge and Control* (1971) and other compilations, addressed concerns about authority and control, children's behaviour and teachers' power, the ownership and transmission of knowledge (with an underlying thread relating to the pedagogue as controller). A research focus on pedagogy was paralleled and in some respects overlapped with a focus on the curriculum (for example, Stenhouse 1983; Whitty 1985; Young 1998).

There was no important attempt to carry over this or any other approach to pedagogy into higher education, and the reasons may not be far to seek. The 'situation' is not as stable and total as is that of the school, the politics of the classroom has not been the same. Teaching–learning interaction is more sporadic, and in recent decades has been basically affected, for example, by class size, modularization and extensive curriculum change, various phases of educational technology and ICT. Student learning has become a focus of research and theorizing. The dilemmas of the more complex 'situation' have been governed by policy changes, system expansion, funding issues, changes in student constituencies, the diversity of institutions and of missions. Within all of this, student learning has increasingly ceased to be the product of face-to-face teaching. It takes place not only in the lecture theatre and the laboratory, but also in the computer room, the library, the workplace, in small groups, in student-led seminars, in structures and interaction based on all the strategies subsumed under titles such as 'learner-managed learning'.

It is not too difficult in relation to higher education to theorize, for example, about the curriculum and curriculum change, about management, about the contexts of learning (from social class and gender to preparation for employment). Theorizing, as in the case of schools, about pedagogy has not been seen to be possible, and may indeed not be possible in ways conventionally associated with the term. Its conversion into the terminology of 'teaching and learning' has pointed to all kinds of issues concerning policy, strategy and their implementation, but not to any basic consideration of the teaching/learning interactions and their contexts (but c.f. Armstrong *et al.* 1997). The considerable literature of teaching and learning is therefore not about a comprehensive approach to pedagogy that addresses the linkages between teaching and learning in its 'situation'. There is a research-based literature on teaching methods and on how students learn (including their motivation, and how they are assessed and succeed or fail in the system). There is a recognition in the literature that university teachers have increasingly become 'facilitators of learning' and provide frameworks and support (Brockbank and McGill 1998). In the institutional settings described in the previous chapter it is possible to glimpse important aspects of how universities and their sub-units approach questions of teaching and learning, and though the focus here is on innovation it is important to have a perspective on these institutions as environments both for teaching and learning in general, and for innovation.

These institutional environments contain elements of innovation in teaching and learning broadly at two levels. At one level an institution or a sub-unit may be (not all are) interested in promoting or supporting innovation to serve one of a number of possible purposes, ranging from improved student learning of a particular segment of a programme to a response to national development initiatives or a response to budget difficulties. The most pervasive of these in the recent past have related to the application of ICT, but others have been directed towards, for instance, problem-based, resource-based, autonomous or open and distance learning. In the 1990s ICT was the subject of extensive policy and strategy analysis and recommendations by government and other agencies as well as by academics (for example, Committee of Scottish University Principals 1992; Laurillard 1993), with a high profile presence in the Dearing report (National Committee of Inquiry 1997a). Universities have made enthusiastic, ritualistic or reluctant responses to such developments, but having invested in them have made varied accompanying policy and strategic choices. Some have sought to encourage institution-wide adoption of the technology for teaching and learning purposes, others have relied more on the delegated authority of strong faculties, schools or departments to make their own priority decisions. All of the second-phase institutions visited have pursued policy directions relating to institutional change, whether relating to the technology, the curriculum (Europeanization, for example), staff development or rewards for 'excellence in teaching'. All are keenly aware at the policy level of the importance of teaching and learning (possibly in connection with teaching quality assessment, possibly in response to funding council or Institute for Learning and Teaching developments, possibly with longer historical explanations).

The second level, as we have seen, is that of the individual innovator or change agent, exploring new ways of handling the large class, project or group work or student seminars or presentations, and these also have an extensive recent literature. The two levels are sometimes inter-related. An institution's strategies may be heavily influenced by the work of individuals within it or seek to harness or colonize their efforts. The aim of student autonomy or student-centred learning may belong to an individual or a university committee. An individual innovator's approach may occasionally be coloured by a growing international interest in, say, 'organizational learning', or institutional strategies in other countries.

The institutions

An important element in the summaries of institutions-as-environments in the previous chapter is the growing emphasis on developing frameworks for teaching and learning. All five of the universities visited had at some point, mainly in the late 1990s, designated someone at senior level to be responsible for teaching and learning – at Glasgow, for example, a new Vice Principal (Learning and Teaching), at Middlesex the Deputy Vice-Chancellor, at The Open University a change in the distribution of responsibilities resulting in the designation of a Pro-Vice-Chancellor for Learning Technologies and Teaching. In all five cases a committee structure also targeted course quality and the intention to enhance teaching and learning. At Salford, from the time of the merger, a Teaching and Learning Committee with a Teaching Development Sub-Committee was established, and at Nottingham from the end of the 1980s a Teaching Committee and from 1995 a Teaching Enhancement Committee were also created. Out of these structures and responsibilities came policies relating to teaching and learning. Glasgow produced the discussion paper 'Towards a learning and teaching strategy for the university'. Middlesex developed a policy commitment and practical strategy for the development of students as 'autonomous learners'. The Open University developed an 'Institutional learning and teaching strategy' that was seen as becoming 'an evolutionary document'. The importance of such developments in the late 1990s here lies in the changes they represent in institutional preoccupations and therefore their implications for innovations. Policies, strategies, attitudes, implementation and support are all crucial concepts in this connection. The reasons and outcomes for the changes relate to national and domestic issues (and in the case of institutional 'strategies' they became a priority development for the funding councils). The relationship of such institutional developments to the practice of sub-units and individuals raises questions of the nature of institutional cultures, and we return to these in the next chapter.

Nottingham provides a useful point of reference here, since, as we have noted, it is a case of innovation within a context that contains strong emphases both on research and on policies and structures directed towards teaching and learning. The University's 1998 version of its *Teaching and Learning Strategy* points to academic staff being 'actively encouraged to develop existing and new approaches to teaching', and also to the provision of strong support 'whilst still being sufficiently flexible for the institution to respond rapidly to changes in the external environment' (University of Nottingham 1998: 3, 5). The complex processes at work illustrate the presence of both innovations that are the product of individual initiative and those that are part of 'guided' or 'directed' innovation relating to policy, financial or other incentives or pressures. Inevitably, in arriving at policy in this area the University's leadership and committee structure determine priorities, themselves to one extent or another in response to national policies and opportunities. The prospectus inviting bids for funding to support teaching and learning projects in 1999 reflected the substantial change from 'ground-based' applications for funding to ones 'which seek to ensure that the University is well placed to meet changing conditions over the next decade' (University of Nottingham 1999: iii). At an early stage the senior management committed itself to the use of information technology throughout the University. This is one form of 'institutional innovation', though one within which 'departmental' or even individual innovation could take place in the form of projects 'guided' or 'directed' centrally – though these and individually generated innovations may overlap considerably. Individuals, here and at other universities, find a direction for innovation, for example, in a wider programme to promote the use of computer-aided learning (CAL) or student-centred learning. Though priorities everywhere may be increasingly determined at the centre, there are funding opportunities for all kinds of innovation – including the 'blue skies' variety. Varied sub-structures also have their own priorities and provide different levels of opportunity.

Policies relating to teaching and learning can, therefore, reach in a variety of directions, including, as at Middlesex towards autonomous learners or resource-based learning that have relevance to its vision of higher education for lifelong learning: 'It will focus its efforts upon developing learning environments that foster learning and create self-motivated, self-managed and enquiring learners . . . supporting innovative methods of learning' (Middlesex University 1996: 11–12). As part of this mission Middlesex has in fact been moving resources from central services to schools in support of student-centred learning; reviewing quality assurance procedures with the aim of reducing unnecessary bureaucracy and workloads; attempting to clarify the University's position to resolve the conflict between teaching and research; reassuring staff on the outcomes of the annual promotion round, and strengthening the Centre for Learning Development. All five of the universities studied have in fact accepted, in addition to the need for explicit policies on teaching and learning, the need for strategies to develop collaborative and authoritative support mechanisms. A key role in the implementation of Nottingham's policies on teaching and learning is that of the Teaching Enhancement Office (TEO), the Director of Teaching Enhancement and the Teaching Enhancement Advisers seconded part-time to work with the TEO in the faculties. Staff views of the work of the TEO ranged from critical and neutral to highly complimentary. One described having a lot to do with TEO and its having 'quite a bit of influence'. Another thought it 'very important', with liaison very close over the implementation of the teaching and learning strategy, as well as with individual staff on projects. The Education Development Unit at Salford administers the Teaching and Learning Quality Improvement Scheme (TLQIS), which is not unlike similar funds at the other universities studied. An interesting feature of the Salford Scheme, however, is that the annual budget it currently spends on 'proposals for innovative educational development' and disseminating 'examples of innovative practice' is made up of sums from a staff development budget but also from each of the faculties. One dean commented that faculty funding of the TLQIS 'ensures their commitment'. In one department there was an internal competition, and the department 'supports one to go forward'. In another case the faculty executive acts as a general filter for bids ('but it is open to all staff to submit'). Some staff commented, however, on the lack of time to go through the application procedure, given pressures of other kinds.

Implementation of policies on teaching and learning, and staff attitudes towards them, are conditioned by a wide range of issues relating to change and the reasons for resistance. Responses to policy pressure for greater use of ICT vary from the most enthusiastic to the most sceptical or hostile. Institutional policy for teaching and learning now almost inevitably focuses to a great extent on its potential for change, including strengthening student recruitment and enhancing student attainment, and it therefore affects the climate for innovation. Even the 'lone ranger' engaged in technological innovation is subsumed in new, collective developments (Taylor 1998). The Teaching Quality Assessment of the 1990s also had varied repercussions in terms of change in teaching and learning. Some innovators thought that TQA had heightened the interest in teaching and learning. At Nottingham there was a feeling in some areas that TQA had had little effect, as the University already had good teaching methods, but some, as we have seen, thought that it had helped them to 'tidy up' what was happening. At Glasgow the TQA system was frequently described as detrimental to teaching, creating huge amounts of paperwork and stress. Some staff went further and complained that the TQA process restricted academic freedom, reduced risk-taking and inhibited innovation.

The most serious problem for innovators in this field was in those parts of universities especially dedicated to maintaining or attaining high ratings in the next Research Assessment Exercise (RAE), or in those universities where it was most clear that promotion and career enhancement depended on a strong research profile. At Nottingham and Glasgow, the two most successfully research-oriented universities studied in the second phase of this research, the balance did not widely inhibit a commitment to new initiatives in teaching, or reduce commitment to excellence in teaching. At Nottingham a commonly expressed view was summarized by one person suggesting that if one asks about the priority given to teaching and learning vis-à-vis research the answer will 'depend on which day you ask the question', and at the time it had to be the RAE. This did not prevent a search taking place for 'the most efficient use of staff time in teaching, our most important resource'. As one senior member of the University put it, emphasizing a commonly held view: 'we are a research-led university, but that gives us better teaching'. At Glasgow it was made clear that the RAE had become the priority, but that staff took their teaching seriously. Reflecting on his first year in office at the University and the emphasis on learning and teaching in the Dearing report, the Principal commented that teaching standards tolerated in the past in British universities were no longer appropriate. Commitment to research or teaching was not in fact 'an either/or option. At Glasgow they enjoy joint priority'. The University had explicitly adopted the goal of the 'well supported academic', encouraging staff to commit themselves to both teaching and research' (Davies 1997: 2–3). In the cases of Middlesex and Salford it is important to remember that their recent history of institutional mergers and the combination of traditions had helped to prolong institutional uncertainties about direction. The commitment to high quality teaching in both universities competed with pressures, which were often fragmentary and felt differently around the institution. A 1997 Salford report on promotion on the basis of teaching excellence conceded that 'it is widely agreed that, in reality, research is the dominant culture' (University of Salford 1997). Although Middlesex had defined its overall priority in terms of providing a high-quality learning experience for students and played down the centrality of research, there were still parts of the University locating development priority in research.

It is not surprising that perceptions of the value placed on teaching and learning in practice, compared with research and administrative responsibilities, differ amongst and within institutions, and even within departments (as we shall discuss further in Chapter 8). Since the lecturers interviewed in the second phase were randomly selected they were not necessarily sympathetic to innovation. Whatever their view of the immediate or wider university environment and their university's policy claims, they did, in all these universities present a uniform personal commitment to their own teaching and their students, even while describing some of the constraints. The latter are also common in higher education – 'we are crippled by marking' being a frequent theme. Although some lecturers and heads of department referred to relatively traditional teaching taking place (sometimes in the context of a variety of approaches), even then there were illustrations of how skills are incorporated, how lectures and seminars are supplemented by active workshops, or how students are challenged in one way or another. As one Salford lecturer explained: 'Even traditional lectures now involve more student presentations – they are more like workshops'.

We have discussed (in Chapter 3) some of the reasons why individuals choose to innovate. Departments are clearly likely to develop innovative or active teaching methods as a result of their subject matter and curricula – for example, in the performing arts or where fieldwork or projects are involved. Teaching methods sometimes change as a result of curriculum re-packaging due to structural changes – notably modularization and semesterization (though such changes in teaching are not necessarily innovative, and may result in reversion to more traditional methods). In both phases of this study there were examples of departmental (as well as individual) innovations, including the use of group projects and 'enterprise', 'real' or 'live' projects undertaken by students for employers or in community projects.

In some of the universities visited policy implementation for teaching and learning often appears to be extremely haphazard. Such 'policy' is sometimes equated with general statements in student handbooks or other documentation: 'There isn't an explicit teaching and learning strategy in this department, just some philosophical statements'. A department may have an away day at which teaching and learning issues are discussed, or be aware of the impact of a teaching quality assessment, or trace its teaching and learning initiatives back to the incentive provided by EHE. Confusion between institutional 'policies' and implementation 'strategies' began to be addressed by HEFCE in a consultation paper in 1998 on raising the profile of learning and teaching in higher education (HEFCE 1998), but more directly in announcing its Teaching Quality Enhancement Fund in 1999, and linking funding for each institution to its possession of an adequate learning and teaching strategy:

> *An effective learning and teaching strategy will outline what an institution wishes to achieve with regard to learning and teaching, how it will do so, and how it will know when it has succeeded.* The strategy will be designed to develop the character, and enhance the quality and delivery of learning and teaching, and to improve the educational experience of students across the whole institution. (HEFCE 1999a: 9, italics in original)

University faculties or schools may also have implementation plans, such as the 'Learning development strategy' contained in the School of Social Science 'Academic Plan' at Middlesex University. Its goal was to enhance the quality of the student learning experience and to make more effective and efficient use of staff resources. Elements in this were the establishment of a 'Core skills and capabilities strategy' for the whole School, a student 'Portfolio of core skills and capabilities', a 'Resource based and student-centred learning strategy' and a staff development strategy addressing curriculum and learning (containing a detailed practical commitment for each of these). Universities set out (as we shall see in Chapter 8) strategies for implementing promotion policies directed towards 'good teaching' or 'teaching excellence' (and sometimes relating these to innovation also).

Strategies for teaching and learning are therefore coats of many colours (often perceived by staff as either threadbare or the emperor's new clothes), but teaching and learning strategies have firmly entered macro-policy with a link to funding. The Dearing report recommended that 'with immediate effect, all institutions of higher education give high priority to developing and implementing learning and teaching strategies which focus on the promotion of students' learning' (National Committee of Inquiry 1997a: 116) – with aims strongly supported by the Scottish Committee set up by the Dearing Committee (National Committee of Inquiry 1997b: 50–2). HEFCE commissioned a report on *Institutional Learning and Teaching Strategies* (Gibbs 1999), setting out existing practice, why institutions need such strategies, mechanisms of change and ways of developing appropriate strategies. The universities visited in this study already had (in some cases long established) specific strategies aimed at such improvements, including programmes of training – some linked to certification at various levels – for new or established academic staff. Programmes of this kind were applauded or criticized for a variety of reasons, which will not be covered here. One important observation, however, is that even if these programmes encourage reflection, change and development, staff frequently found themselves constrained by departmental structures and traditions, as well as validation and assessment requirements – and of course the requirements of research. A few who move towards innovative practices do find themselves valued, particularly if their activity is reinforced by external funding. An interest in pedagogical research, perhaps focused on their own practices, is acceptable in some places, and either discouraged or prevented by some department heads or faculty deans. The relationship between policy, strategy and practice is immensely complex, and without considerable clarification may be a persistent barrier to the successful implementation of strategies elaborated at any level. Where this is understood, monitoring is an integral and prominent part of the strategy.

Although the universities visited in the first phase had been chosen because they contained significant numbers of innovators in teaching and learning, the case study visits were not intended to confirm these universities as exemplars of innovative practice. They did, however, present themselves as exemplars of commitment to 'excellence in teaching'. One of the difficulties in this discussion is, in fact, to separate emphasis on such excellence (which may mean excellence in traditional teaching methods) from emphasis on what was variously called the enhancement of, or changes and innovation in, teaching. It is important also that the 'bottom up', randomly selected contacts in the second phase consistently provided challenging insights into perceptions both of innovation and of other aspects of policy and practice in teaching and in student learning.

At Glasgow, in schools of the University, however powerful was the pull towards research, much effort went into teaching during term time. Staff were widely aware of the University's intended development of 'research-led teaching'. Although there was extensive support amongst staff for the genuineness of this commitment, there were also critical voices, notably regarding variations of attitude and practice amongst units of the University. Differences of perception could relate to promotion and status, but also to experience shaped by subject area. Perceptions of a culture relating to teaching and learning also seemed to be shaped by either length of service or recent experience elsewhere. It is important that relatively new teaching staff are less aware than others that there have been significant changes in University policy and operation, and see insufficient prominence given to teaching rather than those changes that have already taken place. New staff may bring with them experience of institutions, or units within institutions, that have moved more quickly than they may perceive to be the case at

Glasgow. Differences of views about the role of the Teaching and Learning Service in helping to implement policy and change can in part also be ascribed to differences in staff background as well as commitment to subject or research. The meanings embedded in these perceptions have an important historical dimension.

In different ways some of these factors were important elsewhere. Staff at Middlesex were often aware of different emphases on teaching and learning in different schools, reflected in the application of promotion criteria, but also related to the distribution of workloads between and within schools, the size and variation of student intake, and the ways in which the schools functioned. At Nottingham some staff saw ambiguities in the policies and their implementation with regard to teaching and learning, but others were more clearly positive. Teaching staff of all kinds clearly invested the necessary effort in their teaching, with the general aim of enabling their students to learn effectively. Some found the situation difficult, some found it enjoyable and exciting. Experienced senior staff, including distinguished research professors, were applauded for their keenness in helping to improve teaching. Younger staff were caught between the research pressures and the needs of their teaching experience – and although there was hesitation about being caught up too much in the demands of teaching, there was evidence that the initial training programme had been 'well received', and that the University's mentoring and other support was welcomed. For a 'research-driven' university, the sought-after balance between research and teaching and learning at all levels was widely endorsed, though not always for the same reasons. An interesting side-light on this issue came at a meeting to launch a new prospectus of financial support for development projects in teaching and learning. The first question from the floor asked whether the purpose of making teaching more efficient was not to make more time for research in preparation for the RAE.

As part of the national move towards greater recognition of teaching and learning, supported by the funding councils and the Institute for Learning and Teaching, many institutions were already, during the period of this study, devising their own ways of providing such recognition. In the first phase of the study there was widespread evidence of universities using excellence in teaching not only as a criterion (alone or in association with other criteria) for promotion, but also for other forms of recognition. Limited term 'teaching fellowships' or advancement up an existing salary scale were two examples. Other universities were advertising for the first time for staff, full or part time, to conduct staff development and in some cases encourage innovation. The University of Dundee was making 'honorary graduate awards for innovative teaching'. Nottingham's version of such recognition is its scheme to make up to ten 'Lord Dearing Awards for Teaching and Learning' annually (awards named after Lord Dearing not only as author of the report that had this emphasis, but also – and significantly – as Chancellor of the University). The awards consist of framed certificates presented at an annual ceremony, and nominations can be made by a head of school, a colleague or a student group. Evidence of a wide range of possible contributions to improving the teaching, learning and/or assessment of students is admissible, and the panel of judges includes student representatives. This scheme was in an early stage of introduction at the time of the second-phase visit and reception among teaching staff was muted and mixed.

Given the particular features of teaching at The Open University many of the above aspects of policy, implementation and perception do not apply in the ways we have discussed. Differences relating, for instance, to the ways in which faculties operate or subject distinctions affect approaches to teaching and learning are features of academic life at the OU as elsewhere. As we have indicated, however, the interdisciplinary basis of much course development (though not necessarily research development) can strongly militate against the rigidity of boundaries. We have emphasized earlier that two of the most distinctive aspects of the OU's approach to distance teaching and learning have been the collaborative development of courses and the public visibility of the outcomes. 'Teaching' is inseparable from the course design and production process, and the OU has invested considerably in researching how distance students learn and in applying the research. To consider in any detail how the policies, strategies, research and course development work out in relation to teaching and learning at the OU would require a separate study. Staff perceptions of these contexts for teaching and learning include some of the elements discussed at other universities, but only in limited areas, including that of research. The OU is no less amenable to change induced by external pressures than are other universities. Research, for instance, is a prominent part of the lives of many OU academics, as well as of research-oriented units, and it has become increasingly so. Some faculties have a comparatively large research income, and others have a more professionally oriented staff who do not come from a research background. The OU itself has had to think carefully about research in relation to its other activities, with the Vice-Chancellor arguing in 1999 for a strengthening of its research commitment in order to continue to place its distance learning operations 'at the cutting edge of the intellectual discourse' (The Open University, Senate 1999: 3).

Open University staff have therefore felt themselves under greater pressure to increase their research, as is the case in other universities, influencing how staff see their career development either at the OU or elsewhere, given the climate of opinion nationally about research as the route to advancement. The pervasive nature of innovation at various levels of course development and delivery gives rise to initiatives by individuals or small groups. These may be connected, given the purposes of the OU, with the technology of information for or communication with students, and the technology of monitoring and assessing students. Innovation in teaching and learning has to do with forms of supported open learning, types and uses of material, students' interaction with one another, and the induction of associate lecturers into existing and developmental roles. Innovation in teaching and learning therefore has a particular resonance at the OU.

Environments

A crucial feature of teaching and learning that emerges constantly in this study is the relationship with the interpretation of contexts. The study of institutions suggests a number of salient features of the external environment that teachers attempt to understand. The experience in recent years of TQA and the RAE (which we discuss further in Chapter 8) has brought important messages into the lives of teachers in higher education, regarding not only quality and its measurement but also the relative financial rewards to institutions and their sub-units – with the highest rewards from achievement in research. The availability of programme funding for teaching and learning projects or initiatives in defined areas, from the funding councils (for example for teaching and learning technology and computing, and in Scotland for innovative curriculum and teaching initiatives), from government departments (notably the DfEE) and from the research councils, has been a context welcome to some and posing difficulties for others who see obstacles to participation stemming from other priorities. These are just part of the context external to the institution. Within the institution teachers have to weigh the advantages of involvement with educational and staff development units and their programmes, and the attractions and burdens of available funding for innovation and development. There is no doubt that many teaching staff find difficulty in 'reading' their position amongst these competing pressures and opportunities.

Teaching staff are not, of course, always responding as individuals. Part of the context is also the unit in which they live and work, and this may be seen as the department, school or faculty as proxy for the institution, or as in the case of The Open University it may be the course team or region. This again provides situations that have to be 'read'. In the immediate context a teacher may be in dispute or conflict since there is competition for, say, department resources or support against rival bids for university funds. A teacher may similarly be out of sympathy with the department's approach to the distribution of teaching hours (for example, protecting researchers with track records) or study leave or assessment, or with a faculty's distribution of duties across different sites. On the other hand any individual teacher may become part of a unit's strategic planning for developments in teaching and learning. This is particularly the case where a radical curriculum change is adopted at, say, school or faculty level. In the Faculty of Medicine at Glasgow, for example, changes in undergraduate education from the early 1990s culminated in the design of a problem-based learning curriculum. Although a 'curriculum change', it involved considerable changes also in the ways teachers were to teach and students were to learn. It involved much debate within the Faculty of which the School is a part, since the move was away from discipline-based, and therefore what had been department-based, teaching and this had implications beyond the School and Faculty. It involved debate within the University, given that this was a major departure from common University practice. The ground was laid, therefore, for individual members of the academic staff to adapt their teaching willingly or reluctantly, or to resist change. In such strategic planning staff do retain their individuality, but are at the same time subsumed into a wider debate and response to internal and external pressures. In this case these included national moves for reform of the medical curriculum, particularly the publication by the General Medical Council of *Tomorrow's Doctors* (1993) as well as existing internal pressure within the School for the curriculum to be decongested and for other improvements in the preparation of doctors.

Something similar may be the case also in those many units in various universities that have adopted ICT strategies in relation to the delivery of courses, affecting how individuals perceive themselves within the changed environment and expectations. The environment is not only the department or the course or the school or faculty, it is also the wider university and the discipline or profession within which an academic is likely to operate. The subject and its modules are now increasingly cross-disciplinary and open to students from an increasingly diverse range of programmes. Staff therefore have comparisons of method and status to make with colleagues in other parts of the institution. They may also share the teaching of a module with colleagues from the same or another unit, and one difficulty regularly signalled in discussion was that of the younger teacher interested in adopting new methods, when co-teaching with a more senior colleague who might be resistant to change. Within a broad strategy (for example regarding final-year student projects) sub-divisions of a school or faculty may try to arrange their projects autonomously rather than as part of the larger structure. A major, nationally funded project (concerning, for example, skills or the teaching of a specific subject) within a department or school, may be widely envisaged as 'belonging' to a particular teacher or small group and either have little influence or be a source of conflict.

All of this takes us into a context for teaching and learning and innovation that is not simply located in the formalities of structure or responsibilities. Whether it is the Dearing report advocating 'the stimulation of innovation in learning and teaching' (National Committee of Inquiry 1997a: 126) or HEFCE pursuing a variety of strategies through funding for the improvement of teaching and learning at individual, subject and institutional levels, the advocacy and the policy enter a kaleidoscope of supportive and resistant attitudes. The individual innovator also has to interpret these attitudes and messages that are themselves often uncertain and unstable. At whatever level and in whatever forms, approaches to teaching and learning and to innovation are developed, debated, negotiated and resisted within a complex interplay of cultures.

6

The Culture of Institutions

Structure and culture

Innovators, like all other teachers in higher education, work within structures, though not all work with the same degree of consciousness or comfort. The relationships between teaching and learning and these encompassing structures have become particularly apparent and sensitive in a period in which most of the institutions visited (and all four of the campus universities in the second phase) have been through a period of significant restructuring. Allegiances to departments, schools and faculties have come under considerable strain. The operation of, and attitudes towards, committees, policy makers, managers and support structures have resulted in often sceptical views of their impact on teaching and learning. National assessment and funding regimes have also produced mixed, sometimes positive and often strong negative, reactions regarding the direct and indirect effects on teaching and learning. To what extent, however, do established and changing structures explain innovators' experience and the life histories of innovations?

In obvious ways they do. An innovator needing financial support for an initiative and deterred by bureaucratic structures and procedures from seeking it would be one example. The weakening of a departmental/subject commitment within an unwelcome school structure that combines disparate or even cognate subject-based departments and introduces new forms of authority and decision making would be another. Placing one's classroom or laboratory or other teaching dilemmas in the context of the development possibilities of a new national funding initiative would be yet another; as would be the relationship between staff morale and institutional strategic changes. Many of the judgements about the organizational contexts in which teachers perceive their roles have been couched in terms of increasing centralization or managerialism governing the structures. Centralization and centrally-driven policy or initiatives are seen as encouraging institutionally related directions of change, but discouraging or failing to support others held to be important in the teaching situation. Nevertheless, structures are people. People in structures debate and decide. Structural change itself is a response, generated by people, to a range of factors, including funding levels and criteria, the 'market' for student recruitment, the potential impact of performance in the RAE or teaching quality assessment. Even more widely, people in structures anticipate directions of the economy, demography, social and educational policy.

Understanding structures is important, but not sufficient. Knowledge of structures provides what one American analyst described as clues to those aspects of an organization commonly discussed in terms of 'an organizational culture – but not accurately or reliably. As a consequence, an organization's behavior cannot be understood or predicted by studying its structural or systems elements' (Ott 1989: 3). The point at issue is that of deeper insights into such behaviour that require an understanding of the basic values and assumptions, explicit or implicit, which influence people and are transmitted or modified by people in organizations. Decisions to take initiatives in teaching and learning, to sustain or abandon them, to support or discourage them, are not influenced by formal structures alone. Questions of whether an institution has 'a culture', how to define or disaggregate it and how to discuss the work of individuals in relation to it, are therefore important here, since they place innovators and teachers generally in a more interactive situation than is involved in their relations to formal structures. Although there is a voluminous literature, much of it American, on institutional or organizational culture, and much of it helpful to such a discussion, it has to be treated with some caution. It tends to derive from research on industrial and commercial firms as organizations and it is not necessarily applicable to higher education, with its different aims, constituencies, sources of finance and relationships. Important at this point is the fact that the kinds of questions asked in that literature about innovation and its contexts are nevertheless similar to the ones under discussion here.

In the universities studied in this investigation these questions produced a number of salient perceptions of what teachers and others understood by the culture of their institution, or, if different from the whole or other parts, the culture of the part with which they identified. All of this raises a preliminary question about an 'overall' culture: is it possible to talk about *a* culture? A typical definition of culture in relation to organizations reads:

> The set of values (what is good and bad) and assumptions (beliefs about human nature) that distinguishes a particular organization from others ... norms (ground rules for behavior) and artefacts (such as who gets the corner office) that guide actions in the organization. (Beckhard and Pritchard 1992: 46)

Whether sociologists, business and economics analysts and others view an organization as *having* a culture or *being* a culture, the issue of whether it is in fact possible to talk, in the singular, of the accumulated characteristics of 'a particular organization' and a 'set of values' as a culture remains the same. The issue is often resolved by allowing for different categories of organizational cultures.

One approach begins by asserting that 'organizations *are* cultures'. It treats culture as a 'metaphor of organization' and views organizations as 'patterns of meaning, values, and behaviour', all of which are amenable to change. If culture is more than just the system of planning, structures and management, it is implicit, and in order to observe it 'the researcher must find its visible and explicit manifestations' (Meyerson and Martin 1987: 623–4). These 'windows' are discussed commonly in terms of such vocabularies as 'saga, heroes, symbols, and rituals' (Masland 1985: 160). These 'patterns' and 'windows' vary by organization and category. A common typology applied to business organizations looks at four types of culture: the 'power culture', which depends on a central power source; the 'role culture', often stereotyped as bureaucracy, working with logic and rationality; the 'task culture', which is job or project oriented; the 'person culture', where structures exist only to serve professionals working in association, such as barristers' chambers or architects' partnerships (Handy 1985: 186–96). Another such attempt offering a typology of 'changing cultures of universities' divides them under four labels: collegium, bureaucracy, corporation and enterprise, all of which 'co-exist in most universities, but with different balances among them' (McNay 1995: 105–6). All such approaches accept that there is in some way a detectable culture of each institution, whether or not separable individually or by category.

At any historical moment there are, of course, ways of broadly defining general characteristics of organizations, including universities. In a memorable analysis of the American university in the early 1960s Clark Kerr highlights two clichés about it: 'the external view is that the university is radical; the internal reality is that it is conservative'. It is conservative in a dynamic environment, and historically has made serious changes only under irresistible pressure from outside (Kerr 1964: 94–108). Eric Ashby, in Britain, extended the argument a decade later, on the basis of a biological analogy:

> It is characteristic of higher education systems that they are strongly influenced by tradition. They display what a biologist calls phylogenetic inertia. This is not surprising, for one of their functions is to conserve and transmit the cultural inheritance. It is characteristic of them, too, that from time to time they adjust themselves – sometimes painfully – to the social environment which surrounds them. (Ashby 1974: 136)

An unstable equilibrium is established, often undermined and requiring attempts at a new equilibrium. By the mid-1980s the President of Harvard University was describing the American university in general terms as 'large, decentralized, informal organizations with little hierarchical authority over teaching and research' (Bok 1986: 176). Kerr and Ashby were describing an accelerating process with an international resonance, but given the directions in which state, political and public pressures were going in Britain and elsewhere Bok's description was no longer applicable to end-of-century universities in Britain and many other countries, including even swathes of universities and colleges in the United States. Such analyses are time-dependent.

Many of the approaches to organizational culture in business and industrial environments in recent decades are either not transferable to universities, or carry limited messages, given the differences. Despite the new managerialism and commercial realities, universities' funding, monitoring, professional configurations, and policy making, relationships among management, staff and students are on a different basis from that of other types of organization. In a simple sense, therefore, universities are distinctive. Their teachers have (with whatever variations) loyalties to their profession, their discipline and therefore – however much the opportunity is weakened by recent restructuring – their department or other subject unit. A 'higher education culture' may be located in the shared value of commitment to scholarship. Loyalty to the institution may be of the same order, but this may also be simply a form of connivance – in recruitment and retention of students, efforts to attract funding and to survive. The definitions are, however, elusive. An underlying, coherent, accepted set of core values such as existed in the old, small, élite university has been replaced in most institutions by the same fragmentation of values as is a feature of the society that serves the university and is served by it.

An alternative way of considering the culture of institutions in this situation is to start from assumptions about either diversity or conflict. Meek, for example, attacks contributors to discussion of norms in corporate culture as resting their analysis on the premise that 'the norms, values and beliefs of organizational members are factors that create consensus, predict behaviour and create unity'. Cultural conflict is, in fact, most obvious

> in professional organizations – large teaching hospitals, research laboratories, tertiary education institutions . . . Just because group interaction within an organization is based on norms and symbols, it does not necessarily follow that consensus and cohesion, based on shared and internalized value systems, are the result. (Meek 1988: 457–8, 461–2)

Emphasis on the increasing loss of such consensus and cohesion in the recent past is realistic, but raises the difficulty of how far to carry the interpretation of culture on this basis. A culture of diversity and conflict could point also to a culture of chaos unless there is, as some American work on higher education has particularly suggested, an accompanying understanding of the elements that help to manage chaos – a state of affairs on which to thrive, in Peters' account, or 'anarchy' as some influential contributions on higher education define it (Cohen and March 1974; Peters 1987; March and Olsen 1994).

One way of presenting the culture of an organization is through the concept of a dominant culture, which is associated most clearly in the literature with the study of 'corporate culture', which is itself sometimes related to style of leadership. In the highly competitive conditions of recent decades there has been a search for the factors that shape the successful company, enable it to innovate and secure the loyalty of its staff. One popular study of American businesses describes all of them, indeed all organizations, as possibly having a culture:

> Sometimes it is fragmented and difficult to read from the outside – some people are loyal to their bosses, others are loyal to the union, still others care only about their colleagues who work in the sales territories of the Northeast . . . On the other hand, sometimes the culture of an organization is very strong and cohesive; everyone knows the goals of the corporation, and they are working for them. (Deal and Kennedy 1988: 4)

The argument *of* a strong culture becomes an argument *for* a strong culture, for strong cultural bonds to enable what has become the dispersed, 'radically decentralized atomized organization' to hold together (ibid.: 193). Identifying what originates and frames such a dominant or strong culture has inevitably meant addressing the nature of leadership, whether central or diffused. The range of views in this connection is wide, and as with many other literatures on organizational culture, it is primarily American. At one end of the spectrum, as we have seen, is an analysis such as Schein's, affirming that organizational culture has been 'the result of entrepreneurial activities by company founders, leaders of movements, institutional builders, and social architects', and that culture changes as a result of 'the centrality of leadership – the ability to see a need for change and the ability to make it happen'. This affirmation is based within a view of the existence of dominant cultures, companies – even multi-national companies – having cultures 'that were sometimes strong enough to override or at least modify local cultures' (Schein 1985: ix–xi). A rebuttal of this view of the power of leadership expressed in these terms comes from the other end of a spectrum: 'Most anthropologists would find the idea that leaders create culture preposterous: leaders do not create culture, it emerges from the collective social interaction of groups and communities' (Meek 1988: 459).

Between such views of an organization as a 'social construction where participants constantly interpret and create organizational reality' (Chaffee and Tierney 1988: 10) and that of the creative, even heroic leader, has appeared a considerable literature exploring the relationships between different types of leadership and the cultures that they may help to create (and that can also help to create them). Fullan, in Canada, discusses change and innovation in schools and the role of the school principal as a 'collaborative leader', interpreting the pressures for change, but at the same time working to maintain stability (Fullan 1991: Ch. 8). In relation to change in the European university, de Woot argues for leadership with vision 'at every level' (de Woot 1996: 24). Cohen and March in their classic American study of *Leadership and Ambiguity* define a multiplicity of metaphors for the ways in which colleges and universities are governed (including the administrative, the democratic and the anarchic). They suggest, nevertheless, a necessarily ambiguous view of presidents, who

> come to the presidency in a manner that assures both variety and substantial normative homogeneity. Although there is a variation among them, presidents have reasonable attitudes, reasonable backgrounds, and reasonable aspirations in terms of the student population and the major participating groups in the college or university. The process is standard social filtration. (Cohen and March 1986: 29)

From a discussion of leadership at institutional level in British higher education, Middlehurst goes on to conduct an analysis of departmental headship, concluding that the necessary equilibrium between the two depends on skilful management and leadership at both levels (Middlehurst 1993: Ch. 7). The analysis of leadership, viewed in these examples on different bases, is not necessarily the same as an analysis of a strong culture. The two were often coupled, however, in the discussions conducted in the samples of innovators and universities for this study.

Subcultures

A crucial constraint on the formal cultural profile of a higher education institution is the proliferation of academic disciplines on which it is based. One of the clear outcomes of recent work on academics in higher education is an emphasis on the generally primary commitment to their discipline (or in many cases sub-discipline). One of the most vivid descriptions in the United States is that of Burton Clark, discussing 'the organization of the system around subjects' and 'the ascendance of disciplinary cultures and subcultures, now catching the attention of researchers internationally'. Looking at the 'factory floor' of higher education, 'what we see are clusters of professionals tending various bundles of knowledge' and it is this concentration on knowledge that academics have most in common – though 'common knowledge' is what they have least in common (Clark 1984: 107–9). Although academics' work is organized in other dimensions also, it is this disciplinary fracturing that tends to command the main loyalty and to determine national and international networks. Clark goes further: 'With work organized by subject, disciplines that rationally pursue their individual objectives encourage their departmental representatives to turn nominally unitary universities and colleges into confederative gatherings' (Clark 1987: 147). Loyalty to the subject is also loyalty to the department as proxy for the subject, and comes face to face with some of the restructuring that sees substructures as serving other purposes.

It is not surprising if greater centralization of policy making and authority and the combining of subjects, with or without a departmental boundary, into larger and stronger schools and faculties give rise to the kind of tensions and uncertainties we have seen in this study. It can also account for resistance to change. Becher, in Britain, looked at the various possible reasons for such resistance and suggested, from his research into academic communities, one 'straightforward motive . . . for standing out against new ideas':

> In many fields it takes time and trouble to acquire the necessary expertise to make a significant research contribution. People who have spent some years . . . building up the vocabulary and conceptual structure demanded of a specialism in mathematics such as homotopy theory, or undergoing training in Freudian psychoanalysis in order to use it as an approach to literary criticism, understandably see themselves as being committed to a sizeable intellectual investment. (Becher 1989: 72)

Van Vught in the Netherlands similarly discusses 'knowledge areas' as the 'building blocks' of higher education, shaping the typical organizational structure of institutions, where 'fragmentation is abundant' (Van Vught 1989: 258). Disciplines culturally transect institutional culture and the higher education system. As subcultures they are likely to change less radically than the institutions and systems that build on them.

The case studies

It is important to follow through how these interpretations of organizational or institutional culture and its components and constraints match our case studies of the five universities and the perceptions of their academic and managerial staff. This will bring back into the discussion the understandings of teaching and learning, research and the operation of university structures. At the core of the discussion, as of all approaches to institutional culture is the rapid change that has taken place in recent decades in assumptions about participation in or membership of an 'academic community'. The notion of community – used exclusively of scholars, or inclusively of students and all other members of an institution – also reaches out into changes in assumptions about the aims of higher education and its institutions. These wider changes and assumptions are reflected in this analysis, but are not the focus of the discussion.

Middlesex

At Middlesex University responses to a question about institutional 'culture' or 'subcultures' generally focused on the prevalence and impacts of rapid change, including the outcomes of recent restructuring. For some respondents, culture was in fact equated with how the institution decided on and managed change. Middlesex, as we have seen, has undergone, and is still undergoing, what one senior member of staff described as a 'transition', and many of those interviewed pointed to the difficulty of keeping up with the 'current reality'. A good deal of this difficulty was seen as resulting from ways in which restructuring was managed, and there was some feeling that Middlesex was probably not unlike other 'new' universities in this respect. Discussion of these difficulties often focused on the tension perceived between research and teaching, though the University's approach to research was predicated strongly on support for learning. The reception of this policy on research 'that supports learning' indicates, as at other universities, the power of sub-units and individuals to implement central policy differentially, depending partly on the preferred strategy of a school or the academic group, partly on individual preference and interpretation of the motives behind the policy.

This had also been a feature of Middlesex University's history, employing younger, research-oriented staff from other universities, working alongside older staff who had been under pressure to develop research, and all of whom were being asked to give greater attention to the processes of teaching and learning. Some staff saw a division between researchers and teachers, some received mixed signals – deriving, as they often saw it, to a large extent from the zigzags of policy and its formulation since university designation in 1992. Where there was a strong research group in a specific subject area within a school the tension was most apparent. In some schools of the University lack of a research tradition or a poor rating in the last RAE had reformed the 'school culture' – either in the direction of a better performance next time, or in line with University policy to support teaching with appropriate research. In the latter case there was mention in one school of 'very small residual opposition to "utilitarian research"'. Much of the literature on innovation and change points to resistance by established 'traditional' staff (Clark 1987; Becher 1989; Burton and Haines 1997), but this does not seem to be as important in a university that is less research-oriented than those analysed in most of the literature. Resistance to and uncertainty about policy and what it reveals about the institution come from various directions and are more a feature of rapid change than embedded values.

Comments by staff about the University's 'culture' and its meaning to those who work in it differed amongst those at the same level of seniority, and in the same school as well as in different schools. Within one school it was said by one curriculum leader to be 'exciting, there are people in the institution with progressive ideas' (though there was a core who saw the curriculum as having been diluted and who had not taken on board what one person described as 'the aspect of increasing student diversity'). In the same school a senior lecturer described the job as 'satisfying, working with great people' (though with a lot of pressure as a result of increased student numbers). A senior lecturer in another school thought the work was 'interesting, stimulating, hectic' and that he had a lot of control over his own work with a high degree of autonomy and power. A lecturer in the same school 'feels privileged' to work at Middlesex. Another thought it was 'a very challenging place to work', but found the consultation process sometimes 'frustrating and exhausting'.

In these schools there were criticisms of what teaching staff often saw as the impact of University 'centralization' or 'bureaucracy', including the lack of campus identity for some students and a lack of collegiality, 'which has an impact on delivery and teaching methods'. Whilst making some strong criticisms of the institution one lecturer said that 'the immediate environment is brilliant', and that she enjoyed working there, with support- ive colleagues. Such perceptions may be analysed in terms of individuals, their personalities and status, backgrounds and aspirations. Alternatively, or additionally, they can be explored within subject and site cultures. They can be set in the context of more general reflections on University culture offered by several of those interviewed:

> There is a culture of innovation in teaching and learning led very much by the Deputy Vice-Chancellor . . . It comes across very clearly, creates an environment, legitimizes and encourages . . . It is a fragmented culture, however, not present throughout the University . . . (Dean)

> It doesn't strike me that there is a University culture. Areas are dif- ferent, do need to develop in different ways, but central control is a strong feature. (Director of curriculum, learning and quality)

> The 'culture' of the school relates to its changing age structure . . . The increasing proportion of younger staff has worked well with the older staff. Restructuring has gone well, though there are still some 'teething problems'. (Director of curriculum, learning and quality)

> The University is planning to become more corporate at the end of the process but . . . there is an intrinsic tension. Schools have more auto- nomy, funds are devolved to them . . . The position is one of centralism plus devolution . . . The centre keeps reminding everyone it is one institution. School cultures are variable . . . Middlesex as an entity is influenced by its ex-polytechnic history, which is stronger in some schools than in others. (Professor)

The contexts that staff recognize and accept, resist, seek to influence or turn aside from are complex and intricate. Structures may offer clues but are not themselves explanations. Strong central control structures, for example, may be welcome as a stabilizing and encouraging presence, or are seen as bureaucratic and authoritarian. Substructures may themselves be subcultures or may accommodate further group subcultures, where 'the people discover, create, and use culture, and it is against this background that they judge the organization of which they are a part' (Van Maanen and Barley 1985: 51).

The problem with such approaches is that, for whatever level of culture or subculture, they posit shared values, norms and assumptions. Between and within these levels, however, the culture is often, as in the case of Middlesex, the 'unsharing' of values, differences of perception, misreadings of policy or happenings, struggles to understand. If there is *a* culture or multiple cultures within an institution it, or each of them, is as much a pattern of uncertainties and disagreements as it is one of common assumptions. The crucial and very clear message from all levels at Middlesex was the sense that a 'culture' of the organization could only be sensibly discussed in terms of 'change', its directions and implications. Academic staff related most salient issues to that focus and only incidentally to the longer history or identity. Often, however, they identified their unit culture with either the subject or the site, and addressed the ways in which institutional policies and expectations were translated into their local reality, including its management and the preservation of any sense of 'community'.

Salford

The University of Salford had also been through a period of changing realities and searches for identity. Restructuring was a continuing part of the attempt to make the University more responsive to the aims it was defining for itself. Given that restructuring of some kind was a feature of other universities visited, the reservations or opposition to structural changes at Salford were not unusual. Such reservations were often based, with strong emphasis, on distinctions between departmental or disciplinary loyalty on the one hand, and institutional objectives on the other hand – including their embodiment in the creation of larger schools. Anxieties among academic staff related more often than not to these competing loyalties and to uncertainty about the directions in which organizational change pointed.

Since differences of emphasis between teaching and learning and research had been highlighted in the institutional merger and later developments at Salford, the cautious but strong policy focus on research as the dominant culture was inevitably, though with differences, in many people's minds when approaching the issue of organizational culture. Research-oriented staff would accept the policy statement that 'research is the main feature which distinguishes universities from other institutions of higher and further education and which distinguishes universities from one another' (University of Salford 1997: 17). As a justification of Salford's efforts to establish itself more firmly in the national research picture, this also raised difficulties for those staff who did not have a research background and saw themselves as undervalued in the culture of the University. Salford's commitment to industrial and community partnerships, important as they were, figured less prominently in discussions of culture than did the issue of research.

The various forms of commitment to the management and enhancement of teaching and learning were important components of the discussions. It is difficult, however, to take responses in terms of policy, strategy and action and translate them into a culture. How these are debated, developed and perceived within subject-based and cross-disciplinary units and groups helps to shape the cultural explicitness of the organization. One approach to

Salford in this respect is to accept the possibility of something that we might call a 'culture of extreme diversity', linked to continuing historical institutional characteristics, and the focus of sustained pressures as changes take place. Centrally, the directions may concern levels of recruitment, financial viability and institutional survival, and these may be intended to accompany fairness and support for students and staff. Staff respond with understanding or suspicion, but any distrust is accompanied by loyalty to courses and to students, to subject and to the possibilities of initiative and change. The thrust to the world outside is reflected most explicitly in engineering, business and other strongly employment-oriented areas, but the entrepreneurial focus is the subject of mixed views in other areas.

This raises the important question of department, school and faculty cultures, a question widely commented on in the interviews. The dean of one faculty said: 'there *is* a faculty culture, departments decidedly belong, it is not just a random collection of departments, though that seemed so at the beginning'. Nevertheless 'the department is the main loyalty base'. What was distinctive about the department, commented a lecturer in another department, was 'its sense of collegiality', in danger of being lost in the new structure. Positive comments about the department related to this sense of loyalty to it – as proxy for the discipline – and the consequent traditional identification of the department with the social advantages of the small unit. The split that there had been between the research institutes and the teaching departments could raise a tension in this respect. One lecturer explained: 'There are pressures from the institute to do research and make us think like an individual, whereas the department needs teachers and makes us think like a team'. The culture of the department was very strongly influenced by the style of the department heads, described in discussions on an axis from, at one end, friendly and open to ideas about teaching, and at the other end lack of interest in teaching and concentration on research. Staff attitudes to the institution were therefore also influenced by the operation of the department, and perceptions of what the 'centre' was doing to it. Whether they approved of their department or were critical of it, it was generally speaking where staff felt they 'belonged'.

Perceptions from the faculty level, however, could be different. Departmental boundaries could be seen as artificial and capable of being 'packaged' with opportunities and disadvantages in a variety of ways (and often arousing opposition to the particular packaging being adopted). Cultural differences between the faculty and the University were obviously in some cases a residue of pre-merger differences: 'This faculty has a separate culture from the rest of the university. The very strong clash of cultures from 1996 is still around'.

The institutional culture has changed four times in the past 20 years. First there were the 1981 cuts, with the V-C as a heroic figure, saved the University and did radical restructuring. Next came a V-C moderator, who stabilized the University and brought about the merger. Then there was the merger itself. Now comes restructuring. The culture is not just driven by the V-C. A number of competing cultures wax and wane . . . People are continually striving to apply their definition of what the university is. There are always dominant coalitions, but their membership changes, and the culture they subscribe to changes. (Senior lecturer)

Salford is like an old university in that you are appointed to a post for a number of years, but there is a cultural shift going on, a compromise. Market forces have moved us towards the ethos of the former University College and the College of Nursing . . . Old university culture is a traditional community of academics . . . do research when one chooses, publish and eventually retire. (Dean)

These are attempts to reflect on what they see as the constant kaleidoscope of an institution under perpetual internal and external pressures.

The culture of a university like Salford has almost inevitably to be disaggregated into interlocking subcultures. There are, of course, shared values that one would hope are representative of higher education in general – such as commitment to critical scholarship, professional responsibility and successful student experience. It is not clear that these can represent a kind of cultural superstructure, and by its very nature the University cannot be homogeneous enough to represent such a culture. The University's recent history explains why this is particularly so at Salford, but other universities are not very different. At faculty, department or school level it may be easier to recognize research, enterprise or external partnership as approximate shared visions. Given the rate of change, the cultural contexts of teaching and learning are most usefully approached in two ways: first, the complex and confusing accounts that people construct of institutional behaviours, and second, the most local, most immediate environment – which may itself be a stage for complexity and conflict. Perhaps the best final word at Salford is that of the dean who, having commented on the nature of the recent restructuring, deduced that now 'there will be a renegotiation of cultures'.

Nottingham

The notion of a dominant culture fits the University of Nottingham more easily than Middlesex or Salford, although its absorption of a school of nursing has raised some similar questions. Given its national and international research profile, this permeates the University. Although in many respects it is in competition with teaching, there is a considerable and widely accepted effort in the University to ensure that research coexists with and underpins teaching. Contemporary conditions make for much of the confusion and tension that exist in higher education. The 'teaching-and-research burden', as one head of school described it, 'does cause immense strain. New staff know that they need to attract research grants as well as completing the

Postgraduate Certificate in Academic Practice (PGCAP) and doing their lecturing'. The pattern of TQA-plus-RAE-plus-PGCAP could nevertheless be a useful one: 'at different times it is necessary to make time for one or another'. At senior management levels commitment to quality teaching was seen as 'a moral duty to students', but despite this commitment, research is undoubtedly seen by staff as the overwhelming basis on which they are judged. Nationally, the question of support for teaching and learning provided on a subject basis has been addressed prominently and securely by HEFCE's subject-based programmes (beginning with Fund for the Development of Teaching and Learning (FDTL) and continuing through subject support centres and other means of supporting teaching improvement). How far such strategies can impinge on Nottingham (as on other universities) is not clear, since, as one senior manager put it, 'there *is* a conflict of loyalties towards the institution and the discipline'. Research and research-based teaching make this subject identity inevitable, and it is reflected in the way Nottingham's Teaching Enhancement Office bases much of its activity on working closely with faculties and schools.

The structures and procedures for quality assurance also have potential for confusing or fracturing the culture of the institution. We have previously noted a warning in one meeting against Nottingham ruling by 'central diktat' as was suspected of being the case in the new universities, but 'we cannot allow everyone to "do their own thing"', as could become the case in the transition from the former TQA procedure to a new 'continuation audit' process. The relevant structures and people responsible are having to tread carefully between the two extreme options of 'diktat' and anarchy. The importance of such processes lies in the background of what many have seen as an increasingly 'institutional' rather than 'sub-institutional' culture, more hierarchical, more centralized, more managerial, less consensual, less collegial. Such perceptions were not uniform, but they did often surface in discussion. In some cases they were directed at specific, centrally determined policies, in others against the general climate in which the University operated. A school culture could sometimes be described as informal or democratic at the same time as central management was seen as more prescriptive. Many interviewees were aware of radical changes that stemmed from the strong leadership of the Vice-Chancellor. Even such leadership could be perceived in different ways, helping to move the University from a 'staid' to a more dynamic culture, as providing a vision, as strongly supporting the teaching function of the University alongside that of research, or as interpreting the University in more managerial terms. There was certainly a widespread sense that, for whatever reason, the University was being driven more 'from the centre'.

A culture is, however, more than these features and perceptions. It has to do with the certainties and confusions members (if that is how they see themselves) feel in their membership of all the parts of the institution and the system in which they operate – including a school, a committee and a professional or a disciplinary association. It is important to retrieve from the complexities the sense that within all the constraints staff enjoy what they do. They have confidence in their ability to provide what students need, and within limits to couple the importance of their teaching with that of their research. It is not unusual regarding issues of institutional culture for differences of perception between newer and more long-serving staff to be visible. Younger and less experienced staff feel the tensions acutely and do not have a sense of relevant institutional history. It took an experienced and senior member of staff to describe the University of Nottingham of some years ago: it used to be 'extremely dozy, self-satisfied, middle of every table, safe, saw a great virtue having huge financial reserves and an established clientele. There was no reason for change'. The cultural shift had been the outcome of a combination of changes resulting from the historical circumstances of the 1990s, and initiatives by the Vice-Chancellor. A settled culture had been eroded.

Glasgow

The directions being taken, planned or under discussion at the University of Glasgow concern structures and processes that are an important environment for innovation. With implications not unlike those at the other universities, change was an important element in discussions of organizational culture. It was difficult, however, to detect how deep and radical proposed changes intend to be or are able to be. Despite the many clues that emerged it was not possible to make reliable judgements about the strength of some of the shaping forces of the University, including what some felt to be a conservative underpinning to its cultural patterns. This is important for understanding judgements regarding the present and future position of learning and teaching, commitment to which is generally held to be a crucial feature of the culture of the University. Argyris and Schön established an important and influential distinction between 'single- and double-loop learning'. By single-loop learning 'we mean instrumental learning that changes strategies of action or assumptions underlying strategies in ways that leave the values of a theory of action unchanged . . . the values and norms . . . remain unchanged'. By double-loop learning 'we mean learning that results in a change in the values of theory-in-use, as well as in its strategies and assumptions . . . in such a way as to lead to change in the values of organizational theory-in-use' (Argyris and Schön 1996: 20–1). In both individual and organizational learning this is an important distinction. Changing strategies and assumptions and changing values may be simultaneous or consecutive processes, and the latter may simply not occur. The 'transitional' status of aspects of Glasgow's organizational culture appears to involve 'single-loop' changes, but it is not clear how far changes can go across the University as a whole.

The culture of the University was often associated with the nature of 'leadership', which might be identified with the steer provided by the

Principal, the role of the recently appointed Vice-Principal with responsibility for learning and teaching, the roles of Senate and its senior committees, and delegated powers – particularly of deans. Not all writers on leadership agree on how or whether it operates to change institutional culture. Some would see a need for ways of changing values before radical changes can be introduced, otherwise there is the problem of attempting to impose innovation without internal receptivity (Kimberly 1981; Rutherford *et al.* 1985). Others see as a central feature of leadership 'the ability to see a need for change and the ability to make it happen. Much of what is mysterious about leadership becomes clearer if we separate leadership from management and link leadership specifically to creating and changing culture' (Schein 1985: xi). Such formulations isolate a view of reality that does not seem to fit Glasgow. Here the process has been one of some complexity, involving incremental experience and pressure; critical national and institutional changes making it possible to proceed more rapidly and differently; identifying and consolidating a constituency of 'change agents', and action taking account not of institutional culture, but of the variety of institutional subcultures, together with central attempts to make things happen. Policy changes and organizational cultural changes emerge as interlocking 'top down' and 'bottom up' processes. 'Creating and changing culture' is not simply the result of some preliminary process of changing values, nor of 'leadership' intervention.

There is a certain ambivalence about the power of faculties, the leadership of which may see them as less powerful than elsewhere because the 'move to managerialism' was more recent at Glasgow than many other places, yet also as the locus of decision making on serious issues. We have seen, however, the powerful emphasis on the role of the department in teaching and learning and as a crucial environment for innovation. It is therefore the department that is the focus for discussion of the cultural contexts perceived by teaching staff. Central University intervention has not significantly altered the role of the department in representing the subject and protecting the loyalty of teaching staff to it. Senior managers recognized the strength of the discipline base. Many members of staff were engaged in Scottish or wider disciplinary networks. Staff development activities, including those of the Teaching and Learning Service, were seen by interviewees as most effective when carried out in conjunction with individual departments. The boundary is particularly strong round units (as much a school or a faculty in this case) concerned with professional preparation, as was particularly evident in Dentistry and Medicine and national discussions concerning their curricula (for example, CVCP Independent Task Force 1997; General Dental Council 1997). This, again, leads into the international literature concerned with areas of knowledge as 'building blocks', and disciplines and fields as 'social communities with their own history, language, values and norms' (Van Vught 1989: 258, 264, citing Boys *et al.* (1988)). It is in these sub-groups, to repeat a comment previously quoted, that people 'discover, create, and use culture, and it is against this background that they judge the organization of which they are a part' (Van Maanen and Barley 1985: 51). Subject-based departments have their own cultural identities, also described in the United States as a form of 'quiet fanaticism' (Clark 1984: 107–9). This is true of the working of sub-units at Glasgow, but it also matches a wider British experience.

The Open University

We have emphasized that discussions of The Open University involve elements prominent at other universities, but also some that characterize the quite different history and forms of operation of the OU. Interviews at the University offered some interesting perspectives on the culture of the University and reports of the notes taken on some of these can usefully be quoted at length:

> There is a strong ideological framework in operation. There is a heavily consensual system because openness and distance are embedded in the system. It also has something to do with where people feel they belong, and they might feel they belong to a department or a faculty or a region. There are few people who don't get the 'OU thing', which has to do with innovative curricular development that involves new thinking and constant re-examination . . . There is not such a strong subject loyalty as in other places because research boundaries at the OU are not so fixed. OU academics are more hybrids. (Sub-dean)

> There is more than one culture – including administrative and academic. Large numbers think that it is research that matters but still sign up to the OU's mission. Most would say that their commitment is to students. The experience of working in the OU is of endless debate and discussion. Academics have lots of scope for change and acting on their own initiative, but those in administration have a more rigid experience. (Pro-Vice-Chancellor)

> The OU is a captivating place. The staff turnover is very low. There are massive organizational structures. On the one hand the decision-making process is democratic – we need to consult the world and his wife, but finally the power is vested in people like myself. Sometimes it is necessary to be very authoritarian, because of the horrendous deadlines, and some staff feel as if change is inflicted on them. (Dean)

> The OU has founded its reputation on being innovative – it is in the blood. This is an infectious atmosphere where new members of staff come in and work on course teams that are always trying to do something new. There are no lecturers employed in this faculty who do not work on a course team in some capacity. Course teams used to be much more laissez-faire, now they feel much more linked with the whole

higher education system. Distance learning is becoming more prevalent. (Sub-dean and course chair)

There are two aspects of culture, the ideology and mission or vision, which is a shared value, and also the immediate environment. The first is what we are here for. The second will depend on who you talk to. A lot of people don't know who the PVCs are, what the Academic Board does. Probably only 10 per cent of academics take part in University-wide workshops. (Pro-Vice-Chancellor)

The OU has many different cultures, but one thread that runs through is a real commitment to students, student-centredness. Technology is a sub-culture, it is a controversial area with some who think it can resolve everything and some who don't want us to do it at all . . . Graduation ceremonies are special, they connect everyone, there is a real sense of achievement shared by students, associate lecturers, central academics. There *is* a core culture, which is coherent to the whole University. (Regional staff)

Neil Costello's earlier study of the OU as an insider, noted importantly in 1992:

A strong over-arching culture exists in the university . . . However, it became clear from the research interviews that the organizational distinctions . . . were also the repositories of significant cultural differences . . . a multi-cultural analysis would capture the richness of the University more thoroughly and . . . we must consider the features of different sub-cultures. All parts of the University are influenced in substantial ways by the over-arching culture but there are significant differences between the broad sub-cultures . . . The predominant culture is one in which issues are put on the table for debate and where debate is expected before decisions are taken . . . Partly the OU position arises from the undoubted pleasure which comes from teaching enthusiastic, committed adult students, and partly it comes from the University's mission as a university providing opportunities for educationally under-privileged people. A high proportion of the University's staff, at all levels, readily volunteer their commitment to such values. (Costello 1992: 22–4)

Costello's 'broad sub-cultures' relate to the creative areas (typified in our discussion here by the course teams), the operations and administrative divisions (including materials production and the processing of student assignments), and the regional organization. It is clear, however, that there are other possible typologies of subcultures – for example, research oriented and non-research oriented, pro- and anti-technology. One head of department thought that 'there *is* a departmental culture, though it does not come through very strongly'. There were differences, not only based on research, between the 'more academic' faculties and those more involved with professional preparation.

There is, however, a sense in which an 'over-arching' culture can coexist with a culture of difference. One active course member and chair commented that 'there is enough freedom in the system so that people can attach themselves to projects. People want to work on new things and there needs to be enough slack in the system to enable them to do so . . . The institutional culture is a collaborative culture'. There are two ways of interpreting a collaborative culture within a system described in this way. Collaboration may mean subscription to the basic, shared values of the University, alluded to by some commentators. Collaboration in this sense surmounts more 'minor' differences and criticisms. However, a collaborative culture may also mean a 'distributed' collaboration, in the sense that each course team, or department or whatever is an essentially collaborative but discrete unit, with its own subject, ideological or other parameters. Both meanings point to the need of the culture and the subcultures to overcome or manage conflict. The latter meaning appears to imply a tolerance of fragmentation, but this would be a superficial reading. As we were reminded in various ways the OU can only operate on the basis of the interdependence of its parts, the stronger-than-elsewhere interdisciplinary work of its teams, within what one senior manager called the OU's 'heavy freight of idealism'.

Concepts are not constant, though some are more so than others. Staff were described as 'dedicated', but dedication in an older sense may be modified by newer pressures for research, or by an atmosphere of constraints within which risk-taking becomes a weaker component of dedication. The University describes itself as 'open' in a number of senses, one of which is 'open as to people'. Openness, as was explained in one discussion, is a key value of the OU, but the University has hitherto seen itself as *passively* open. The assumption has been that any student can come, but there are obstacles and what is needed is the more active establishment of the conditions that can enable students to come. The organizational culture of the OU, it was emphasized, should be more about 'how to *deliver* openness'.

Despite the emphasis on interdependence, it was also clear that there are difficulties in achieving cross-faculty collaboration: 'Most faculties would not dream of going to another for advice about some new idea, even though they may have tried something similar, so there is some reinventing of the wheel' (a familiar situation in other universities). In such cases both innovation and collaboration lose some of the assumed meanings, affecting the analysis of cultures and frameworks. There exist what appear to be constant paradoxes, built into the recent history. In one faculty the comment was made that 'the culture has changed over the last 20 or so years, it has become more cost-conscious and cost-efficient . . . The University is a hybrid involving an academic sub-culture and a producer/publisher one . . .' In the same faculty a stern critic of aspects of the University felt nevertheless that in his experience 'there *are* innovative reflexes', and he was totally committed to it as a 'wonderful institution'.

The vocabulary in which to describe an institutional culture at the OU is in some of its features not unlike that used of other institutions, and given the importance of the OU in the overall picture of higher education in the UK it is worth setting out the main elements:

- a set of central ('over-arching') values to which most staff are strongly committed, expressed most frequently in terms of commitment to students and to the OU's 'mission';
- an array of 'immediate environments' to which staff are dedicated with varying degrees of strength (an array within which staff may also make unstable choices of where 'to belong');
- an increasing contest between individually controlled choices and institutional or sub-institutional pressures (relating to research in particular);
- a culture of the tolerance of diversity, on which the University tries to build, but around which it has increasingly to impose frameworks, stemming from various internal and external factors (expressed most directly in terms of financial constraints and planning needs);
- an understanding of the differences between the OU's practices (in course preparation, teaching and innovation) and those of other institutions of higher education, although with a sense of convergence as distance learning becomes more 'prevalent';
- a sense of both threat and opportunity in cumulative changes relating, for example, to course teams, collaboration of other kinds, relationships amongst 'broad subcultures', the ability to carry through 'innovative reflexes', the impact of technology as a catalyst of change and the strength of the centralizing impulse.

The OU illustrates the possibility of an influential institutional culture within which strong subcultures also exist. The commitments of the participants, in all areas of activity in the University, to the central values and to their immediate working environments, are in many respects greater than in the campus universities visited. If other universities reveal a 'core culture' it tends to be of a different kind – including research-orientation in some, regional or community-orientation in others. Inner-city post-1992 universities have competed successfully with the OU in attracting educationally disadvantaged and mature students, and change at the OU is partly in response to these and other changes in the 'market'. It is difficult to compare the OU with other universities. It is, however, an important case study in British higher education of how 'innovative reflexes' can (but may not always) inform development; how collaborative processes work and their relationship to established procedures; and how balances between the priorities of individuals and the institution are struck. Above all perhaps it illustrates how staff, even when critical of aspects of it, can remain 'locked on to the University's mission and its heavy freight of idealism'. In some senses, as was claimed in discussion, the OU represents a culture 'stronger than anywhere else' in higher education.

Perceptions

The experience of these five institutions suggests that innovation depends on a configuration of vital elements: how an institution's culture is interpreted by a range of constituents; the degree of conflict and consensus within it; the pattern of attitudes within which initiatives are received; the nature of and reasons for change and the ways in which it is managed; relationships between the centre and the periphery; and views of what needs to be sustained, adapted or abandoned in the historical moulding of an institution and its substructures.

The perceptions articulated by teaching staff in relation to institutional cultures and subcultures, of change and its causes and management – and in some cases of failure to change adequately or at all – seemed to be strongly influenced by age, length of service and experience of other institutions. Leadership and perceptions of leadership both proved to be more important in relation to institutional culture and to teaching and learning within it than was originally assumed in conducting this study. Amongst structural factors the most striking one was the importance attached to the department or other basic unit. However, the distance generally felt by teaching staff from 'the university', 'the institution' or 'the culture of the institution' was great, and it is this distance – in higher education as in other organizations explored in the literature of corporate culture – that is the main basis for what are often identified as myths and symbols (for example, Allaire and Firsirotu 1984; King and Anderson 1995). This may apply to familiar symbols to do with parking or architecture or dress codes, but both symbols and myths may surround the promotion and reward system, the decision-making system, the interpretation of policy. Departments are the real presence and filter of wider institutional behaviours and meanings (schools are too recent a phenomenon in the case study universities to have such a clear role). An important role in many cases is played by the faculty dean as the go-between of centre and periphery. Given these diverse maps of the ways institutions work and are perceived, including the tensions that pull in many directions, teaching staff have understandable difficulties in locating themselves and their approach to teaching and learning, and in some cases innovation, in an 'institutional culture'. Such difficulties can engender anything from apathy to cynicism towards the institution, but, in the case study universities it is important to repeat, not towards the teaching interaction with students.

7

Enabling and Inhibiting

Innovation and community

Within organizational or institutional cultures there are different balances of forces encouraging and resisting particular kinds of initiative and change in general, balances that Becher describes as 'the apparent coexistence of radical chic with entrenched conservatism' (Becher 1989: 71). Becher's focus, like that of most commentators, is on the latter, on 'inborn' resistance to new ideas or ways in which 'chic' is neutered by establishments. What this study suggests is that the conditions of recent years have made it more difficult to judge whether there are impermeable cultures of resistance to change. Not only do patterns of innovation change, but so also do the roles of policy makers and the structures they inhabit. Entrenched conservatism is not necessarily located in leaderships and establishments, but is also distributed unevenly around institutions. At all levels of the universities studied people have had to come to terms with increasingly strong and frequent pressures for change. Although they have responded in widely different ways they have had to recognize that their 'radically chic' colleagues, in however small or large a minority, and wherever they are to be found in the institutional diagram, have some sort of legitimacy within national trends. Radical change, of course, is not necessarily innovative, and the directions of national movements for change are not necessarily welcome to innovators and change agents. Something, however, has been happening. Change has been inescapable at most levels of most institutions.

We have seen the paradox that more centralization has been accompanied by a sense of more directions and more confusion. While there have been kaleidoscopic shifts the same pieces of the patterns have been discernible as one moved from campus to campus (though there are other universities not included in this study that have not necessarily experienced the same sort of kaleidoscope). Locating the factors that enable and encourage or inhibit innovation involves the institutional and departmental cultures we have discussed, and within them various balances of community and conflict, and the persistence and evanescence of opportunities and support.

A crucial feature of this study, as we have underlined, has been the link between innovation and the nature and direction of institutional change. The ways in which change is managed are identified by innovators as closely related to encouragement or inhibition. It has been important for this discussion to distinguish between abrupt structural changes and the more complex and difficult changes in institutional culture, which is rooted in tradition and personal and group interest. Lueddeke suggests:

> Effecting change relating to teaching or curriculum improvement at a fundamental or cultural level in higher education is difficult. Vested interests, inertia, clinging to existing satisfactions and role ambiguity all play their part . . . Many organisations that have reached organisational 'maturity', which seems to be the case for the 'older' universities, are finding that their 'culture becomes a constraint on innovation' and that this state may lead to decline of markets and increasing internal stability or stagnation. (Lueddeke 1997: 163)

It is, however, only certain kinds of innovation with certain kinds of institutional implications that are perceived by managers as contributing to institutional progress in the academic market-place. Where a culture of innovation becomes at all visible it goes beyond this limited perception and embraces innovation as relevant to the whole identity of the institution or the unit. Innovation in this case is recognized as directly relevant to interactions amongst teachers, students and learning environments. Its launch and trajectory depend on the professional confidence of teachers and the way this is created and renewed in the circumstances. Innovation confronts concerns about the implications for all participants of consultation on the implementation and impact of change, and their relevance for established individual, group and institutional identities. Institutionalized change can prevent innovation, promote a narrow understanding of the levels at which innovation is desirable, or enhance innovation opportunities at all levels.

What encourages and inhibits innovation is to be found, therefore, in the cultural environment of the institution. This environment used to be spoken of in terms of 'community', the identifying concept – often idealized – of a university. However trimmed and modified, the concept remains present to varying extents, from its strong emphasis in the Oxbridge college or the religious seminary to the struggle to keep alive what remains of the attempts at coherence of more recent generations of university foundations – redbrick, plateglass or some other version of what came to be known as 'higher education' in the second half of the twentieth century. The subuniversity 'college' concept copied by York or Kent at Canterbury in Britain, or by the 'cluster colleges' plan of Santa Cruz in California, was an attempt to preserve within the mounting increase of scale the core values and experience of 'community' or 'collegiality'. The residential unit was intended to enable people to know one another on a sustained basis, to trade academic debate or gossip, and enjoy a 'manageable' environment.

The Oxbridge model, and to some extent the nineteenth-century college or university, offered versions of community within which the elements of their culture were easy to understand – a shared recognition of the purposes, strategies and style of academic life, the backgrounds from which most students and tutors came and the range of world views they mostly espoused, and the unquestioned symbols of the transactions of learning. The undermining and disintegration of this coherent culture were accompanied by the confusions, divergences, tensions and conflicts that became features of academic institutions in the late twentieth century. Higher education shared the uncertainties of the diverse society of which it was increasingly seen as a part, a society that increasingly influenced the diversity within higher education. The distinctive nature of the higher education institution itself became the subject of increasing controversy, and its procedures for access, teaching and learning and responding to the needs of the parent society became prominent topics for internal and external debate.

Innovation was just one part of the processes of change. Established understandings became reinterpreted as resistance to change. Leadership involved not just management but also the management of change. What emerged widely was something that might be termed proleptic versions of culture – appeals for acceptance of new forms of community that did not exist. The basis could be technological, procedural, based in hard planning or millenarian announcements. Leadership meant seeing the new shapes, followership meant failure to recognize them. 'Change' in such situations can mean, as we have stressed, centralized and structural change, or diffused change initiated by individuals or teams. All of these attitudes surfaced in this study, but it is support for, or resistance to, individual innovation that is central to this discussion.

Drives and obstacles

Other recent studies have looked at how participants have viewed these fundamental shifts in institutional behaviours and attitudes. An analysis by Drummond *et al.* of the problems of implementing good practice relating to personal transferable skills (PTS) in higher education began by identifying where the internal drive to promote such a skills programme tended to be located, in the context of external national 'driving forces':

> The most common situation . . . was one where a small number of committed individuals, who had typically been involved in initiatives such as the EHE programme, were struggling to effect meaningful change. It is clear enough that however committed and well informed such individuals might be, their potential to produce the types of widespread change required for PTS programmes to be really effective is necessarily

limited, especially as they tend to be marginalised within academic departments. (Drummond *et al.* 1997: 8)

Barriers encountered to implementation at an institutional level included 'institutional inertia', as well as 'the systematic prioritisation of research' in universities. At other institutional levels the research found, for example, that 'traditional systems of departmental management make sustaining long-term development initiatives difficult in some institutions'. A 'structurally defined emphasis on research' undermined interest in and commitment to teaching issues, and whilst 'many institutions claim to have reward systems . . . which recognise and support a culture of innovation in teaching, these frequently lack any real credibility'. Wherever the drive for change originated, in national pressures or individual initiative, conditions could be 'difficult and inhibitory'. At the heart of the issues raised in the research was the significance of 'the potential to manage change effectively' (Drummond *et al.* 1997: 8–14). This is a case of a change need identified at national, and in many cases at institutional and individual levels. It presents the confused nature of institutional cultures and the barriers raised by aspects of institutional structures. It exemplifies the confrontation of old and new in the dramatically altered picture of higher education institutions.

A research study by Burton and Haines of innovation in the teaching and assessment of mathematics in 15 UK universities outlined the competing demands on lecturers by their schools and faculties, resulting not only in the devaluing of teaching, but also in resistance to the research project itself:

> Indeed, some senior academics questioned the rationale and potential effectiveness of this project upon which we are reporting, a questioning which might be understood in terms of the devaluing of teaching and learning within the university culture. (Burton and Haines 1997: 273)

Concern about the mathematical knowledge of graduates reflected the state of teaching, learning and assessment 'to which these graduates have been subjected throughout their educational history, and ultimately about how change is viewed and managed within University departments'. The research parallels in many ways that on skills, but in this cases focuses strongly on the role of the department, and particularly the head of department:

> promoting and managing change is a necessary component of managing a department . . . In some respects, rather than considering how the teaching and learning environment for mathematics could change, perhaps one should ask why mathematics departments are so resistant to change . . . We have drawn attention to the role of the university departmental manager in helping to meet this challenge to manage change, a role which it appeared many managers do not understand or implement. (Burton and Haines 1997: 273–90)

Again, the picture is of an established understanding of teaching a subject, of the centrality of research, and of the role of a department and its 'manager' coming into direct conflict with new approaches to student learning and attainment. Emphasis on the student as central and emphasis on the need for new approaches both encounter resistance.

These two examples illustrate how, in practice, higher education institutions are faced with drives and directions that make it difficult to redefine a culture, or more precisely to confront the scrambled values of an institution and understand what is now meant by a 'community': 'I have argued that the university is subject to a range of forces which may effectively dissolve its claim to be a community in the sense of a unit with an internal cohesion and inherent bonding force' (Schuller 1992: 38). In the present study, even in the universities we have visited that have the most settled identities, change can be widely seen as a puzzle or a threat. What these examples and our previous discussion emphasize is the absence of community in the traditional sense and problems innovators face as a result. The traditional academic community was not without its confusions and conflicts, but the scrambling of values has transferred them to different and deeper levels. The absence of community now means an intense competition for power and influence, and in the case of individual teaching staff a confused competition for rewards. It has also meant the imposition of frameworks and very often, notably those dealing with research or policy and action plans, the exclusion of many innovators from mainstream activity and support. It has in many cases faced innovators (and others committed to the improvement of teaching and learning) with the problem of negotiating often turbulent currents of authority leading upwards from those at the level of the department. The paradox is often the need for some sort of innovation to take place, but the difficulty individuals sometimes, or often, have in taking the initiatives.

Both phases of this study produced substantial information regarding how the enabling and inhibition of innovation were perceived by teaching staff in the universities, mainly in connection with funding and policy. In the first phase, across the 15 institutions visited, 85 people responded to a question as to how their innovation had been funded or how their institutions supported initiatives. Of these, two-thirds (64) felt that funding was needed to implement an innovation and only seven thought that their project could have occurred without funding. Half (42) had received support from internal funds (usually teaching and learning or academic development funds), and 11 people had tried without success or with difficulty to obtain such funding. Sixty-eight people commented on the still resonant memory of EHE in response to a direct question, mentioning it in relation to external 'push' factors, as a welcome source of funding or as an element in project ideas and development. All but four of these responses were positive, describing EHE as 'opening doors', raising the profile of teaching and learning, or accelerating the pace at which something had happened. Another positive feature of the responses related to Teaching Quality Assessment. Of the 64 responses that mentioned TQA, 61 per cent (39) described it as a positive force for innovation in teaching and learning, leading people to think about teaching and learning for the first time, or strengthening innovative activity in departments. Negative judgements about TQA came from 22 per cent (14) and the remainder made neutral remarks about TQA visits.

In this first phase perceptions of institutional policies, support or encouragement were largely negative. Fewer than half of those interviewed commented on this area, and of these 24 had a negative view (and seven of these thought that teaching and learning innovation was not discussed, valued or adequately resourced). Several people also commented on receiving greater recognition from outside their university than within it, or saw both strengths and weaknesses in the line taken by central authority. Where people applauded support, it was in connection with funding or the work of an educational development unit or the like. More substantial in these responses was the largely negative battery of comments, by 55 people, on the attitudes of their colleagues, considering innovation to be unnecessary, too time consuming or threatening (four people commented that the very term 'innovation' was interpreted as threatening). Twenty respondents reported mixed reactions amongst colleagues, 18 described them as supportive. Responses by students were described in very mixed terms. Twenty innovators reported positively, as a result of student feedback ('most find the process very liberating'), 16 talked of variable responses from students, and 11 commented on resistance or criticism from students (including those who would prefer 'chalk and talk').

Attitudes

The range of innovators' views, including harshly negative comments, about other people's attitudes, is worth pursuing further. It is important to remember that these comments derive from interviews in the first phase of the study, mainly with those who have themselves introduced innovations. In their replies to questions about their experiences with regard to innovation they identified the sources of encouragement, apathy and opposition that they had encountered. Being first-phase responses, we can code the interviewees as before, by their 'O' (old) or 'N' (new) university and a number that indicates their institution. The kind of innovation is indicated for each respondent. What follows is a form of extended case study of attitudes, expressed in transcribed notes made during the interviews, or in direct quotations.

Colleagues

For nearly a fifth of interviewees who mentioned their colleagues (17 of 89), the examples given were predominantly expressed in terms of encouragement, support and praise. For most the positive reaction came as a result of success in their innovation:

Staff who were initially sceptical are now helpful, for example in writing software. Only one member of staff is still hesitant, but he sees the service it provides. (O13.12 Pharmacology, computer simulations)

Some resistance from old staff to new methods, they hated the idea of all the paper work, but most of them have now been convinced partly through the course review process (every module, every semester) – a prominent opponent was convinced by reading the course review – he reckoned the students liked it, he was surprised, but he'd go along with it. (O4.9 Music, group project work)

It is possible to innovate. The software is accepted by the department, the faculty and the University as 'manifestly a success', in terms of student reaction, the interest of other . . . departments, and its marketing potential. Apart from an overseas contract there are other contracts, which the department went out looking for. One other British university has bought it. This software is 'what I get the biggest buzz out of now'. (O4.13 Environmental Studies, computer-aided learning)

The University's reaction is positive. When it began, at examiners' meetings there were questions like 'What's this?'. Staff came to accept it, as a different way of looking at economics. Students' enthusiasm would be 7 or 8 on a 10-point scale. Agriculture are doing something similar. (O15.9 Economics, role play/group work)

Other staff respect the method knowing that student work does not suffer. Other people are taking it up. The first year coordinator asked each member to submit ideas for interactive tutorials, and there was a lot of support for participative tutorials and exercises. The same is true of the enormous strides made in medical education. (O2.4 Sociology, group work/presentation)

Other innovations were backed by senior managers from the outset, for example:

With the European project he took a risk, since it went through no quality assurance procedures. The Dean and the Head of Department said go ahead and do it. He ignored the opposite quality assurance advice not to do so on the grounds that there was no formal examination. He convened a key skills group and the strategy required a phased implementation, and opposition appeared in stages two and three. In the latter, the staff agreed but the students resisted. There are now other University initiatives in the skills area, and some other faculties are collaborating. (O2.6 Law, group essay)

New staff were given the chance to be innovative in some institutions:

Colleagues were astonishingly receptive, humouring him as a new boy. He had to convince Undergraduate Teaching Committee. (O3.9 Chemistry, group project work/presentation)

Others received support from the discipline community, backed up by external funding:

His colleagues are extremely sympathetic. In the discipline of archaeology there is now a culture of using IT this way for the teaching of archaeology students. The national culture has become stronger, with innovative uses of computers, and the electronic library. It is data rich and graphic, and his impression is that it is becoming more so. Most archaeology departments have an IT specialist, not necessarily using simulation. As a result of the TLTP development each archaeology department had an interest in using computers in their teaching. Each department developed its own module under TLTP – relating to bones, geophysics etc. The take-up is still developing, and he doesn't know how much of the material developed is being used nationally. He put in a bid to the Innovations Fund to explore what material is available elsewhere, but was not successful. (O1.3 Archaeology, computer simulation)

Over half of the innovators who referred to the reactions of their colleagues (47 of 89) did so predominantly, however, in terms of resistance and opposition. Some new staff found it hard to break through the patronizing attitudes of their seniors, with gender being a factor in at least one case:

She was seen as an eccentric, but 'that's normal in this department. Older colleagues are a little threatened, "It will all fall down around your ears, my dear". They see what I'm doing as completely different but provided it is a success, that's OK.' (O13.2 History, problem-based learning/IT)

Opposition could be based on the nature of the innovation in terms of its pedagogic merits:

The arguments have not yet been won in open and distance learning, partly because of the loss of face to face contact, and partly because they do not feel the need for it. (O4.1 Teaching and Learning Support, distance learning)

There is a slow chipping away at staff resistance to innovative teaching and learning methods. Mostly still a didactic lecturing method – those staff who were younger and with industrial experience realised that with a wider range of ability and more students they needed to adapt teaching and learning methods, for example in terms of training for employment in the chemical industry . . . It is easier to assess individuals than groups – the biggest resistance to novel methods is the desire to be fair and rigorous with regard to individuals. (O8.4 Chemistry, project work)

Initially (before Enterprise in Higher Education) people were surprised. She proposed developing 'presentation skills', someone laughed, others smiled – who could do that? It might be OK if someone could teach it, but who had the skill to do it? (N10.7 Law, transferable skills)

Colleagues were reluctant to take on added teaching responsibilities, feel no time left for ornamental skills which should be acquired in later professional life – which is a defensible position. (O8.8 Chemistry, project work)

Opposition could also be based on financial constraints:

The department is in deficit and discusses teaching on the basis of cost. Colleagues say that student projects are expensive and want to go back to lab reports. He is opposed to this and is fighting to keep projects alive. His physics/electronics students are the only ones who do projects in all three years. (O4.2 Physics, group projects)

Some innovators were opposed by their own senior or middle managers:

Has had positive feedback from students but from higher up the organization have had criticisms – seen as not theoretical enough and too challenging. Those higher up too ready to dismiss without knowing enough about it. (N5.11 Business Studies, using novels for management studies)

He is keen to innovate, but there is opposition from senior staff. (O2.5 Urban Studies, transferable skills/IT/group work)

Struggle to become involved in Enterprise at all, superiors very opposed, but opposition now broken down. Faculty very slow to get involved. (O8.7 Classics, group and project work)

As mentioned earlier several innovators referred to the 'fear' factor, or innovation as a 'threat' or a 'risk':

Colleagues feel threatened – resource-based learning, which is group-based and sharing is seen as taking away their ownership. They think putting everything on computers will mean no reason to attend lectures. Fear. In another module tried without lectures, but new member of staff came in, wanted traditional teaching and assessment and reverted. (N6.11 Business Studies, resource-based learning)

They are used to working with books and with text. 'To be honest, my work is seen as a threat, danger.' Course always has had positive feedback from the students, is recognized as an exciting course, others worried that as an elective it will become too popular. (N6.14 English Literature, active learning/'verbal skills')

The students received a briefing in industry, and were then engaged in forecasting for industrial firms. This was seen as a threat by other staff, some of them seeing it as 'no way to teach economics'. (O12.14 Economics, case studies)

Other staff have resisted the development, feeling threatened by it. Students regard it highly. 'Lecturers complained that my students were overworked and this interfered with work for their modules, and they threatened to stop it but the students defended it'. (O12.17 Environmental Science, project work)

Alone in conducting the course in this way. A lot of staff (and some students) opposed the idea (and still do). The staff felt threatened and worried they might be made 'redundant'. Putting the material on the Internet, removing the need for tutorials – and this is another difficulty with his colleagues. (N7.18 Business Studies, student-centred learning)

Part of the problem was the fact that staff were overwhelmed, asking how they could cope, cancelling tutorials, but remaining opposed to change. Staff took Teaching and Learning in Higher Education units but few went on to take the certificate. 'Training yourself to teach' is not popular in higher education. Those who do may become change agents. Many staff however saw innovation as a risk. (N9.5 Education, resource-based learning)

Many respondents perceived a general antagonism to change:

Has had battles to change culture – innovation means more work and giving away control. (O8.2 Anatomy, group work/transferable skills)

Her idea to innovate in this way, not encouraged by others (indeed strongly discouraged by colleague). (O8.6 Law, project work)

With colleague set up biological education group – small number of staff interested in teaching and learning, important had strong support from Director. In the main staff very suspicious – 'load of codswallop', 'suck it and see', 'we'll do what we know works'. (O8.12 Biology, group project work/transferable skills)

Some colleagues are 'usefully sceptical' ('why bother?', 'why invest time in . . . ?'). There is opposition from programme managers. Staff development enthusiasts are like a club. (N10.11 Agriculture, learning logs)

Barriers? Attitudes of some staff. Luddite elements in the university – give lecture handouts and go – rife in this department. Very low attendance for staff development and sharing of information. Considering this, has received more support than expected. (N10.12 Marine Studies, using the Internet and simulations)

Deputy VC was supportive if it was faculty-wide. From colleagues there was some suspicion and opposition, seeing it as a threat or as 'a substitute for lecturing'. With time more people became supportive. In the faculty there were perhaps 10 per cent for, 10 per cent against, and those in the middle didn't think about it. (N10.18 Civil Engineering, peer-assisted learning)

There was little chance of getting more resources. He felt that in the University most staff had a contempt for teaching. Given that there were so few people chasing money for innovation and teaching and learning, if you showed any interest at all you were likely to get some and they had exploited that . . . Very difficult, however, to get other departments to pick up on their ideas, the departments were sort of very tight, very difficult to convince them to pay any attention to things learnt elsewhere. It took so much time to bring about any change. (O12.1 Chemistry, computer-aided learning)

He has met resistance from technical colleagues. (O12.4 IT, students as teachers)

Engineers were not used to anything like this and what he was doing was unpopular. He was 'excommunicated' in the department, and seen as an 'odd ball'. Traditional lecturing was what the other lecturers understood whereas he wanted a more interactive situation. Half the students loved it, half didn't. (O12.13 Engineering, active learning)

There was indifference, not necessarily reflected outside the institution:

Staff within the School/University don't enquire much about it. (N10.5 Business Studies, group work)

No one had ever approached her directly for help, or to offer an input of this kind. She thought that many people in the department still didn't know her work, although she had worked with a number, talked to them, designed things together. From elsewhere in the University she had had contact with Educational Development Service staff, but hadn't had too much contact with anyone else. (N7.17 Health Studies, reflection/active learning)

Some innovators are painfully aware of how they are perceived by their colleagues:

He has taken part in other initiatives . . . He sees innovation as 'part of the job' . . . His colleagues have often seen him as 'a bit lightweight'. The staff are 'very traditional creatures' though many (a minority) engage in a lot of good practice. He has sometimes been seen as a 'chancer' at the time, but the others are also having to change as numbers continue to increase. (N11.7 Biology, group work)

It is an 'unusual' position, and some colleagues run away when they see her coming. She tries to move at others' acceptable rate. She keeps trying but there is a lot of resistance. (N9.1 Psychology, group/project work)

Just over a quarter of interviewees (25 of 89) identified mixed responses from their colleagues, giving both positive and negative examples. Many of them felt that time was on their side and they were winning the battle, even if it was a far from easy task:

There was opposition from some colleagues who thought it meant losing a traditional part of the course. Now they are fairly content. (O13.12 Pharmacology, computer simulations)

Other colleagues in engineering departments are suspicious of innovation and change, but over the years the number of innovations in engineering departments has grown. At international conferences papers are given about all sorts of innovations in engineering education. In some cases change results from desperation. Where there has been a massive increase in student numbers change has been obvious. (N10.18 Civil Engineering, peer-assisted learning)

To begin with very little of what she did rubbed off on colleagues, though they helped with the video. Originally it was a lot of work and they didn't want to be involved. Through CAL she tried to interest others and one of them became involved and teaches it. Her colleagues do other things and 'are not antagonistic', but what she does is 'not their thing'. The others are dragged in as personal tutors. (N7.16 Pharmacology, computer simulation)

Coming as he does from commerce, he had no preconceptions about how to teach. Accountants are conservative people. The most important aspect of it all is how it is presented. If people see the benefit you can carry them with you. There are satisfactory outcomes in student performance. Many of them see the benefit with hindsight. At the time they might prefer the traditional method, but afterwards they defend his approach. (N7.18 Business Studies, student-centred learning)

The skills unit is seen as innovative, and hostility to it is on the wane. There has been some ripple effect to other units. She has spent a lot of time working on colleagues who were 'likely to moan'. Even the diehards are committed to good teaching. (N7.21 Life Sciences, study skills)

For some innovators isolation was a factor:

Other staff in the department don't know what she does, and it isn't discussed – it's OK if the results are OK. (O13.11 Maritime Studies, interactive lectures)

One interviewee identified three kinds of reaction to innovation, here expressed in terms of the EHE:

Three groups: (1) interested in Enterprise, tried it; (2) antagonistic but learnt the language, good at the process; and (3) old fashioned – need to give the students as much info as possible. (O8.5 English, learning journals)

The mixed response was sometimes founded on a tension between the desire to meet what were seen as the needs of students and a reluctance to tie education too closely to the needs of employers:

She felt that staff who wanted to adopt this system wanted it to provide support for students, they saw education as transformatory, they saw this approach as student-centred. For her it was basically a question of whose best interest is being served by this device. She would want it to promote autonomy to promote reflection but she was worried about it being highjacked for other purposes. She felt that in a student's view, what was really important for them was that they acquired the skills because they felt that these were skills that employers wanted. She felt that students wanted to be able to pick the appropriate units which would give them those skills, but this conflicted with some teaching staff who felt that this was too instrumental, it was incompatible with what they saw as learning for learning's sake. There were some staff who were concerned that degree courses were being too much tailored to the needs of employers. (N7.13 Education & Communication Studies, profiling)

For several a measure of success in winning over their colleagues had been gained at a personal price:

Some staff support it, some still have misgivings. It's difficult to be innovative – some staff see me as a joke sometimes... (N7.22 Mathematics, computer-enhanced learning)

Students

The reactions of students, of course, varied. Of the 47 interviewees who referred to the reactions of their students, 11 did so in mainly negative terms and a further 16 in a mixture of positive and negative. Clearly, some students needed persuading:

Students' response is variable, and they need to be sold the need for things like communication skills and why students should do things for themselves. Some of them have asked 'Why can't you just lecture at us?'. Students' attitudes have changed, however, and more of them are now used to working in groups in schools, and more conversant with team effort. (O4.6 Pharmacology, group work/presentations)

Those who start in the second semester want passive learning – the students from the first semester will explain it to them. Those who've had passive learning first prefer it until persuaded. (N6.11 Business Studies, resource-based learning)

Some student resistance to shift from the dependency mode they are getting from other colleagues. He has carried group work into his normal teaching. Now has a three-hour practical class, students read up area and report to one another, prepared as groups throughout course. The students didn't see value of group work until they got into third year. He doesn't agree with 'happy sheets' with tick-a-box evaluations geared to lectures – a fair percentage of students said drop the group work, they wanted a more didactic approach, but when the third years have met employers, they then say don't drop it. It's more difficult because other staff have adopted a didactic approach. (O8.2 Anatomy, group work/transferable skills)

A failure to persuade the students could lead to the collapse of the innovation, particularly if it was already vulnerable through lack of support within the department:

He tried to introduce the scheme in the business accounting unit of the undergraduate degree, but students were opposed, and he couldn't get it accepted without management support, which was not forthcoming. His mistake was in not starting by showing what the benefits would be. (N7.18 Business Studies, student-centred learning)

Some students were more suited to new teaching and learning methods than others, which were also more appropriate for certain areas of the curriculum:

Students like a mixture of CAL and other methods – it suits some, not others. Needs to be integrated into the whole. Extremely favourable response at first, achieved its objectives, but degree of response has tapered. Suits certain areas of the curriculum, not all. Need face-to-face discussion for some parts. (O3.6 Accounting, computer-aided learning)

Students were said by some staff to be reacting negatively to 'innovation overload':

Students find it quite a relief to go to normal lectures by non-innovators! Can have too much innovation, can go too far. (O4.7 Geology, core/transferable skills)

Fourth years were complaining about the number of in-company projects. (O3.5 Management Studies, computer-aided learning)

Students' opposition was often described as composed of several elements:

Students put up some resistance to being marked by other students . . . Teaching occupational psychology to students in their final year she did not set essays but got them to write a report and there was resistance from the students. (N9.1 Psychology, group/project work)

It did not continue because the students complained that it was too much work and more than other students were expected to do. (N9.6 Geography, problem-based learning/field trips)

She had addressed the problem of how to deliver PBL in a traditional curriculum. What she did was not popular with students, who were unhappy at the lack of lectures . . . Students see this process as too late in the third year. Some don't like the work in groups and some regret the lack of formal teaching. (N9.15 Law, problem-based learning)

However, just under half of those who referred to student reactions to their innovations (20 of 47) gave overwhelmingly positive accounts of their responses:

Colleagues foresaw disaster with students faffing around choosing, but in practice hasn't happened. She's done an introductory module with them first and they know what they are taking on. OK once they get started. (O13.2 History, problem-based learning/IT)

Students are very responsive. She coaxes them, cajoles them, it's fun. (O13.4 English, interactive lectures)

Students accept and enjoy the method. (O13.9 Law, student-centred learning)

Have many opt-ins. Students like being treated as human beings in their first year. They come over from some other subjects where they are treated like rats or where it is all mass lectures with no tutorials. (O4.8 Philosophy, student proctors)

'We felt what we had got was useful to students because they told us it was.' They came to tutorials of their own choice – students were being looked after by computer until the tutor could get there. It helped the introverted student, who could ask the computer. (O3.1 Mathematics, computer-aided learning)

A minority want chalk and talk, but most students find the process liberating. (O2.4 Sociology, group work/presentation)

His programme was successful and students 'love it'. (O12.22 Maths and Computing, project work)

Indeed, there was some evidence that students themselves were exerting pressure for change:

There was increasing pressure from students particularly those who had done HND, to adopt new methods. These are students who go into their second year of the degree programme, 2+2 type qualification. Students liked the new approaches and therefore there was some pressure from them on traditional staff. (O12.1 Chemistry, computer-aided learning)

A good deal in these responses clearly depended on a combination of the innovator's approach and the nature of the innovation, as well as on the students' prior experience and the attitudes of other staff. Innovation often meant risk taking and unpopularity, with innovators even being branded as dangerous. Difficulties were not necessarily the result of taking radical initiatives. Even what elsewhere might be seen as a simple departure could in some situations be regarded by colleagues as threatening to established practice. Attitudes described by these respondents could be not only supportive or hostile but also ambivalent and capable of reversal. In the case of colleagues' attitudes, enabling and encouraging or resisting and discouraging are not always pure categories. The complexities of the institutions reach down into these relationships.

Making judgements

Other versions of support and obstacles became clear from the general investigation of the 15 universities. There was much discussion amongst innovators and managers, for example about the reality and symbolism of the investment by many institutions in supporting continued curriculum change and innovation in teaching and learning after the end of their five years of Enterprise funding. One old university had committed £860,000 to such support and development since the end of its EHE funding, and senior staff pointed out that TQA ratings had benefited. A former polytechnic invested £150,000 in the same way in 1994–5. The establishment of new support structures through units concerned with educational development, teaching enhancement or learning support was a feature of many post-EHE developments. The encouragement for innovation brought about by such investment, as well as by the accompanying staff development activities, was mentioned often enough to constitute an important feature of higher education in this period and the staff development was represented in many instances as a major factor in culture change. The funding involved, and its distribution by a special committee or by the educational development unit, was important enough in one university to cause some unease at the level of the heads of schools that their authority was being undermined.

In the second phase of the study, with its focus on the inner life of five universities, these features were largely confirmed and others surfaced. In terms of enabling innovation two particular emphases emerged. The first is the important role often ascribed to either an interested vice-chancellor or a deputy or pro-vice-chancellor. We have seen in previous chapters how such senior managers are sometimes identified as champions of teaching and learning, and of innovation, perhaps even while being associated with centralizing tendencies and widely unpopular structural reform. The direction of senior management energies towards teaching and learning, and a widespread acknowledgement of the influence they exercised, was particularly interesting at Glasgow and Nottingham, given the coexisting research orientation of the universities. A strong commitment to and responsibility for the enhancement of teaching and learning were vested in a pro-vice-chancellor at four of the five universities, and a Deputy Vice-Chancellor at Middlesex, and whatever the problems faced by individuals and units in pursuing innovation, recognition of the importance of their roles was undoubtable.

The second important emphasis that emerged was that of the crucial importance of interdisciplinary and inter-unit collaboration at The Open University. We have highlighted the view that innovation at the OU is located to a large extent in the culture of collegial interaction and collaborative planning and development by course teams. Although collaboration is not absent from other universities the particular form and strength of collaboration is unique to the OU in the universities visited, and clearly has much to do with the modes of operation of a distance learning university and the nature of its 'teaching' responsibilities. Future discussion of change and innovation in relation to the curriculum or to teaching and learning can usefully take greater account of the collaborative basis on which this one university locates its experience of innovation.

The discussions with innovators in the first phase of the study tended to emphasize the lack of organizational support and recognition, and colleagues' negative attitudes, as the two main discouraging factors facing innovators. In the second phase these were confirmed and extended. The discouraging features of universities included tensions between the department and the university that placed would-be innovators in some difficulty, and the specific lack of technical support at university or departmental or other level that prevented the launch or the successful completion of some kinds of initiative in teaching and learning. We have seen also that the increasing lack of collegiality, not just the attitudes of specific colleagues, was identified as an obstacle to innovation. Such a lack intensified the feeling of staff committed to the improvement of teaching and learning that they ran the risk of becoming even more of the 'loner' in a restructured academic universe. What '*they*' would say could be, and sometimes quite distinctly was, ignored by innovators, but more generally a private enthusiasm could be seen as having a variety of unwelcome consequences.

This points, in the universities visited in both phases of the study, to the sense of a fragmented culture that we have considered. In the secure boundaries of research (either in a department or in a 'confederation' of similar departments across higher education institutions) the fragmentation is less noticeable or less important. Broadly speaking, however, throughout this study the fragmentation has for large numbers of people meant differences of priority and behaviour amongst schools or departments, different perceptions of the fair operation of old or new structures and procedures. Modules and semesters are sometimes referred to as contributory factors, but mostly the causes are seen in the commercialization of the institution, competition within the institution and between institutions, the increased bureaucracy staff see as resulting from national pressures and requirements, increases of scale, the uncertainties arising from interpretations of an institution's position in the higher education system and the wider society.

The study by Drummond *et al.* referred to above placed attempts to introduce personal and transferable skills in institutional contexts at three levels, at each of which barriers to change were encountered – institutional, departmental and individual.

1. At an institutional level barriers included: 'Problems in promoting and managing change in any large organization, which is sometimes referred to as institutional inertia', the 'systematic prioritization of research' and concerns about the role of higher education and issues such as academic freedom. (The first two of these replicate what was found in this study, but the third was replaced by the rather different issues of centralization, managerialism and the place of the individual in the changing institutional culture.)
2. At the departmental or school level the barriers consisted of resource implications affecting the ability to respond to changing demands; a 'lack of awareness of the scale and breadth of the changes involved in implementing good practice in . . . teaching and learning'; 'traditional systems of departmental management', which made it difficult to sustain long-term initiatives; modularization and its impact on 'the continuity of the learning experience'; reluctance to adopt 'innovative approaches to teaching and particularly to assessment'. (Most of these featured in the present study but with different degrees of emphasis.)
3. At the individual level the 'inhibiting factors' included: the career path of many academics being research focused; the pressure of short-term contracts for many staff; 'high levels of commitment to the academic discipline', seen as weakened by an emphasis on skills; academics without training lacking the 'expertise, experience and confidence to adopt new approaches to teaching'; failure to motivate students. (Since the present study focused in its first phase on committed innovators, some of these considerations did not apply, though the research issue was everywhere present.)

Drummond *et al.* deduce from this analysis that 'to date, very little attention has been paid to how changes in teaching and learning practices in HE can be most effectively managed' (Drummond *et al.* 1997: 9–10, 13). This analysis is, of course, directed at the implementation of a policy-driven, and even externally-driven, type of change. Broadly speaking, however, the typology of 'barriers' is similar to the kinds of inhibitions identified by innovators in the present study. How changes in teaching and learning practices can be 'most effectively managed' was not quite the same focus in this study, but the picture of the higher education institutions examined by Drummond *et al.* contains many identical or similar elements to those of the study of innovation.

A discussion by Lueddeke of a possible model to help guide the process of change and innovation in higher education is based on an analysis of the existing literature of 'organizational change and diffusion of innovation in higher education' and not on a direct study of institutions. There is interest here, however, in Lueddeke's proposed 'generic framework/model for change' that would need to include the following:

- *Integrate experiential and dynamic praxis (interrelating theory, practice, and experience)*, ensuring that change initiatives in higher education are rooted in 'authentic' and problematic experience . . .

- *Encourage collegial and collaborative (vs. managerial) decision making,* emphasizing linkages and relationships, not structures . . .
- *Demonstrate a capacity to adapt to existing practice and to changing circumstances . . .*
- *Focus on reflective, generative and transformative activity* . . . [and the kind of change efforts] providing a plan for a guided journey and not a blueprint for change . . .
- *Ensure credibility (meaningfulness and acceptability) to the academic 'mainstream'. . .*
- *Function largely within ambivalent teaching/learning environments* (Lueddeke 1999: 244–6. Author's italics)

Although Lueddeke's hypotheses are not grounded in the kind of experience innovators and others have reported in this study, they mirror some of the underlying characteristics and concerns that we have discussed. His emphases, relating to a close analysis of the international literature, are on, for example: a recognition of ambiguities and the problematic; the need for close attention to curriculum and student learning processes in approaches to change; a combination of the collegial and the managerial (which is a kind of update of Becher's description of the coexistence of radical chic and entrenched conservatism). Wherever, in the present study, the focus is on obstacles to innovation, the understandings offered by innovators also concern, as in Lueddeke's model, the failure of institutional initiatives and strategies to address a number of factors. These include 'authentic' and 'problematic' experience, the loss of a significant 'collaborative' element in decision making, and the absence of management and support structures that make possible adaptations that make links with existing practice and changing circumstances.

The portrait of higher education and its 'barriers' established by Drummond *et al.*, and the model of guidance for change and innovation suggested by Lueddeke, correlate usefully with the deductions that emerge from this study. The correlation is between a concern with how change is managed and the experience of teachers wishing to introduce change primarily at the level of teaching and learning interactions. This study has been directed primarily at individuals choosing, launching and sustaining initiatives, or failing to do so in their circumstances, and those aspects of their institutions that provide or withhold encouragement. Although offered in terms of innovation at the level of the individual teacher, these conclusions regarding innovation have messages for teaching and learning generally in higher education, as well as for institutionally driven innovation policies. What we conclude from the study with regard to the factors that enable and inhibit innovation is as follows:

Innovation in teaching and learning is most likely to take place when:
- the innovator feels a degree of security within an understood community or cultural context, recognizes the need for change and has encourage-

ment or support from the head of department, dean or other person in authority;

- the institution has a policy establishing parity between research and teaching and learning, including for purposes of promotion, and the policy is reflected in practice;
- colleagues and people in authority show an interest in disseminating the outcomes of innovation;
- resources are available through the department, an innovations fund or similar fund, and an educational development or learning support unit.

Innovation is most likely to be obstructed by:
- low esteem of teaching and learning, compared with research;
- lack of recognition and interest by colleagues and people in authority;
- institutional or other policies and action plans laying down firm directions that preclude individual initiative;
- excessively bureaucratic procedures for approval, support and resources;
- quality assessment procedures or other procedures that inhibit risk-taking.

8

The Competitors

Teaching, research and administration

For academic staff in UK universities roles are generally defined in terms of the triumvirate of teaching, administration and research, although 'enterprise' (including links with industry and potential employers, marketing and sponsorship) has also entered the vocabulary of roles in some universities. The bulk of the funding by the higher education funding councils is devoted to the support of teaching and learning. Thus, the Higher Education Funding Council for England (HEFCE), gave £2694 million for this purpose in 1998–9, which was 70 per cent of its funds. Despite this, a perhaps surprisingly high priority is given by universities to research, which receives substantially less, though the 'dual' system also adds research funding through the research councils. This funding imbalance has partly been a result of the structure of competition and rewards built into the funding system. The money for teaching has been distributed by means of a predominantly formulaic system that is based on an institution's student numbers and the kinds of courses taken.

Relatively little funding has been allocated to reward 'excellence' in terms of teaching and learning. The major example of this is the Fund for the Development of Teaching and Learning (FDTL), which allocated £12.4 million over the period 1996–2000. The FDTL was established by HEFCE to support projects aimed at stimulating developments in teaching and learning and to encourage the dissemination of good teaching and learning practice across the sector. Bids could only be made by those institutions that had demonstrated high quality in their educational provision through the quality assessment process, the first time that the Council had linked such results to its allocation of funds. In 1999, under its Teaching Quality Enhancement Fund (TQEF), HEFCE announced that from that year it would allocate £89 million over a three-year period for its learning and teaching strategy: 'The TQEF introduces an inclusive approach to funding which ensures that funds will be provided to all higher education institutions (HEIs) to encourage development and enhance the quality of learning and teaching'. This was to be achieved by funding at three levels: recognizing and rewarding high quality teaching by individuals; at subject level a Learning and Teaching Support Network (LTSN) and a continuation of FDTL; and at institutional level, in addition to TQEF funding, £90 million over two years to improve the technology infrastructure of learning and teaching (HEFCE 1999a: 4).

Research, however, has overwhelmingly been financed according to the principle of 'selectivity' or has been awarded by means of competition via bids for funding to various providers. Thus, in 1997–8 UK universities received £2617 million of research income, £883 million of this coming from the funding councils, over 90 per cent of which was allocated on the basis of the Research Assessment Exercise (RAE). Of the rest, £534 million came from the research councils, £399 million from charities and philanthropic organizations, and the bulk of the remainder from UK government bodies, industry, commerce and public corporations and the European Union.

For academic staff with hopes of building a research career the RAE has been *the* measure of success. Even the winning of external grants from research councils, charities or industry has often been most celebrated in terms of the likely effect on RAE ratings, partly because these are given so much publicity. Indeed, it seems that some universities enter fewer staff for grading in the RAE than they might in order to maximize their quality rating, even at the cost of lower research income as a result (through lower volume). Research careers are built on RAE success – researchers are promoted to readerships or professorships to reward them for their contribution to the last RAE or to keep them for the next RAE, or are awarded to new staff recruited specifically to boost the chances of future success. In some universities with strong RAE ambitions, redundancies or early retirements have been the penalty for those who have failed to live up to expectations in terms of research outputs – though some of these staff are re-allocated to mainly teaching roles.

The RAE is a process whereby the research output of university departments is judged by peer review (involving a panel of experts in each subject) every four or five years. Submissions in 1992 had to quantify all publications, but in the 1996 and 2001 exercises the emphasis has been on quality rather than quantity with just four outputs having to be identified per 'active researcher'. Information also has to be given on numbers of research students and bursaries, research degree completions, external research funding, general research culture and future plans. Departments in each subject area are then given ratings according to the extent to which their output meets standards of 'national' or 'international' excellence. In 1992 this was a five-point scale. In 1996 this was expanded to a seven-point scale to include a 3A and 3B and a 5 and 5*, slightly amended for 2001. Funding flows to universities on the basis of a formula which rewards both high ratings and high volume (the number of active researchers entered), although in practice there is a trade-off between these, with universities reducing volume and entering only the best of their active researchers. There is a separate Unit of Assessment (UOA) for education research to which researchers on teaching and learning in higher education may be submitted. In practice, however, academic staff in non-education departments prefer to submit their work to their own subject panels. There is little evidence so far that these have rated research on teaching and learning in higher education on a par with subject-based research, although RAE 2001 may be different in this respect if the 1999 guidelines are put into practice (paragraph 1.10 in HEFCE 1999b: 7).

The former polytechnics entered this competition for the first time in 1992 and some of them have invested heavily in climbing up the RAE league table (*Times Higher Education Supplement* 1996: xvi). This has meant a significant heightening of the importance of research for the academic staff of 'new' universities, the great majority of whom previously saw themselves predominantly as teachers. The 'old', or pre-1992, universities have long given a higher priority to research, a position made possible by government funding allocated to them for that purpose. This 'core' research funding was invested in these institutions in such a way as it enabled them to establish and preserve staff:student ratios far superior to those prevailing in 'new' universities. The 'old' universities have therefore been under pressure to secure high levels of research funding to maintain staffing levels – any drop down the RAE ladder can have drastic consequences, even if the old universities are still relatively well-funded compared with the new universities. For the latter, funding council research money from 1992 onwards has been welcome, but their staff:student ratios are still much less favourable, meaning that extra research responsibilities often have to be taken on in addition to already onerous teaching duties.

Amidst all this, academic staff are expected to make some contribution to the administration of their institutions. Some, of course, are in management roles where they are responsible for the work of others, student admissions, external relations, running departments, courses, research centres or laboratories, for example. For others, a proportion of their time is inevitably devoted to responding to the demands of the bureaucracy that caters for such processes as students' progress and assessment, or records staff research outputs also for RAE or other purposes. Despite the employment of specialist administrators, much of the information to make the system operate still has to come from academic staff, some of whom take on considerable administrative burdens. Although such work is frequently resented by those whose priority is teaching or research, for others the route to promotion is in fact through taking on administrative or managerial responsibilities. Again, the amount of time spent by academic staff on administrative work is partly a product of the overall staffing position – the more teaching and research income received the more specialist administrative staff can be employed, and the better the staff:student ratio the less the burden of administrative work per member of academic staff.

How, then, are these forces experienced? Is research seen as underpinning or undermining teaching? What are seen as the relative weightings accorded to research, teaching and administration? What are the favoured paths to promotion? How does all this affect the willingness of academic staff to devote themselves to innovation in teaching and learning?

Research and teaching

In the first phase of this study, research issues were discussed with 92 members of staff at the 15 universities visited, all of whom had been involved in introducing new methods of teaching and learning. Many told us that research was given a higher priority than teaching in their institutions, although this was not necessarily the case for them or their department, if, for example, there existed a priority link with practice in the professions or other employment:

His concern is that too large a proportion of resources is directed to research at the expense of teaching (and this is true of other disciplines also). (O13.12)

'We are research led'. Most people are motivated by their research . . . This university is very concerned with research – it's the core activity . . . (O3.12)

The old polytechnic system was geared towards teaching. Since becoming a university research has become paramount . . . The institution is now more interested in teaching and learning, but still has a research culture – 95 per cent emphasis on research, 5 per cent on teaching. (N10.8)

The aim is to keep staff teaching time at a minimum, everyone to be an active researcher, research comes first. (O4.7)

There was evidence of teaching being given a low priority by some:

A lot of his colleagues 'think research' and find teaching an 'irritant'. (O4.2)

The prevailing culture wasn't, in this university, just about research, although for quite a few people research was the priority and teaching was seen as the necessary pain. That wasn't true throughout the university. (O12.10)

There were frequent references to the influence of the RAE on teaching developments, even though these interviews were taking place in late 1997 or early 1998, at least 18 months after the last RAE (April 1996) and two or three years before the next (April 2001, although at the time of interviewing this was expected to be in 2000). Many of the comments related, for example, to disappointing performance in the last RAE, and pressures – even requirements – to concentrate on doing better next time:

At a managerial level, everything is geared to RAE 2000. (O4.12)

From now on it is expected of all staff that they be active researchers, as she is. (O4.13)

The department is taking less notice of opportunities to use computers in teaching and learning – it's taking the RAE more seriously. He has been asked what papers will be published for next RAE many times – the pressure is on and that is the priority. (N5.12)

If the department doesn't get a 4 in the next RAE there is a chance the department will disappear. (O4.6)

There is now research pressure – in reality there are too many demands to be able to innovate. (N6.8)

The RAE hit the University in very significant ways. It pushed people out who were very experienced and good teachers. There is so much pressure on them to get PhDs and do research. A lecturer will lose a job if not an active researcher. (O15.6)

How well we do in the RAE is the key to the future of the department – there is a fear of funding crashing with negative effect on number of staff, and on the quality of staff and of teaching. (O3.4)

The general staff response to teaching and learning is 'We've got RAE to think about!' People are not being rewarded for teaching in a real sense. (O2.13)

The last two years have been good for teaching and learning, but now academic staff have been called off for RAE work. (O8.1)

All that matters is research, 'our teaching is OK anyway so we've nothing to worry about' is the attitude. (O8.2)

Support from his colleagues started off well, but lately it has been dropping because 'they have gone off to work for the RAE'. (O8.3)

The department didn't do as well as anticipated – it got a 3B. The postmortem aimed at the perceived deficiency in research. There is still a feeling that teaching will happen anyway and the real focus is research. The whole future of the department is on the line so this emphasis is not surprising. For the RAE it is recognized that everyone needs to pull together. (O8.4)

Her own priority is research not teaching at the minute. 'Research is everything'. They got a 4 in 1992, but dropped to a 3A in 1996. It was a total priority to get the 4 back . . . 'Research is absolutely everything, now we are not into teaching.' There was an actual memo from the Director – teaching mustn't be an excuse for not writing. (O8.6)

The RAE is a huge focus – so much money flows from it, inevitably an intense focus. In the midst of this we have tried to think of ways of enhancing teaching and learning. We think we have done very well in Teaching Quality Assessment . . . We have done less well in the RAE. We can say that this university is student-centred and has done well in teaching and learning, but there is an intense focus on what needs to be done to lift RAE ratings. (O8.11)

It was clear that new staff in some universities were made aware that research had to be their top priority:

The departmental Teaching Committee contains only older staff. Younger staff are expected to devote themselves to research, and have only a light administrative and teaching load. This is necessary for their careers. (O4.6)

His main initial preoccupation as a new lecturer was to establish himself in research and for the first couple of years that was the bulk of his effort. (O4.15)

'We are being forced into a research culture – this is for the good.' If people coming in haven't got research degrees they will get them. Staff development encourages them to go on to get PhDs. (O16.2)

To get through probation he needed to show he was an active researcher. When he started he had 160–200 hours teaching, a high load for a probationer, plus a lot of administration. He wanted to make teaching more efficient and effective. He wrote articles on accountancy and finance education, which counted as research. (O3.6)

However, the possibility of being entered in the RAE as a researcher in education, rather than in their subject, was only available for some and not for others:

For RAE 1996 she was entered in business studies, all four outputs in substantive area. RAE 2000 likely to be the same again. She could submit an education output, but won't as she needs to make progress in her substantive area. (O3.5)

She felt that every time she tried to develop research she had been prevented in doing so, she was taken off research and told that what she was doing was useless for the RAE. Her own research had been concerned with the relationship between learning and the design-making process, in particular how that ties in with the development of self-confidence which she thought was very important for learning. All of this, she felt, related very strongly to teaching and learning approaches. When she was trying to do some educational research she had been timetabled to the full extent possible. When she dropped the educational research her timetable was reduced. Basically her head of department had told her to stop doing it or else, so she did. (N7.5)

In pharmacy his teaching orientation has worked against him. In the 1980s there was a pendulum swing away from teaching in science-based disciplines towards research, in the way university financing was directed. In his case his research was education-based, but it satisfied the requirements, and it contributed to education's RAE rating going up. (O13.12)

If he wanted further promotion to a chair he would need to write another three or more books, ideally on history, not the teaching of history. His department is very supportive, he has written on staff development, etc. and has done research on the teaching of history (the latter after the head of department checked with the RAE panel that this was acceptable). (O15.1)

In one university the use of the education UOA to bring together researchers in teaching and learning from across the university had evidently been given a high priority, with submissions being made in 1992 and 1996:

The RAE brought together those doing research in teaching and learning in higher education, they were previously isolated . . . He has fought in his own department to have what he is doing seen as research – which has been an uphill struggle. In the early stages he had to fight to make it clear that he was actively researching. This was confirmed by the last RAE and this university has confirmed education research is an important activity. It seems totally relevant to pursue his research interest in education alongside staff from other departments – this has become the 'Education Research Grouping'. Through the Innovation Programme . . . there are special interest groups for staff from across the university: assessment method; web technology; distance learning. The research circle overlaps with these – these projects act as a stimulus for research. (O3.6)

A strategic decision was made to set up an education UOA, all participating departments had to decide on its own group to be entered. They were aiming to raise the level of teaching and learning through it for RAE 2000, but this was not the main driver – basically it was intended to support new developments. They have established a 'Research in Innovative Learning Group' for active researchers entered in 1996 and others who have since joined. (O3.8)

For the next RAE we will have an education UOA. How people learn through interactive on-line networks is an important research area which the university will invest in. (O3.12)

However, entering research concerned with innovations in teaching and learning in the RAE, whether in the subject or education UOA, still presented difficulties:

He was entered in his own subject area in RAE in 1996. His teaching and learning innovation was not used in RAE as an output but it had a bigger impact than things that were. 'If we don't develop these things others will (USA) and we'll have to pay.' (O3.3)

Research on teaching of the subject doesn't count in English. (O8.5)

There is anger with RAE panels on their reluctance to credit research in teaching and learning in the subject area. (O8.11)

He was entered as an active researcher in the education UOA. But it has to be subject-based research to be fully recognized. If staff did action research on teaching and learning in their subjects they should ideally be included in their subject UOA. (O8.12)

Research was not, however, the priority for all:

This was still a teaching department, not a research-oriented department. Student numbers have fallen so there are more opportunities for research, but in the past and even last semester he had 16 hours teaching per week, so research was unrealistic. (N5.3)

In modern universities lip service is paid to research. He was originally employed to improve University research but now, of necessity, he spends less than 5 per cent of his job doing it. (N6.4)

Ironically, some staff were told to give the highest priority to their teaching in order to maximize their departments' chances of success in the next RAE:

The last RAE was unsatisfactory – they got 3A as a school, an extremely tough panel. The university is focused on getting as many 5s as possible – this is the primary aim. For the next RAE the university will be looking carefully for good outputs and record of research money. The university has decided those members of staff who will not be RAE active are to be encouraged to specialize in teaching and learning and teaching and learning innovation – he has accepted. Now there is no pressure on getting research grants and he can spend time on other developments . . . Six in the school have taken the offer and moved sideways, they are no longer expected to demonstrate research capability. (O13.13)

She wasn't included in last RAE, she has more output now but the threshold for inclusion is higher. There is talk of putting some staff on teaching-only contracts – it is hard to avoid this being seen as a punishment. (O8.5)

RAE money goes to those who are successful. It can be divisive – some people are taking on bigger teaching loads to allow others to concentrate on research. (N10.9)

Staff would have to have four publications as the RAE entry ticket or undertake more teaching to free those that do. (O3.10)

He doesn't do much research because he is much involved in teaching and teaching innovation, with the support of his head of department ... RAE has driven out all else for some. His teaching load releases others to do research. (O3.11)

However, a number of interviewees made statements that rejected the zero-sum notion of a trade-off between an emphasis on research and on teaching, arguing the case for complementarity:

His research and teaching have fed into each other, and his teaching has benefited from his business insights. (O4.2)

Staff who want more time to research must teach more effectively ... In philosophy you are a good teacher partly because you are a brilliant researcher, plus 'it's natural', at least for some. (O4.8)

Design and problem solving were part of the subject so provided he published in appropriate journals with theoretical under-pinning there was no problem about inclusion in RAE. His own bias was towards research, but he enjoyed teaching and bringing research to teaching. (N10.14)

She liked to get students to talk aloud, to offer their immediate reflections, to offer their reflections after undertaking the work and she liked to interview them about their reflections. She thought that by doing this research, she gained an awareness of the learning that had taken place, in depth, and that the students came to realize this as well ... She knew that some staff felt that there was some sort of conflict between research and teaching, but she didn't think so. Maybe some of the old polytechnic staff who saw themselves first and foremost as teachers may see research as a threat, but not her. Everyone that she was working with was doing research ... Her own research is highly qualitative, really she is trying to capture the voices of those qualifying in her field. (N7.17)

Insofar as teaching and research were competing with one another for the attentions of academic staff, however, a key signal of institutional priorities was likely to be given by the system of promotion and rewards.

Promotion and rewards

First phase

All of the 15 phase-one universities visited had formal policy statements about promotion, which gave some recognition to the contribution that could be made by excellence in teaching, often in terms of being one (and very occasionally a required one) amongst the other factors. In seven of these universities particular prominence was given to teaching and curriculum development activities, especially with regard to promotions at the lower levels, but also in terms of senior lectureships in old universities and principal lectureships in new universities (which were at similar pay levels to readerships but did not entail the same status or degree of release from teaching or administrative duties). Even for readerships and professorial appointments, some mention was often made in the procedures of taking account of contributions to teaching or curriculum development, but these appointments were predominantly seen as rewards for significant research output, although the performance of administrative or managerial duties was sometimes significant for professorial appointments.

However, two of the new universities included in the first phase of our study had established routes to promotion to the equivalent of readerships explicitly based on excellence in teaching and learning and involvement in innovation. Only one of these had implemented the system prior to our visit – a new university, with an overall research profile towards the bottom of the top half of the RAE 1996 league table of new universities. The initiative was part of an institutional policy designed, in its own words, 'to provide parity of esteem and financial reward for lecturing staff who focus their career on teaching and related activities with those active in research who already have the opportunity for promotion to "Reader"'. This was to be done by appointing 'staff to posts of equivalent status for those who have a leadership role in curriculum design and development, teaching and managing student learning within their subject area.' These 'Reader in Educational Development' posts were designed to enable appointees to 'a) achieve recognition for their scholarship, skills, commitment and their importance to the institution; b) devote themselves to improving the quality of teaching and learning in their department and faculty; c) disseminate good practice.' This system had been established less than a year before our visit, so that we were unable to gauge its impact on the priorities as seen by academic staff, although we were able to talk to some of the first appointees, one of whom spoke of the significance of the post in the following terms:

> It has raised the profile of teaching. She thinks the Readership is important in the University because a lot of new staff are appointed because of their research and many new staff see teaching as merely a burden. 'We can now say that the institution does reward teaching, so we can start to change that sort of culture.' (N7.20)

Perhaps inevitably, however, especially at this early stage, not all staff saw these positions as desirable. One respondent, who had been promoted for other reasons, saw these readerships as 'spurious'. Another had declined to apply, preferring to aim for promotion in her subject. There clearly remained a divide, even in a new university, between those with strong commitment to their teaching and those who see this as subsidiary to research.

Elsewhere in the same university, however, other agendas were evident, with staff looking for backing from business for programmes that brought in external funds. It should not be forgotten that entrepreneurial activity of this kind was, for some departments in some institutions, the highest priority.

It is important to look further at how these competing claims on academic staff were variously perceived in different sorts of institution and in different parts of the same institution. In the second-phase case studies of the five universities the focus was on the interplay of institutional factors affecting innovation in teaching and learning. It is helpful to consider the reward systems at work, since it is evident that the activity best rewarded by a university is that which it most values.

Second phase

To make sense of the various policies adopted on matters of promotion, it must be understood that the 'old' and 'new' universities differ significantly in their pay scales for academic staff. Simply put, the former employ lecturers (divided into A and B) and senior lecturers, whereas the latter have lecturers, senior lecturers and principal lecturers. A principal lecturer's salary in a new university is roughly equivalent to that of a senior lecturer in an old university. Both have readers and professors, heads of department or school, deans of faculty or school, and senior managers with responsibilities at the institutional level. Part-time staff employed in both sorts of institution are mainly on short-term contracts with little prospect of promotion. In addition there are technical and research staff on different scales who sometimes make a contribution to teaching.

Each of the five universities visited in the second phase had policy statements on criteria for promotion that acknowledged the contribution of excellence in teaching and learning, sometimes with specific reference to involvement in innovation. However, these varied significantly in the degree of prominence they gave to such matters compared with research and, in some instances, to 'entrepreneurial' activity.

The policy at Glasgow was set out for us by one of the Vice-Principals, who pointed out how in practice it was difficult to find tangible evidence of excellence in teaching, whereas this was more likely for innovation:

'We do very genuinely, and have done for a very long time, feel that we should give equal weight to teaching and research in promotion. We have found it very difficult to do so, just because of the evidence base'. The University has talked about portfolios but has not used them, 'largely because we have never seen how to get evidence from a portfolio to the committee in a manageable way'. Titular professorships are 'strictly on the basis of academic leadership', and almost inevitably this means a 'reasonably strong research base'. For many years he sat on promotions committees, and 'if someone could display that they had done something innovative, even better I suppose if they had got some money from somewhere to do something, it looked hard and concrete – a bit like publications or research income, which you could quantify. Whereas if the head of department said "he's one of the best lecturers I've ever come across", how do you know?'

A head of department explained his perspective in terms that gave less recognition to teaching, but rather more to administration:

'If a member of staff is an enthusiastic teacher and does less research than a colleague he will no longer be penalized . . . We are of course all out to get higher ratings in the next RAE, most people in this department are publishing well and teaching well. Some people are given a bigger teaching load. It is true that when it comes, for example, to study leave the researcher will have a better chance, if he has a contract for a book with Oxford University Press before the next RAE. When it comes to promotion I would say that the researcher would have a better chance of promotion to reader. But if your research is more than adequate . . . it is a three-legged stool at Glasgow and includes administrative experience, you have a good chance of getting a personal chair. Some people are obviously promoted to a professorship on the basis of their administrative experience, for instance if one has been a dean or a vice-principal or other senior administrative position.'

A minority of the teaching staff at Glasgow (the 'bottom up' interviewees), were relatively optimistic about the rewards for teaching excellence, as well as the contribution of administration:

She expects that teaching excellence would contribute to promotion, she would think so, she would stress her own strengths.

They are told that there are three prongs – teaching, administration and research. In term-time they are flat out on their own teaching and administration . . . The promotion forms for senior lecturer contain more pages on teaching than for research.

Teaching rewarded? Oh yes, she thinks so – due to the promotion criteria being based on teaching, administration and research ('one of the few universities that state this . . . and what attracted me to come here'). 'The administration load is enormous and it needs to be acknowledged in this way.'

For most interviewees, though, research was seen as the dominant factor:

'All the promotion is based on research' . . . Three of the four lecturers who have put in for early retirement are primarily teachers.

No rewards for teaching. She feels very frustrated. It is not valued enough.

The importance of teaching and learning? 'It is rated very highly within the School. In the university as a whole, the RAE has a much higher profile'. There was no reward for an excellent in Teaching Quality Assessment. Staff do not get rewarded for teaching as promotion is all research-based. She feels very frustrated and under-valued.

At Nottingham the emphasis on rewarding teaching was somewhat greater, but had not yet reached a par with research, at least on some accounts, particularly for promotion beyond senior lecturer. The senior and middle managers interviewed saw it in these terms:

Teaching and learning is an area that does count for promotion to senior lecturer, which is possible with excellent teaching and administration records and at least 'adequate' in research. People applying for promotion in the school are normally, in any case, good at everything. Excellence in research, supported by referees, is necessary for promotion to readerships.

Teaching does feature in promotions, but research is the main driver. For a senior lectureship you require strengths in two out of three (teaching, research or administration). One or two people have been promoted principally through teaching and learning achievements. But in his subject all are active researchers – those who weren't have recently left through early retirement.

'Rewards for excellence in teaching and learning and/or innovation are a major problem. We have been saying formally that we are regarding teaching excellence as important as research excellence in promotion. The problem is that this is extraordinarily difficult to apply. For promotion from lecturer to senior lecturer, the candidate has to demonstrate excellence in two out of three of teaching, research and administration. It is a problem to demonstrate and prove excellence in teaching, being good is not good enough. The value added bit is always on the research end . . . Innovation can make the difference, where the candidate has clearly brought in a new teaching method, genuinely new or if he or she has played a considerable role at institutional or national level . . . Just saying good at teaching and administration is not good enough.'

Teaching is an important part of the portfolio for promotion, even for reader. If a candidate for promotion is a poor teacher he or she won't get it. But it's difficult to judge teaching. 'We are a research-led university, but that gives us better teaching.'

There are no direct incentives for teaching excellence and/or innovation. Indirectly you can get internal promotion up to a certain level if you have been innovative in teaching – he has seen this happen with promotion primarily due to teaching. But you are not promoted to professor on that basis, this sends a message about the relative importance of teaching. It is far more difficult to provide incentives for teaching. In research you can give a percentage of the money to staff who attract research funds, but this is not possible in teaching.

Excellence in teaching is an important part of the process of promotion to senior lecturer . . . He thinks that the promotion process has changed and this is taken more into account.

Promotions are very frequent for those OK at research, OK at administration, excellent at teaching. If very good at research will get a readership. Senior lecturer given if particularly good at teaching, although everyone would have to show some research output, would have to be an active researcher at the required level.

Again, though, the bottom up interviews with lecturing staff showed that most saw research as the dominant factor:

Excellence in teaching is important for promotion but research counts more.

Nottingham is 'rather exceptional' because of being strong on research and teaching . . . but beyond the level of senior lecturer it is research output that really counts . . . 'The old criteria are still there'.

He does not feel valued as a teacher by the management. When he hears them talking about the importance of teaching 'I cringe'. They want it but don't want to pay for it. He has never tried to get promotion as he has felt that his output and publications have been inadequate.

'My publication rate is what really counts no matter how good my report on teaching is.' A colleague (a senior lecturer) advised her recently that to get promotion to senior lecturer one needs a 'national' research standing and to get a readership one needs an 'international' research standing.

'The documentation about promotion is quite different from reality!'

'Anyone who wants to get promoted, it is absolutely crystal clear, won't get there without research. Every young lecturer has got to put emphasis on research . . . Good researchers are often good teachers, but not always.'

He feels cynical. It is only research that is judged. He thinks that there is a threshold of a certain number of publications that are needed before you can get promotion to senior lecturer. He has many colleagues who have enjoyed teaching to the detriment of their research and have not been promoted as a result. It is difficult to provide evidence for good teaching.

However, steps were under way to raise the profile of teaching through the University's 'Lord Dearing Awards for Teaching and Learning'. These were intended to reward those staff working either individually or in groups who made an outstanding contribution to the development of traditional or innovative approaches to teaching. Nominations could come from heads of school, colleagues or student groups. Awards were presented in the form of a framed certificate at an annual ceremony and were intended as a mark of distinction in the University. Views about their impact varied:

> The Dearing Awards were status symbols and were being widely applauded. The attempt was to get the balance right, managing people's time.

> The Dearing Awards? He doesn't know anyone who has been nominated. He is not interested in that sort of thing. In general, staff enjoy their teaching, see it as an important part of the job and get on with it.

> He is being put in for a Dearing Award. Only a piece of paper – would only be a real award if money was attached.

In addition, there were attempts being made to improve the measurement of teaching performance in order to better inform the normal promotions process, although these were strongly resisted by some, for example:

> There is now to be a system of using student feedback in promotions ... Every member of staff has to collect formal feedback from students, a detailed questionnaire, which is done for departmental quality assurance, but for a certain percentage of modules the results go to be statistically analysed outside. People are not happy with university-wide questions, targeted at laboratory experience. Any candidate for promotion must present this statistical analysis. There are doubts about what to do with this when it comes to the Promotions Committee. Students will mark down their views of the subject rather than the teacher, they are influenced by when sessions are timetabled, etc. He doubts that anything dramatic will come of it.

Nonetheless, there is clear evidence here of concerted attempts to raise the profile of teaching and learning in the promotions process, although not yet evidence of how great the impact might be, for example, for those who had been given Dearing Awards or had attained high scores in the student evaluation surveys.

At Salford, senior and middle managers were convinced that teaching excellence and involvement in innovation were rewarded through the promotions system:

> The situation has improved, performance in teaching and learning is now one of the criteria in the promotions statement, but still not enough, not engrained.

> Over the next five years changes would include greater rewards for teaching. A lot was already being done. Before the merger a group of university and college people produced guidelines for promotion on

the basis of excellence in teaching . . . It has been implemented and significant numbers have been promoted on the basis of teaching. Staff need to demonstrate relevance and people were given help to produce evidence, with the aim of achieving comparable treatment with that for research.

Teaching versus research is a big issue in the university in some departments. It is not true that teaching does not count for promotion. Over the past three years there have been many claims for recognition on the basis of strength in teaching (staff provide a reflective commentary, indicate external recognition, submit a portfolio, point to curriculum development). There have been a significant number of cases of promotion on the basis of teaching.

Non-researchers can and do get promoted on the basis mainly of their teaching. He is a member of the Promotions Committee and is confident that promotion via research or administration or teaching or entrepreneurial activity or some combination is a reality – any one of these can be the 'prime mover'. On the basis of teaching a portfolio is required, and admittedly it is more difficult than other areas to provide evidence.

The university is struggling to make the equality between teaching and research a reality.

The last of these respondents added that promotion without a serious research record had become easier, but a number of heads of department disagreed:

The university would deny this but this department has suffered badly in promotions rounds. It is difficult to convince staff that teaching and curriculum development are valued . . . A head of department has responsibility without authority – can't motivate staff when not able to promote them.

Substantive posts in the university have tended to be a reward for research activity. Excellence in other areas is less tangible . . . it has meant that people deliberately set out to avoid teaching, management and administration so as to get on with research. In the department this is changing.

There is a live debate about non-research as a basis for promotion from lecturer to senior lecturer, with a lot of people saying 'it is really based on research'. Others disagree, point to the criteria.

When the three institutions merged the old university culture dominated in terms of promotions procedures. Senior lectureships were awarded on the basis of research capability, with a small number of exceptions . . . Now there are four criteria in regulations for promotion, judged against research, teaching and learning, administration and innovation. They have developed a portfolio system. This has freed it up to recognize teaching and learning. Have to get excellents in two out of four, usually three. Nevertheless, there is still a significant bias towards research. The reality is that a strong research record puts you in a better position than the reverse. He disagrees violently with this bias. For this faculty teaching and learning and management/administration, working with external agencies, and so on, are fundamental to success:

The rewards for teaching excellence and/or innovation are there in rhetoric, but not necessarily in practice. This is not so true in the faculty, but what the faculty can give is extremely limited, this is an old university system. The VC says that in the future there will be a more faculty-based rewards system, the faculty will be able to interpret the words in ways that will reflect the activities and priorities of the faculty.

Bottom up perceptions, from interviews with lecturers, were less divided:

Generally speaking promotion is based on good research – traditionally. However, there has been one exception in the department.

He thinks there are different feelings in the department about the importance of teaching. For him it has equal status to research. However, the rewards still go towards research . . . spending hours on developing a new programme will probably not be rewarded in career terms.

'Just try and get promotion with teaching!'

He achieved his promotion on research and administration, though he felt that he had been involved in producing 'innovative' course materials . . . He feels that it is very hard to get promotion with teaching.

At Middlesex University, the institutional policy on promotions gives great prominence to teaching and learning, as explained by the top down interviewees, who were often nonetheless aware that the general perception of the position amongst teaching staff was different:

With the aim of raising the status of teaching . . . they wrote a document in 1994 entitled 'The measurement and reward of excellence in teaching' – and 'the policy works'. Staff submit portfolios based on their teaching with their applications to the Promotions Committee.

'To get promotion you need research, although that is not the only thing – the University is seeking new ways to promote excellent teachers.' Both good teachers and researchers are getting promotion. They have usually tried new things, but are excellent teachers. To get through to the sort of students Middlesex has needs a more interactive approach.

The promotion policy works, with its emphasis on combining significantly two out of: administration and other contributions of value to the university, research, and teaching and learning. Excellence in teaching is demonstrated through a portfolio, and new staff are having to do the Postgraduate Certificate in Higher Education. A lot of strategic attention has been given (especially in this school) to achieving parity between and teaching and learning on the one hand and research on the other. There are areas of the school with no tradition of research and most applications for promotion from there are on the basis of administration and teaching and learning.

Everyone has to come up to a certain standard in teaching and learning. Then on top of this strong research enhances an application for promotion a great deal.

It is possible to be promoted to professor via research or not as a researcher, and the latter case may include innovation in teaching and learning. A high proportion of promotions are not on the basis of exceptional research, but staff perceptions are different. They still think promotion equals research. There is a discussion about a possible readership equivalent in teaching.

The promotion criteria encourage a pedagogy focus, and applicants are proud to present a portfolio. Some of 'the youngsters are also being enthused' . . . sabbatical semesters for teaching and learning developments are possible.

There is a growing recognition that the opportunities for promotion are changing, and that teaching is a good route to take. This is the corporate view, but most staff still view research as the main way to promotion, coupled with management ability. The university needs to be more explicit and active in this regard.

When it comes to promotion, there are supposedly three areas, candidates must be excellent in two, but he still thinks teaching is the most difficult to judge, but weighted as heavily as research – this is a general feeling in the institution. Innovation is a way of distinguishing yourself in terms of teaching.

Excellence in teaching and learning and/or innovation are the main criteria for getting people promoted. Not enough people in the School are involved in research to get promoted, but in spite of that people will still say there is too much emphasis on research, teaching not rewarded, but she knows this is not true. There is a problem of reversing old ways of thinking.

Although lecturers often acknowledged the support given by institutional policy to applications for promotion on the basis of excellence in teaching or involvement in innovations, they were less certain about the practice:

Teaching and learning are rewarded. Examples of good practice are held up. However, promotion is only really given for research – this is the reality.

> She has recently tried and was advised by the Dean that she needs to do some research though 'you are obviously a good teacher'. Two out of three is the criteria – but people are applying that can offer all three – so they win.

> He achieved promotion to principal lecturer because of his teaching initiatives rather than his research, although it is also fair to say that he has been very involved in administration (committees, etc.) on a university-wide basis. However, most people's perception is that it is still research that is needed for promotion to PL.

> Is excellence in teaching and learning rewarded? Yes and no! No one is likely to get promotion on teaching excellence alone.

There was not here, however, the same degree of scepticism as existed at the other universities about the contribution performance in teaching could make to a case for promotion. Nor was there an assumption that research necessarily counted most, with involvement in administration often being seen as more significant. These differences, of course, reflect the degree of involvement in research of each of these institutions.

The Open University presents an interesting contrast in several respects. The information given in the University's written promotion criteria for academic staff explain that Heads of Units and the Academic Staff Promotions Committee have regard to performance of the member of staff in:

- teaching – 'with emphasis on exceptional contributions and innovation as a member of a Course Team to the preparation, presentation and maintenance of a course'. (Under this heading is also listed postgraduate student supervision, training of tutorial and counselling staff and summer school teaching);
- research activity;
- administration and management – committees, course managers and 'outside liaison';
- 'other work' such as representing the university externally and 'outstanding contributions to the attainment of the objectives of the university and to its corporate life'.

The operation of the policy was explained in the following terms in the interviews:

> As head of department he puts forward people in his department who he feels should have promotion to the Faculty Promotions Committee which then goes on the University Promotions Committee for final approval. For appraisals staff are required to write up their achievements and identify their needs. Teaching is the most important of the four components (other three are research, administration and external activities), though there has been recently a much stronger sense of the importance of research (too much importance, in some people's opinion). He thinks that it is a good thing to be more research orientated

– he feels that there is a good balance now. Promotion can be achieved to senior lecturer without a serious research record, especially when people are considered to be innovative in their teaching.

In order for a young lecturer to get promotion, in most cases, they need to have the experience of chairing a course team and getting publications – this represents both teaching and research. Minutes of course team meetings are taken and opinions are heard by the course team chair and all the members (who often include the head of department and/or dean). Therefore there are many sources of evidence for excellence in teaching. He felt that with regard to promotion to senior lecturer, 'administration can be very meaningful – sometimes more than teaching or research'. However, teaching is 'more meaningful here' than at other universities.

Promotion is still heavily reliant on research though teaching needs to be there too . . . excellent teachers with no research are less likely to get promotion.

In order to get promotion staff must be found to be above average in two of the following areas: teaching (course production); research; administration; external activities. One of these must be teaching. They must be able to show their ability to innovate explicitly.

These responses indicate that a high level of contribution to the work of course teams in terms of course design and management (OU equivalents of teaching with an element of administration), is a vital requirement for promotion. However, it was not necessarily seen as sufficient with strong performance in research being of increasing significance.

From the interviews it was clear that the best routes to promotion have been research and administration, even where the policy announced a 'three-legged' (or in some cases a 'four-legged') stool. Excellence in teaching and learning or involvement in innovation has been important for some, but these have been the exception. For the majority of those who had gained promotion, adequacy in terms of their teaching has been a requirement, but little more. Involvement in innovation, particularly when this has been given a high profile nationally, and especially when it has brought in external funding, has helped. However, taking on running a course or a department, obtaining a big research grant or publishing leading works in the field are the established routes to success.

This disparity has partly been a product of difficulties in recording contributions to teaching, although these are now being overcome in some of the universities visited where portfolios of achievements, student and peer evaluations have all been employed to this end. Interestingly, innovation in teaching and learning emerges again, though infrequently, as an identifiable 'measure' that can be taken into account in the promotion process – obviously with a particular emphasis at The Open University. For many of those interviewed, however, the reality of the situation has not shifted greatly from that we have described above, where the RAE is seen as the very highest priority with other tasks being seen as necessary but not sufficient to guarantee success. The alternative goal of success in quality assurance, with its associated league tables based on TQA scores, has to some extent counteracted this tendency. None of those interviewed in fact cited success in such terms as the basis for having made a case for promotion, whereas individual research output that contributed to RAE ratings was frequently used in this way. For many of the old universities visited, high TQA scores could in any case be expected on the basis of their relatively high levels of resource in terms of buildings, equipment, libraries and staffing – advantages partly gained from previous RAE success. For those universities that saw themselves as big players in research terms, the RAE was always high in the list of priorities, losing out to periodic subject reviews as part of the quality assurance process, but regaining prominence once the next RAE came close.

Other universities were faced with the choice of diverting already scarce resources into research to raise their profile to get in amongst the big earners, or to concentrate more on their 'bread and butter' activities. More often such institutions were able to sustain research ambitions in some parts of their subject portfolio whilst in practice abandoning them in others. A key factor here has been the availability to some departments in new universities of funds stemming from the RAEs of 1992 and 1996 – where these have been present the chances of research being a high priority have been greatest. Some old universities, including at least two of those visited in phase one, which had departments that have lost such funding have shed staff (sometimes those with the heaviest teaching commitments), closing subjects and merging departments, or bringing in new staff with higher research profiles. It is highly doubtful if any department would survive even at Nottingham if it had had strong TQA scores and attracted funding for innovative programmes, but if it did not also have high RAE ratings. For Middlesex, although the RAE is still important, there has been a clear shift to give a higher priority to teaching. It is important that in different ways each of the second-phase universities saw its particular level of research as support for teaching (part of what Glasgow called 'the well supported academic').

The inevitable conclusion here is that promotion policies reflect the funding realities. Innovators in teaching and learning have to read the signals with great care. A small number have managed to penetrate the promotion system without a research profile, including where research is a stringent priority. Finding a match between the purpose and life history of the innovation and the relevant institutional policies and practices is not necessarily something the innovator wishes to establish, but it has sometimes proved possible. This is particularly the case where the institution encourages and welcomes success in obtaining funding from what may be seen as the more prestigious external sources, or where the innovation rests within a framework of something like an institutional 'innovations fund'. Realigning these forces means reconsidering internal funding and policy directions. It also means – as the funding councils have understood – using funding arrangements for higher education to intervene in these processes in favour of teaching and learning. It also means recognizing the importance of the creative and developmental roles of innovation, and raising the level of priority given to the aspects of higher education it represents.

9

Challenges of Innovation

Typologies

At the centre of this discussion has been the innovators and what they do, in the various contexts that they inhabit. So far as innovations are concerned, it is possible to divide them into broad categories according to the types of innovations undertaken (c.f. Chapter 3 and Appendix A) and also by the three levels of sponsorship (individual, guided, directed) that we have suggested. Since the 1960s it is also possible, however, to place innovations in, or directly influencing, teaching and learning in a different kind of rough typology:

- *Individual and group innovations*: classroom and course related, a direct response to student needs and professional concerns (student-led seminars, laboratory simulations, etc.).
- *Disciplinary initiatives*: sponsored or encouraged by subject associations or by professional or profession-related bodies such as the General Medical Council; informal collaboration amongst subject specialists across institutions.
- *Innovations responding to the educational media*: taking advantage of new technologies and acquiring or developing associated materials (software, e-mail, open or resource-based learning materials, etc.).
- *Curriculum-prompted innovations*: to meet the needs of modular and semesterized structures (including new assessment procedures) and in response to the changing content of fields of study and interdisciplinary developments.
- *Institutional initiatives*: including policy decisions of many kinds (regarding information technology, work-based or resource-based learning, etc.) and staff development processes; new structures, including educational development units and similar bodies, teaching and learning committees, and the appointment of senior managers (pro-vice-chancellors, deans, etc.) to oversee the developments.

- *Systemic initiatives*: including government creation of new and, in various ways, different kinds of institution (The Open University, the 'green fields' universities), the funding of system-wide change (Enterprise in Higher Education, work- and skills-related developments); national agency schemes to extend the use of computers and educational technology; national pressure groups (Royal Society, Higher Education for Capability, Open Learning Foundation, etc.).
- *Systemic by-products*: resulting within higher education institutions from system-wide policies and practices (Teaching Quality Assessment, changes in student funding).

Any such typology, of course, acutely raises the question of whether there is any real meaning to the concept of 'innovation'. An analysis such as one based on 'individual', 'guided' and 'directed' innovation, as we have suggested, overarches such a detailed typology, but both approaches point outwards from the innovative event to the nature of structural and policy changes in institutions and the system. The ultimate meanings ascribed to 'innovation' have to be sought in national policy and politics and in institutional responses and aspirations. A different typology might be constructed based on conceptions of 'conservative' and 'radical' innovation, polishing or undermining the status quo (Ayscough 1976; Boyle 1978; Berg and Ostergren 1979; Levine 1980). The pursuit in depth of any typology would also mean considering the profound differences of approach to teaching and learning, and to forms of innovation in general, amongst institutions with different histories, statuses and ambitions.

Different types of innovation call for different requirements in relation to financial and moral support, and different opportunities for access to both in different types of institution. These institutional differences also account for the position of innovation in teaching and learning, in competition with traditional or innovative approaches to the promotion and conduct of research and other commitments of academics within their institutional and disciplinary cultures. The study of innovation in teaching and learning is a study of interactions, attitudes, institutional policies and practices, national contexts and the consensual and confrontational characteristics of all of them. 'To stimulate innovation' means asking not only 'what kind of innovation?', but also 'whose innovation, in whose interests and in what, if any, policy contexts?'

Change

The underlying effects of change of many kinds and at many levels have pervaded this discussion. In general, change in higher education is driven by a number of forces including the demands of employers, government policy initiatives and attempts by teachers in universities to meet the changing needs of students and to reflect the changing nature of their subject matter and the technologies available for teaching and learning. Inertia, or resistance to change, is also heavily supported by a range of factors. For certain traditional institutions the nature of their intake has remained more or less constant, the demands of employers fairly distant and the temptations of government-advocated reforms generally resistible, despite the necessity of some minimal effort in response. The higher education sector is, of course, highly differentiated, with the obvious divide between the pre- and post-1992 institutions, well illustrated by the league table of RAE performance, with a fairly neat division between them in terms of quality ratings at about the half-way point. Although there are such divisions between the old and new universities, they do not alone account for differences of approach to teaching and learning and to innovation. There are also important divisions within institutions and even within departments. In the most research-oriented of old universities there are lecturers who see themselves primarily as having a teaching role, and in the most progressive of new universities, aiming at becoming student-centred learning centres, there are nevertheless those who strongly aspire to international levels of research excellence. For many 'academics' – perhaps those who would much prefer the term to that of 'teachers' – their subject remains paramount and their expertise is measured by their research commitment, grants and outputs rather than the quality of learning experienced by their students.

Yet, even in the more traditional parts of the UK's higher education system there has always been some room for individuals to innovate in what they teach and how they teach it. On occasion both 'academics' and 'teachers' have experimented with new modes of delivery or more interactive methods of learning. Individual innovation has sometimes benefited from a lack of institutional attention to such matters, but any gains from this neglect have been haphazard and isolated. Even when sources of funding for innovation such as EHE have encouraged such innovators to come out into the open, their exposure has often been short lived, with good ideas not being taken up elsewhere in the institution and often their own schemes being shelved once other priorities reassert themselves when the external funding has come to an end. On the other hand, major institutionally driven initiatives, such as semesterization and modularization, have had a profound impact in most, but not all, universities (year-long modules, for example, may simply mean a change in prospectus vocabulary). However, the drive towards segmented curricula has been to some extent tempered by the new enthusiasm for generic skills, or 'key graduate attributes', which supposedly transcend subject boundaries. What Bernstein (1971) would call a 'collection code' with strong boundaries between contents has occasionally coincided with weak 'frames' where the relationship between teacher and taught, learner and subject matter is more fluid, as represented in work-based projects, group presentations and collaborative learning of various kinds. It is noteworthy that the tendency towards the standardization of outcomes in some institutions has led to centralized core skills provision along with the proliferation of module choice.

Amidst all this, 'individual' innovation has been encouraged by some institutions, discouraged or ignored by others. The 'guided' innovation of the kind sponsored by EHE, with increasingly strong indications of suitable directions for research and development, was often reinvented in its application by innovators who had different sorts of agendas from those who established and funded the programmes. Increasingly, though, it seems that we have moved towards 'directed' innovation. The result is that institutions are driven by the need to maximize the returns from their investment in information and communications technology, to compete with other providers for increasingly discerning customers aware of the costs of tuition. The tendency has been sometimes towards 'niche curricula' to attract students, or more often towards a more standardized curriculum in areas of study together with the possibility of a more individualized pedagogy (which is at least the hope of the advocates of information and communications technology and computer-mediated communication).

One of the biggest problems confronting universities, however, is to convince their teaching staff, who so far have not been tempted to jump on the innovation 'bandwagon', of the desirability of the new directions now advocated by senior managers. The mix of motivations that drove the individual innovators or 'lone rangers' (Taylor 1998), who were in the minority in their own institutions, is unlikely to be so effective with the majority who are all too persuaded that MacDonald (1974) was right in his description of innovation as a 'hearse'. For the latter, innovation will not be adopted without considerable struggle unless they can be convinced that the improvements in student learning are real, that their other professional priorities will not be undermined, and that the risks outlined by MacDonald can be avoided. Failing that, they will need to be persuaded that change is the best means of advancement or the only means of survival.

The diversity of approaches to teaching and learning that has resulted from other sources of change and from responses to them has in recent discourse sometimes been discussed in terms of the conditions of postmodernity. New, if modest, changes in teaching and learning have some earlier twentieth-century ancestry, but the post-modern analysis sees the end-of-century changes as more fundamental, and as Menon describes the phenomenon, with quite different origins:

> The increased importance accorded to the experiential aspect of education under post-modernism . . . has encouraged an increase in the practice of problem solving, open learning, and experiential learning in contemporary higher education . . . The new forms of learning are thought to liberate individuals from rigid learning structures and allow them to learn through their own, different, and diverse approaches to the acquisition of knowledge.

The resulting increase in students' mastery of their own learning is paralleled by the disapproval from academics, as part of their 'resistance to the post-modern orientation in education'. Such resistance is accompanied by

'a questioning outlook . . . towards the forms of teaching and learning promoted by a post-modern orientation in higher education' (Menon 1997:
107–9). For our purposes here, however, the origins, conditions and
orientation do not have to be circumscribed in this way. The intentions of
innovators are influenced by scale as well as diversity, the numbers and
heterogeneity of students as well as the pursuit of differences of knowledge
and the means of acquiring it, a commitment to the value of learning as
well as doubts about grand educational narratives. It is certainly the case
that the initiatives taken by innovators are rooted in experience, with the
intention of introducing deliberate change. Fundamental to the notion of
innovation and the boundaries of its operation and interpretation, however, is the fact that the experience and its outcome are not concerned
purely with what teachers do and the procedures they adopt and make
available to students. It is a planned process within perceptions of policy
related, structural and cultural change, as well as in its immediate, operational sense of the need for change.

Incentives

The underlying intention of innovators is invariably to encourage and
support students to develop more effective learning, but the incentives
to innovate are in fact varied, and initiatives are taken at different levels.
The question is therefore – whose innovation is one talking about? At one
extreme an innovation can be that of Dr X on his own in a corner of
department Y, and at the other extreme it can be contained in a policy and
strategy adopted by senior committees of Z University. The reasons for a
particular innovation can be widely diverse, for instance:

- It may have a national context, for example a national report or a new
  funding initiative.
- It may stem from a realization that teaching and learning for students'
  immediate success in a degree is important but not enough for the longer
  term, and it may be directed towards the improved employability of students and new work patterns.
- It may come from the creation or adaptation of new technologies.
- It may result from an awareness that an old way is not working, and that
  a new way is needed to enable students to be autonomous and more able
  to take responsibility for their own continued learning.
- To improve learning and access to learning, it may mean changing the
  format and rhythm of learning in order to cater for mature and part-time
  students, to make it possible for students to interrupt and resume their
  studies.

There is a spectrum. At one end an innovation, such as introducing
student-led seminars or the varied use of a timetable slot originally scheduled
for a lecture, comes from the interaction of tutor and students. At the other

end is an institution choosing to adopt a strategy for work-based learning, skills development or ICT, with institutional investment in initiatives steered towards such targets that are consistent with the institution's overall aims and requirements. Departments or faculties also adopt action plans and priorities and innovators face the choice of working within them or pursuing their independent path. Tensions are often produced, therefore, between individual initiatives and the collective priorities of national and institutional direction making. For innovators there are also more immediate tensions. An innovation is often seen as threatening by colleagues and senior staff, challenging old routines and assumptions. Innovators, as we have seen, have often described themselves as isolated, or as being seen as 'dangerous', 'eccentric', responsible for 'a load of codswallop', and have seen colleagues as feeling intimidated, or senior staff as unsympathetic. They meet with opposition and hostility, being 'excommunicated' in the department, amongst colleagues who are 'sceptical' or have 'contempt for teaching' and see research as the overwhelming priority.

Fortunately that is not the whole picture. There are situations where the success of an innovation has depended on the support of colleagues or senior staff, and this has been forthcoming. There are other situations where initial scepticism and resistance has been overcome and has turned into support (though sometimes support which means 'It's OK as long as you're doing it, but it's not for me'). The decision to innovate and the position of the innovator therefore depend considerably on the institutional culture, its declared and operational priorities, the reward structure for staff, the availability of resources, the prevailing assumptions about what is best for students and for the institution. For individual innovators the issue is one of how best to provide for increased numbers or changed constituencies of students, how to respond to the interests and expectations of all the partners, how to 'read' the difficulties and opportunities of the institution and of higher education. As we have also seen, staff may have great difficulty in reading the signals and placing themselves and their intentions with regard to teaching and learning in the cross-currents of the institutions. The most stable feature of their responses is their commitment to improving the interaction with students and the learning outcomes.

The challenges

For the purposes of this study we have assumed that we are not necessarily talking about major, path-breaking initiatives, but about what people do that is new *in their circumstances*. Although the discussion has encompassed 'guided' innovation – the encouragement or temptation to move in a particular direction, and 'directed' innovation – with its tighter definitions of acceptable directions in which to go, the focus has been primarily on what individuals have done and have found it increasingly difficult to do in the new climate of higher education. Individual innovators are mostly people who have thought of taking an initiative of some kind in response to their present circumstances – including increased student numbers, changes in the pattern of recruitment and student motivation, the pressures of traditional forms of assessment, or some other set of factors in the teaching situation or the wider teaching environment. This study of the situation of the innovator and innovations suggests eight significant challenges:

1. There are obvious problems about *what sort* of innovation and its *purposes*. What someone sees as an innovation to improve student learning may be seen by someone else as ideological or budget-cutting or a waste of time. The challenge here is what *can* be done, possibly because the old way is simply not working, or there has been a radical change in student background and diversity. The challenge is to individuals.
2. The second challenge is to know whether an innovation may be beneficial for students, particularly given changing student circumstances, constituencies and expectations. This is a difficult personal challenge because the judgement cannot be made on the basis of market research or any other research. The challenge is to translate into a workable process a hunch or a hope or a conviction that students will benefit, though there may, of course, be resistance from some students to non-traditional methods.
3. There is a challenge connected with the institution itself, the kind of institution it is. Institutional cultures, statuses and priorities are profoundly different, depending on their histories, the ways in which they have responded to the pressures and requirements of recent years, their place in 'the market'. Of course in some cases there is no challenge at all, where traditional methods may remain intact or at least dominant and relatively *un*challenged. The challenge is to judge the position of teaching and learning and of innovation in the institution as it has been or as it may become in the rapidly changing world of higher education.
4. There is a serious challenge to be faced, therefore, in terms of the priorities and plans of the institution or the faculty or the department. Does the innovation fit within their rolling plans and the directions that these define for financial or other support? Can it therefore be done? Even if innovation involves or may result in research on teaching and learning this is still part of the challenge. 'Non-discipline' research is still rarely accepted as respectable, and admissible for the RAE (or for institutional purposes), although this may change following the encouragement given by the guidelines for RAE 2001, which state that 'research into the teaching and learning process within higher education (pedagogic research) . . . will be assessed by all subject panels on an equitable basis with other forms of research' (HEFCE 1999b: 7). The impact of this, however, is still far from certain.
5. There is also a challenge, therefore, to know what kind of support, if any, may be needed, what obstacles may need to be overcome. Is it available, likely to be forthcoming?

6. Thinking about innovation raises the question: 'Should I be tempted by the *available* funding, which may determine the direction I can go?' Since the early days of EHE this has become an increasing challenge, as institutions have themselves become more directive or prescriptive and the challenge may be in balancing one sort of personal commitment and unfunded innovation against another sort that may attract resources. The challenge may be one of choices between what we wish to do, which may raise all kinds of difficulties, and what can more easily be done because there are institutional or external funding opportunities.

7. There is a personal challenge to do with recognition, including promotion. Not only innovation in teaching and learning, but an interest in teaching and learning as such may reduce promotion prospects. The increasing emphasis nationally and in institutions on equal recognition of teaching and research raises a major challenge – that of judging how real such policies are in practice (even if in theory an institution promotes the enhancement of teaching and learning, and innovation may be considered to help promotion prospects by providing tangible evidence). Nevertheless, extensive comments have been heard in this study, such as: 'All the promotion is based on research', 'Staff do not get rewarded for teaching as promotion is all research-based', 'My publication rate is what really counts no matter how good my report on teaching is', 'Just try to get promotion without research!'

8. Finally, the challenge is to answer the question: *Why should I bother?* The answer to which may be:
   • The RAE lies ahead and I still have $3\frac{3}{4}$ articles to write.
   • Everyone in authority wants me to do something else.
   • I have too much administration to do and no time.
   • Innovation generally means an up-front investment of time, and though there may be sabbaticals for research, I won't get one for teaching and learning.
   • People think I'm eccentric, or worse.

These are salient issues for innovators or would-be innovators, and we have found them in one form or combination or strength or another in all the institutions visited. Of course, some of these issues may not be challenges at all. For example, what an institution or faculty wants may turn out to be what an innovator wants, and there may have been consultation about the policy or the plan, which the innovator has been able to influence. Teaching and learning policies may be serious, debated and flexible. On the whole, however, we have found innovators and innovation projects relating to teaching and learning to be often treated as low status and with suspicion. This is particularly true in the context of the drive for research success as described at some universities in both phases of this study – though there are important exceptions. Universities that in many respects look similar may have very different approaches to the extent of support they wish to give, and be seen to give, to the enhancement of teaching and learning.

The challenges that arise from the study and the experience on which it draws therefore point in a variety of directions:

1. Challenges to whom?
   - To the individual teacher, to make difficult decisions.
   - To the department or other unit, to support individual and/or collective initiatives.
   - To the institution to balance its policies on its needs and the experience of its members.
   - To students to understand the purposes of innovation.

2. About what?
   - Teaching and learning (in competition with research and administration, in relation to career opportunities, etc.).
   - Everyone's priorities.
   - The meanings of 'higher education'.

3. From where?
   - The whole context of higher education.
   - The nature of institutional policy and funding.
   - The demands of the discipline.
   - Personal dilemmas.

4. To do what?
   - Be tempted in another direction.
   - Go ahead and do it.
   - Do nothing.

Those, broadly speaking, are the kinds of questions that people engaged in innovation or committed to improving teaching and learning, in many disciplines and different types of university, seemed mostly to be asking about the challenges.

Innovation and its environments

'Innovation' is sometimes seen as necessarily radical, or as comfortingly liberal. Or as a dirty word. In teaching and learning it relates, as we have clearly seen, to a range of competing assumptions and priorities within institutions and more widely. At the time of writing, therefore, there is contained in these complex challenges an interesting question about whether anything is seriously changing. That there have been profound changes affecting innovation over the past decade is beyond doubt, given the shifts in funding and accountability and quality machineries, the greater centralization of decision making, a new managerialism, the loss of community and collegiality – all of which and related vocabularies have been regularly used by those interviewed during this study. It is important to note that critical comments of this kind are sometimes accompanied by recognition that the real problem lies with policies and pressures coming from outside the institution. But the question is whether we are now on a plateau, or whether there are real prospects of change? Things *are* happening:

- Teaching and learning *are* being talked about and made the subject of national and institutional policies, and obviously the Dearing report and responses to it have played a part. Staff development strategies have gathered momentum (including the appointment of staff to support 'academic', 'curricular' or 'learning and teaching' innovation in universities where such vocabularies have not previously existed). There are many instances of staff in departments or faculties having a remit to promote an interest in teaching and learning, and also quality assurance mechanisms that are levers of increased attention to teaching and learning.
- Structures to support teaching and learning are in place in most of the institutions visited. These include the appointment of pro-vice-chancellors responsible for teaching and learning, and committees for teaching and learning at institutional or faculty or other level, and though structures do not necessarily tell us a great deal, they do indicate significant changes of emphases in the recent past. People who do the teaching, however, often see these departures as having minimal relevance or impact.
- In support of such developments the Institute for Learning and Teaching has come into existence, and despite pronounced initial teething difficulties has moved in the direction of reinforcing the above trends and particularly the accreditation of staff development.
- The Higher Education Funding Council for England has seen the need to put more, albeit still relatively modest, funds into support, including subject support, for teaching and learning (modest by comparison with the funding of research). This is probably the clearest pointer to an understanding of the need for change in the status of teaching and learning in the system, and in the position of innovation.
- The Economic and Social Research Council in 1999 launched an initially £11.5 million Teaching and Learning Research Programme, an ambitious and potentially enormously valuable programme with significant opportunities for links to innovation. This is not a programme purely for higher education, and there is much that is positive in that fact – given the opportunities for linking teaching and learning in higher education and in the remainder of the formal education system, as well as in all the other locations of the 'learning society' where teaching and learning take place.

It is an interesting challenge to know whether this accumulation of developments means a real shift in the environment for innovation in teaching and learning, or whether it is just a temporary recoil from the excesses of the RAE and the growth of dominant, even obsessive, research cultures. This takes the discussion back to the difficult concept of 'community' in the changing conditions of higher education. As we have noted, there have been attempts in recent years to redefine the meaning of a 'community of discourse' or a 'community of scholars'. Even when 'community', in the élite university conditions of the nineteenth and first half of the twentieth century, focused on the small tutorial, sherry and the 'conversation' of tutor and taught, the community also extended, for the upper echelon of academics, to their trans-institutional, often trans-national subject-related invitations or collaborations. It is clear from research on such areas as the external examiner system and threshold comparability that if these operate at all convincingly they do so at subject level. The community as represented by the subject association and its conferences, external examining, the professional journal and research interaction, are viewed by large numbers of academics as their 'real' culture. Despite the also increasing peer competition for research and other funds, the subject-based community of discourse is a means of stepping aside from institutional pressures. More and more self-consciously, teaching staff are under a tension at the meeting point of formalized institutional and disciplinary cultures.

The concept of 'community' is a difficulty present in much of the American, European and other literature on the issues surrounding teachers in higher education. American analysts have done battle since the 1920s over the meanings and possible strategies of 'general education', linked to the problems of a society increasingly bereft of the processes and symbols of solidarity and community. In the famous Harvard report on *General Education in a Free Society* in 1966, the emphasis was clear:

> a supreme need of American education is for a unifying purpose and idea. As recently as a century ago, no doubt existed about such a purpose: it was to train the Christian citizen . . . The student's logical powers were to be formed by mathematics, his taste by the Greek and Latin classics, his speech by rhetoric, and his ideals by Christian ethics.

Hence the growth of a part of the school and college curriculum devoted to general education, a somewhat 'vague and colorless' term, but used 'to indicate that part of a student's whole education which looks first of all to his life as a responsible human being and citizen' (Harvard Committee 1966: 43, 51). A Carnegie Foundation publication in 1981 reflected on general education that it was

> rooted in the belief that individualism, while essential, is not sufficient. It says that the individual also shares significant relationships with a larger community. In this manner general education affirms our connectedness. It is the educational tool we reach for in our search for renewal of the frayed social compact. (Boyer and Levine 1981: 18)

What the American debate in its various phases suggests is a struggle to match a revised curriculum with the needs of greater social 'connectedness', and the role of the teacher has not been ignored in the literature. Academic specialization and its effects are the focus of Damrosch's *We Scholars: Changing the Culture of the University*. Without attempting to 'wish away' specialization, Damrosch suggests that 'within academia, we need to do better at talking across the lines of specialities and identities . . . We should give renewed attention to the ways in which we can bring together differing perspectives and the people who hold them . . .' (Damrosch 1995: 8). Fundamental to this argument is the inevitability of specialization, and though the contours of the American debate are different from those in this study they reveal the same set of difficulties – a 'frayed' sense of community (in society and the institution) and the tension between it and, in this case, the specialization and isolation of the scholar.

It is not clear to what extent this picture will be significantly changed by the new technologies, but the impact on how academics position themselves at this point of tension is bound to increase in various ways. The trans-institutional disciplinary network and discourse will go on becoming increasingly global and immediate, and the notion of 'institutional community' is already undermined at every new technological step.

The institution-subject tension is likely to continue to figure prominently in debate and action. Where *students* position themselves in this respect is a very different discussion, varying considerably across different types and statuses of institutions. Their commitment to 'subject' is vastly different under modularized and unitized structures. Their sense of community is a function of size, campus dispersal, relationship with the institution as part-time or distance education students, age, part-time employment and a host of other factors. The structures representing the knowledge base and the cellular subject structure of institutions are not frameworks within which students in most institutions see themselves. The disciplinary 'community of discourse' excludes students. The 'community of scholars' is not conceptualized in terms of students. For most students the 'community' is no longer the institution. Nor is it a continuing constituency of subject-based fellow students, since the constituency changes at the end of every module. For students there are few of the landmarks that distinguish the dual culture of academic staff. The scale of the institution, its increasing diversities and disparities, the increase in mediated communication, mean that the 'community loyalties' of students may be to activities and symbols with more meaning than anything 'institutional'. This may be the bar (often pub rather than students' union), personal relations (based on anything except the academic programme), a community *outside* the institution (given the proportion of older and part-time students). Only in tightly defined professional preparation programmes do students have a different perception. All of this has implications for the ways in which teachers perceive and relate to students, and the kinds of initiatives in teaching and learning that they wish to take – with or without formal institutional support.

There is an important final emphasis. The different kinds of innovation and levels of decision making for innovation will continue to raise the question of whose innovation we are talking about. All of these recent and current moves could end up with more *institutional* or *system-wide* innovation, not necessarily with any greater opportunity for individual initiatives. This does not mean opposing institutional or system-wide innovation. There is of course a strong argument that it is essential to harness the energies of individual innovators for wider, possibly institutional initiatives, given among other reasons the difficulty of individuals disseminating their work. Such recruitment of individual energies for wider, planned innovation and dissemination has a great deal to commend it, but it is only one consideration. At the heart of the kinds of innovation explored in this study is the experience of teacher–student interaction from which innovation arises. Individual teachers need to be able to say 'this isn't working', to ask what are the reasons relating to the teacher, the students and the situation, and to decide on action. It would be good to think that the individual innovator and the individual initiative will be able to survive and to influence how teachers teach, how students learn, and how institutions and the system enable them to do so.

Appendix A: Types of Innovation and Frequency of Occurrence amongst those Interviewed in Phase One

1. Making use of computers   **77**
   (*Web, Internet, Intranet, computer-aided learning, computer-based learning, computer-mediated communication*)

2. Skills   **45**
   (*personal, transferable, key, core, employability, communication and problem solving*)

3. Team projects, group learning   **40**
   (*co-operation and collaboration*)

4. Student presentations   **16**
   (*individual or group*)

5. Interactive seminars or lectures   **16**

6. Work-based learning   **16**

7. Problem-based learning   **16**

8. Resource-based learning   **14**
   (*packages, booklets, etc.*)

9. Distance learning or open learning   **12**

10. Peer tutoring, mentoring or assessment   **9**

11. Others   **18**
    (*for example, student-directed learning, learning journals/portfolios, profiling, reflective practice*)

Appendix B: Institutions Visited

Phase one
University of East London
University of Glasgow
Heriot-Watt University
University of Leeds
University of Lincolnshire and Humberside
Middlesex University
University of Nottingham
Oxford Brookes University
University of Plymouth
University of Portsmouth
Queen's University of Belfast
University of Salford
University of Wales, Cardiff
University of Wales College of Medicine
University of York

Phase two
University of Glasgow
Middlesex University
University of Nottingham
The Open University
University of Salford

Appendix C: Subject Identity of those Interviewed (Phase One)

Category	Frequency
Clinical and Pre-Clinical	4
Science	39
Professions Allied to Medicine	8
Engineering and Technology	19
Built Environment	8
Mathematical Sciences, IT and Computing	19
Business and Management	13
Social Sciences	15
Humanities	17
Art, Design and Performing Arts	3
Education	9
Central Management	20
Support Services	47

Appendix D: The Sampling Procedure for Phase One of the Study

Method

Since the focus of the first year of the project was to be on innovators and innovations in teaching and learning at the undergraduate level the initial task was to decide at which higher education institutions there were clusters of likely people. This was done by scanning as many sources of information as could be found for what they identified as innovations. The number of references revealed at which institutions there were significant clusters of innovations, mainly sponsored or conducted by individuals, as defined by the authors, editors and others concerned with these sources. An initial selection of universities was made on this basis (no non-university higher education institutions showed up significantly in this process), modified slightly by later information (relating, for example, to TLTP and FDTL projects) and the need to ensure adequate representation of types of university and regions of the UK. From this selection, therefore, of *innovators* and *innovations*, approaches were made to *institutions*. In all cases contact persons at the universities concerned were then asked to suggest other names of people known to be, or to have recently been, involved in innovations of interest to this project.

The main sources of information are set out below. For full publication details see Bibliography.

Directories

Brown, S. (1991) *Students at the Centre of Learning* (SCED).
Educational Development Group of the London and South-East Regional Polytechnic Consortium for In-Service Training (1990) *A Directory of Educational Innovations* (SCED).
Exley, K. and Dennick, R. (1996) *Innovations in Teaching Medical Science* (SEDA).
Exley, K. and Moore, I. (1993) *Innovations in Science Teaching* (SCED).
Hart, J. and Smith, M. (1995a,b) *Innovations in Computing Teaching* (SEDA, 2 vols).
Hounsell, D. *et al.* (1996) *The ASSHE Inventory: Changing Assessment Practices in Scottish Higher Education* (Assessment Strategies in Scottish Higher Education).
Houston, K. (1994) *Innovations in Mathematics Teaching* (SEDA).
Hughes, I.E. (1995) *A Compendium of Innovation and Good Practice in Teaching Pharmacology* (Leeds University Press).
Knight, P.T. (1994) *University-Wide Change, Staff and Curriculum Development* (SEDA).
Open Learning Foundation (1996) *Open Learning Case Studies* (OLF, 10 vols).

Partnership Trust (1996) *Partnership Awards 1989–1995.*

Portsmouth, University of, Enterprise in Higher Education (1994) *National Project Directory* (2 vols).

Rust, C. (1990) *Changes of Course: Eight Case Studies of Innovations in Higher Education Courses* (SCED).

Scottish Higher Education Funding Council (not dated) Flexibility in Teaching and Learning Schemes 1 and 2, mimeo, listing with descriptions of projects funded by SHEFC (annex to evaluation).

Towle, A. (1994) *Innovative Learning and Assessment* (King's Fund).

Archives

Two days were spent scanning the archives of Higher Education for Capability.

With the exception of the annual booklets published for the receptions for the winners of the Partnership Awards, all other Partnership Trust records were destroyed before the beginning of this project.

Books

Books, which were in fact compendia of case studies and other material, were scanned. For example:

Boud, D. and Felitti, G. (1991) *The Challenge of Problem Based Learning.*

Gibbs, G. (1992) *Improving the Quality of Student Learning.*

Graves, N. (1993) *Learner Managed Learning.*

Slowey, M. (1995) *Implementing Change from Within Universities and Colleges.*

Tait, J. and Knight, P. (1996) *The Management of Independent Learning.*

Thornley, L. and Gregory, R. (1994) *Using Group-Based Learning in Higher Education.*

Some books were institution-specific (for example, Assiter, A. (1995) *Transferable Skills in Higher Education* (North London), and Sneddon, I. and Kremer, J. (1994) *An Enterprising Curriculum: Teaching Innovations in Higher Education* (Queen's Belfast)).

Journals

Complete files of *Research into Higher Education Abstracts* and *Studies in Higher Education* were scanned and individual items in other journals located.

Other

Conference proceedings and theses were consulted.

Appendix E: Interview Schedules

Outline of topics for phase one semi-structured interviews
Clarify why we are meeting:
- us
- ethics protocol
- their innovation(s) – what, when?

Previous history relevant to the innovation (personal, other) or – was this when he or she became an innovator?
How did it happen? In what context(s)?
Alone, or in collaboration?

Why innovate?
What was the intention? Purposes?
Pressures, inducements, opportunities
Theory

How did the innovation proceed?
Its extent
What support (departmental, institutional, external)?
The implementation process
Responses (colleagues, students, other)
Any evaluation or other reports (for example, external examiner)

Life history of the innovation:
- continuation, or not
- adaptation
- extension/adoption (within the department, elsewhere in the institution, in the subject area in other institutions)

Interest in the innovation?
Publications? Other outcomes. Materials, etc.

Reflection on the process:
- adequacy of support
- opposition/obstacles
- roles of committees, senior colleagues
- did it survive, die, become embedded, change (as a result of what?)?

Personal outcomes for the innovator (any, positive, negative, etc.?)

Lessons:
- Implications for innovation/innovators
- Implications for institutional organization/policy
- Implications for funding bodies
- quality assurance
- and so on

Have they any documentation to give/lend us?
Can they suggest any other documentation we ought to see?
Any other people we ought to contact?

Thanks

Outline of topics for phase two semi-structured interviews

For lecturers ('bottom up')
1. Nature of project, *ethics protocol.*
2. Interviewee's title, *position* and current responsibilities.
3. *What's it like to work here?*
4. What are your *relationships* (professional!) like with other staff:
   - peers
     collaborative/team or group-oriented/supportive versus competitive/individual/isolated?
   - those in positions of managerial responsibility (department/school/faculty/institution/other)
     positive/responsive/supportive versus negative/hierarchical/unresponsive?
5. *How do you get anything to change in this university?* In particular, *how would you go about introducing new methods* of teaching and learning and getting others to adopt them?
   - Have you any experience of this?
   - What helps?
   - What hinders?
   - Is funding available and, if so, is it important? How would you get funding?
6. What *pressures/incentives for change* in methods of teaching and learning have you experienced?
   - Quality Assurance (internal and external)?
   - national initiatives (EHE, FDTL, TLTP, CTI, DfEE, others)?
   - subject?
7. Does the *subject/course/department/school/faculty/institution try and bring about change* in the way you teach? If so, how?
   - Involvement with/perceptions of educational development services.
8. *How important is teaching and learning* compared with other aspects of your job:
   - administration?
   - research?
   (Explore in terms of what the respondent thinks it should be, what the institution thinks it should be and how it actually is.)
9. Is excellence in teaching and/or involvement in innovation in *teaching and learning rewarded?* If so, how?

10. How do you see the *future of teaching and learning in this university*?
11. I'll obviously be very careful not to write up any of this in a manner by which you can be identified. However, is there anything you've just told me which I should be *particularly careful* about? Anything I should check with you first before I use it?

For managers ('top down')
Explain project and ethics protocol if necessary, including assuring your anonymity. Position regarding reporting and gatekeepers.

1. Interviewee's title, *position* and current responsibilities
2. Interviewee's position/*roles in the structure, influence through committee(s)*, etc. (including any connection with teaching and learning service or similar unit). (Assess level of influence.)
3. Can you place *teaching and learning in the priorities of the university (faculty etc.)*? How does it fare in relation to research?
4. Is it a question of getting adequate teaching done, or *is teaching and learning the subject of innovation policy and practice*? Is there a (university, faculty) policy on innovation?
5. Is there *funding to support teaching and learning 'enhancement'*, who is responsible for managing it, are you involved? Do staff proposals have to fit in with a plan/policy?
6. EITHER
There is a literature regarding *'institutional culture' and sub-cultures*. Do those concepts have any relevance in relation to this university/faculty etc.? (Extend this discussion in whatever ways the answer might make possible.)
OR
If you had to describe the culture of this institution what would you say it looked like? Are there any identifiable sub-cultures? (Extend this discussion in whatever ways the answer might make possible.)
7. (If the answer to 6 makes it possible to ask): *Where would teaching and learning and innovation fit* in this culture/sub-culture?
8. *How responsive is the university (faculty, etc.) to external initiatives* relating to teaching and learning (for example, EHE, TLTP, CTI, FDTL, DfEE)?
9. *How important are recent/current national policy initiatives relating to teaching and learning* (for example, HEFCE funding, ILT)?
10. Are *excellence in teaching and learning and innovation rewarded*? If so, which? How?
11. Would it be possible for you to address a conference on the subject of '*innovation in your university (faculty)*'? If so, what might your main points be?

Repeat about anonymity. But is there *anything we have discussed that I should be particularly careful about*? Anything to check back with you before I use it?

Topics for discussion ('focus') groups
1. How would you describe this university as a place to work?
2. What is the biggest teaching and learning issue in this school/department? In the university as a whole?
3. What changes in teaching and learning are currently taking place in this school/department? In the university as a whole? Why, by whom and how are they being introduced?

Appendix F: Ethics Protocols

Phase one

What the project is about

The past decade has seen increased attention to methods of teaching and learning, and the 1997 Dearing report, *Higher Education in the Learning Society*, has further emphasized the need for innovative responses to the challenges facing higher education. The agenda for these changes has included increased student numbers and diversity, the promotion of lifelong learning and a learning society, and satisfying the requirements of employment and citizenship. The project aims to examine and interpret the innovative responses of higher education in the recent period to these pressures and opportunities. It will seek to analyse the sources, nature and implementation of recent and current innovations, the obstacles and life histories. It will explore the meanings attached to innovation as process and product. It will therefore attempt to identify:

- the motives, sources of ideas, successes and failures of innovators in a range of subjects in a variety of institutions, and implications for staff satisfaction and rewards;
- the characteristics of innovations generated by individuals, institutions, internally and externally available funding, external scrutiny, national policies and programmes, international models and research;
- the factors (inter-personal, institutional and structural) which do or do not stimulate and support innovation;
- the contribution of new developments in communication and information technologies to innovations in teaching and learning;
- innovation as creation, adaptation, transfer, development, dissemination;
- the contexts of innovation, including those of finance and institutional scale and structure.

Although curriculum change, modularization, assessment methods, access and emphases on skills and learning outcomes, for example, relate to teaching and learning, these will be contingent rather than central features of the project. The focus will be on those innovations that seek to shape the learning interface of students with teachers, one another, the technologies and materials. These include such processes as problem-based learning, open learning, independent learning, distance learning and computer-based or supported learning.

Who we are
We all work at the University of Plymouth; Harold Silver as a visiting professor in HE, Andy Hannan as Research Coordinator in the Faculty of Arts and Education and Sue English as a research assistant.

Where the money is coming from for the project
We are funded by the Economic and Social Research Council, with some assistance from the Higher Education Quality Council in the first year with other co-funders joining the ESRC for a possible second year.

Confidentiality
Findings will be presented in such a way that no individual can be identified unless he or she expressly agrees otherwise. Similarly, institutions will not be identified without formal permission being obtained. Information already in the public realm is not subject to these constraints, but care will be taken not to link it to data gathered through this research in such a way as to undermine these principles.

Right of withdrawal
All those being interviewed have the right to withdraw at any time, to ask for recording to cease or to require that information given should not be used in any way.

Feedback
Copies of the project report will be sent to all participating institutions and made available over the Internet to all those who contributed.

Phase two

What the project is about
The past decade has seen increased attention to methods of teaching and learning, and the 1997 Dearing report, *Higher Education in the Learning Society*, has further emphasized the need for innovative responses to the challenges facing higher education. The agenda for these changes has included increased student numbers and diversity, the promotion of lifelong learning and a learning society, and satisfying the requirements of employment and citizenship. The project aims to examine and interpret the innovative responses of higher education in the recent period to these pressures and opportunities. The first year of this project (which began in September 1997) focused on innovators and innovations. In this second year we are concerned with institutional contexts for innovation. Our aims are:

- To explore the higher education institutional climates/frameworks that support or inhibit institutional or individual efforts to innovate in teaching and learning.
- To continue the exploration of 'new patterns of teaching and learning' begun in the first phase and needing further understanding in the context of institutional climates/frameworks.
- To consider how higher education institutions embed, or fail to embed, innovations in teaching and learning.
- To explore the role of subject disciplines and departments with regard to innovations in teaching and learning.

- To investigate the impact of national policies on institutional approaches to the funding and support of innovations in teaching and learning.

Who we are
We all work at the University of Plymouth; Harold Silver as a visiting professor in Higher Education, Andy Hannan as Reader in Education and Research Coordinator in the Faculty of Arts and Education and Sue English as a research assistant.

Where the money is coming from for the project
This year we are jointly funded by the Economic and Social Research Council, the Higher Education Funding Council for England and the Department for Education and Employment.

Confidentiality
Permission to include an institution in the project will be obtained from its Vice-Chancellor/Principal. The intention is to name institutions following a process whereby authorization is obtained. The use of information about the institution will be the subject of agreement between a nominated 'gatekeeper' of the university and the project. Permission will be obtained at subject/departmental/school level from a nominated 'gatekeeper' before any report on information gathered at that level is made to others (internally or externally). Findings will be presented in such a way that no individual will be identifiable unless he or she expressly agrees otherwise. If any doubt arises the individual concerned will be consulted. Information already in the public realm is not subject to these constraints, but care will be taken not to link it to data gathered through this research in such a way as to undermine these principles.

Right of withdrawal
All those being interviewed will be given the opportunity at the beginning of an interview to discuss issues raised in this protocol. Interviewees have the right to withdraw at any time, to ask for recording to cease or to require that information given should not be used in any way.

Feedback
Copies of the project report will be sent to all participating institutions and made available over the Internet to all those who contributed.

Bibliography

Abercrombie, M.L.J. (1970, fourth edition 1979, contains foreword to the first edition) *Aims and Techniques of Group Teaching*. Guildford: Society for Research into Higher Education.

Abercrombie, M.L.J. and Terry, P.M. (1978) *Talking to Learn: Improving Teaching and Learning in Small Groups*. Guildford: Society for Research into Higher Education.

Allaire, Y. and Firsirotu, M.E. (1984) Theories of organizational culture, *Organizational Studies*, 5(3): 193–226.

Arbuthnott, J.P. and Bone, T.R. (1993) Anatomy of a merger, *Higher Education Quarterly*, 47(2): 104–19.

Argyris, C. and Schön, D.A. (1996) *Organizational Learning II: Theory, Method, and Practice*. Reading, MA: Addison-Wesley.

Armstrong, S., Thompson, G. and Brown, S. (eds) (1997) *Facing up to Radical Changes in Universities*. London: Kogan Page.

Ashby, E. (1967) Machines, understanding, and learning: reflections on technology in education, *The Graduate Journal* 7(2): 359–73.

Ashby, E. (1974) *Adapting Universities to a Technological Society*. San Francisco: Jossey-Bass.

Assiter, A. (ed.) (1995) *Transferable Skills in Higher Education*. London: Kogan Page.

Ayscough, P.B. (1976) Academic reactions to educational innovation, *Studies in Higher Education*, 1(1): 3–9.

Beard, R. (1970) *Teaching and Learning in Higher Education*. Harmondsworth: Penguin.

Beard, R.M., Bligh, D.A. and Harding, A.G. (1978, fourth edition) *Research into Teaching Methods in Higher Education Mainly in British Universities*. Guildford: Society for Research into Higher Education.

Becher, T. (1989) *Academic Tribes and Territories: Intellectual Enquiry and the Cultures of Disciplines*. Buckingham: Open University Press.

Beckhard, R. and Pritchard, W. (1992) *Changing the Essence: The Art of Creating and Leading Fundamental Change in Organizations*. San Francisco: Jossey-Bass.

Berg, B. and Ostergren, B. (1979) Innovation processes in higher education, *Studies in Higher Education*, 4(2): 261–8.

Bernstein, B. (1971) On the classification and framing of educational knowledge, in B. Bernstein (ed.), *Class, Codes and Control*, vol. 1: *Theoretical Studies towards a Sociology of Language*. London: Routledge & Kegan Paul.

Bernstein, B. (1975) Class and pedagogies: visible and invisible, in B. Bernstein (ed.), *Class, Codes and Control*, vol. 3: *Towards a Theory of Educational Transmissions*. London: Routledge & Kegan Paul.

Bligh, D. (1971) *What's the Use of Lectures?* London: University Teaching Methods Unit.

Bok, D. (1986) *Higher Learning*. Cambridge, MA: Harvard University Press.

Boud, D. and Felitti, G. (eds) (1991) *The Challenge of Problem Based Learning*. London: Kogan Page.

Boyer, E.L. and Levine, A. (1981) *A Quest for Common Learning: The Aims of General Education*. Princeton, NJ: Carnegie Foundation for the Advancement of Teaching.

Boyle, J.D. (1978) Conservative innovation, *Studies in Higher Education*, 3(1): 63–71.

Boys, C.J., Brennan, J., Henkel, M. *et al.* (1988) *Higher Education and the Preparation for Work*. London: Jessica Kingsley.

Brockbank, A. and McGill, I. (1998) *Facilitating Reflective Learning in Higher Education*. Buckingham: Open University Press.

Brown, S. (ed.) (1991) *Students at the Centre of Learning*. Birmingham: Standing Conference on Educational Development.

Burton, L. and Haines, C. (1997) Innovation in teaching and assessing mathematics at university level, *Teaching in Higher Education*, 2(3): 273–93.

Carboni, M., Oakey, D.H. and Sanger, J. (1996) Learning for capability – the experience of the University of Salford. Paper presented at 'Placing the Student at the Centre' conference, Maastricht, 20–2 November.

Carnegie Commission on Higher Education (1972) *The Fourth Revolution: Instructional Technology in Higher Education. A Report and Recommendations*. New York: McGraw-Hill.

Chaffee, E.E. and Tierney, W.G. (1988) *Collegiate Culture and Leadership Strategies*. New York: American Council on Education.

Clark, B.R. (1984) The organizational conception, in B.R. Clark (ed.), *Perspectives on Higher Education: Eight Disciplinary and Comparative Views*. Berkeley, CA: University of California Press.

Clark, B.R. (ed.) (1987) *The Academic Life: Small Worlds, Different Worlds*. Princeton, NJ: Carnegie Foundation for the Advancement of Teaching.

Cohen, M.D. and March, J.G. (1974, edition of 1986) *Leadership and Ambiguity: The American College President*. Boston, MA: Harvard Business School Press.

Collier, K.G. (ed.) (1974) *Innovation in Higher Education*. Windsor: NFER.

Committee of Scottish University Principals (1992) *Teaching and Learning in an Expanding Higher Education System* (MacFarlane Report). Edinburgh: Scottish Centrally-Funded Colleges.

Committee of Vice-Chancellors and Principals, Independent Task Force (1997) *Clinical Academic Careers*. London: CVCP.

Committee on Higher Education (1963) *Higher Education* (Robbins Report), Cm 2154. London: HMSO.

Committee on University Teaching Methods (1964) *University Teaching Methods* (Hale Report). London: HMSO.

Costello, N. (1992) Strategic change and the learning organization. Unpublished MPhil dissertation, Judge Institute of Management Studies, University of Cambridge.

Costello, N. (1993) Organisational cultures and distance learning, *Open Learning*, 8(2): 3–11.

Council for National Academic Awards, Learning Resources Working Party (1981) The use of learning resources in higher education, *British Journal of Educational Technology*, 12(2): 84–92.

Dale, E., Finn, J.D. and Hoban, C.F. (1950, revised edition) Audio-visual materials, in W.S. Monroe (ed.), *Encyclopedia of Educational Research*. New York: Macmillan.

Damrosch, D. (1995) *We Scholars: Changing the Culture of the University*. Cambridge, MA: Harvard University Press.

Davies, G. (1997) The Principal's perspective, *The Report 1996–97*. Glasgow: University of Glasgow.

Deal, T.E. and Kennedy, A.A. (1982, edition of 1988) *Corporate Cultures: The Rites and Rituals of Corporate Life*. Harmondsworth: Penguin.

Dearing Report: c.f. National Committee of Inquiry into Higher Education.

Department for Education and Employment (DfEE), Higher Education: Quality and Employability Division (1998) *Higher Education Development Projects 1998–2000*. Sheffield: DfEE.

De Woot, P. (1996) Managing change at university, *CRE-action*, 109: 19–28.

Drucker, P. (1985) *Innovation and Entrepreneurship: Practice and Principles*. London: Heinemann.

Drummond, I., Nixon, I. and Wiltshire, J. (1997) Personal transferable skills in higher education: the problems of implementing good practice, mimeo. Newcastle: University of Newcastle, Department of Architecture.

Educational Development Group of the London and South-East Regional Polytechnic Consortium for In-Service Training (eds) (1990) *A Directory of Educational Innovations*. Birmingham: Standing Conference on Educational Development.

Educational Media International (1978), no. 3.

Exley, K. and Dennick, R. (eds) (1996) *Innovations in Teaching Medical Sciences*. Birmingham: Staff and Educational Development Association.

Exley, K. and Moore, I. (eds) (1993) *Innovations in Science Teaching*. Birmingham: Standing Conference on Educational Development.

Flood Page, C. and Greenaway, H. (eds) (1971) *Innovation in Higher Education*. London: Society for Research into Higher Education.

Freeman, C. (1974, edition of 1982) *The Economics of Industrial Innovation*. London: Pinter.

Fullan, M.G. (1991) *The New Meaning of Educational Change*. London: Cassell.

Fyfe, W.H. (1950) Lectures, *Universities Quarterly*, 4(3): 239–43.

Garrick Report: c.f. National Committee of Inquiry into Higher Education.

Geiger, R.L. (1986) *To Advance Knowledge: The Growth of American Research Universities, 1900–1940*. New York: Oxford University Press.

General Dental Council (1997) *The First Five Years*. London: GDC.

General Medical Council (GMC) (1993) *Tomorrow's Doctors*. London: GMC.

Gibbs, G. (1992) *Improving the Quality of Student Learning*. Bristol: Technical and Educational Services.

Gibbs, G. (1999) *Institutional Learning and Teaching Strategies: A Guide to Good Practice*. Bristol: HEFCE.

Graves, N. (1993) *Learner Managed Learning: Practice, Theory and Policy*. Leeds: Higher Education for Capability.

Goddard, J., Charles, D., Pike, A., Potts, G. and Bradley, D. (1994) *Universities and Communities*. London: Committee of Vice-Chancellors and Principals.

Hale Report: c.f. Committee on University Teaching Methods.

Handy, C.B. (1976, edition of 1985) *Understanding Organizations.* New York: Facts on File.

Hannan, A., English, S. and Silver, H. (1999) Why innovate? Some preliminary findings from a research project on 'Innovations in teaching and learning in higher education', *Studies in Higher Education,* 24(3): 279–89.

Hart, J. and Smith, M. (eds) (1995a) *Innovations in Computing Teaching.* Birmingham: Staff and Educational Development Association.

Hart, J. and Smith, M. (eds) (1995b) *Innovations in Computing Teaching 2: Improving the Quality of Teaching and Learning.* Birmingham: Staff and Educational Development Association.

Harvard Committee (1966) *General Education in a Free Society.* Cambridge, MA: Harvard University Press.

Hawkridge, D.G. (1978) The propagation of educational innovations, in D. Brook and P. Race (eds), *Aspects of Educational Technology Volume XII: Educational Technology in a Changing World.* London: Kogan Page.

Higher Education Funding Council for England (HEFCE) (1998) Learning and teaching: strategy and funding proposals, mimeo. Bristol: HEFCE.

Higher Education Funding Council for England (HEFCE) (1999a) *Teaching Quality Enhancement Fund: Funding Arrangements.* Bristol: HEFCE.

Higher Education Funding Council for England (HEFCE) (1999b) *Research Assessment Exercise 2001: Assessment Panels' Criteria and Working Methods, RAE 5/99.* Bristol: HEFCE.

Hilgard, E.R. (1964) Teaching machines and creativity, *Programmed Learning,* 1(2): 55–60.

Hounsell, D., McCulloch, M., Scott, M. and the ASSHE Project Team (1996) *The ASSHE Inventory: Changing Assessment Practices in Scottish Higher Education.* Edinburgh: University of Edinburgh, Centre for Teaching, Learning and Assessment.

Houston, K. (ed.) (1994) *Innovations in Mathematics Teaching.* Birmingham: Staff and Educational Development Association.

Hughes, I.E. (ed.) (1995) *A Compendium of Innovation and Good Practice in Teaching Pharmacology.* Leeds: Leeds University Press.

Jones Report (Brynmor Jones, chairman) (1965) *Audio-Visual Aids in Higher Scientific Education.* London: HMSO.

Kerr, Clark (1964) *The Uses of the University.* Cambridge, MA: Harvard University Press.

Kimberly, J.R. (1981) Managerial innovation, in P.C. Nystrom and W.H. Starbuck (eds) *Handbook of Organizational Design,* vol. 1: *Adapting Organizations to their Environment.* Oxford: Oxford University Press.

King, N. and Anderson, N. (1995) *Innovation and Change in Organizations.* London: Routledge.

Knight, P.T. (ed.) (1994) *University-Wide Change, Staff and Curriculum Development.* Birmingham: Staff and Educational Development Association.

Kremer-Hayon, L. and Avi-Itzhak, T. (1986) Roles of academic department chairpersons at the university level: perceptions and satisfaction, *Higher Education,* 15: 105–12.

Laurillard, D. (1993) *Rethinking University Teaching: A Framework for the Effective Use of Educational Technology.* London: Routledge.

Levine, A. (1980) *Why Innovation Fails.* Albany: State University of New York Press.

Lueddeke, G. (1997) Educational development units in higher education: much ado about something?, *Quality in Higher Education,* 3(2): 155–70.

Lueddeke, G. (1999) Toward a constructivist framework for guiding change and innovation in higher education, *The Journal of Higher Education*, 70(3): 235–60.

MacDonald, B. (1974) Safari – An abstract of the proposal submitted to the Ford Foundation in 1971, in Safari: *Some Interim Papers*. Norwich: University of East Anglia, Centre for Applied Research in Education.

MacFarlane Report: c.f. Committee of Scottish University Principals.

MacKenzie, N. (1970) Springboard or scaffold? The Commission on Instructional Technology in the United States, *British Journal of Educational Technology*, 1(3): 173–82.

MacKenzie, N., Eraut, M. and Jones, H.C. (1976) *Teaching and Learning: An Introduction to New Methods and Resources in Higher Education*. Paris: Unesco Press.

McNay, I. (1995) From the collegial academy to corporate enterprise: the changing cultures of universities, in T. Schuller (ed.), *The Changing University?* Buckingham: Open University Press.

March, J.G. and Olsen, J.P. (eds) (1979, edition of 1994) *Ambiguity and Choice in Organizations*. Oslo: Scandinavian University Press.

Masland, A.T. (1985) Organizational culture in the study of higher education, *Review of Higher Education*, 8(2): 157–68.

Meek, V.L. (1988) Organizational culture: origins and weaknesses, *Organization Studies*, 9(4): 453–73.

Meisler, R.A. (1971) Technologies for learning, in S.G. Tickton (ed.), *To Improve Learning: An Evaluation of Instructional Technology*, vol. II. New York: R.R. Bowker.

Melton, R. (1986) Innovation in The Open University. The Open University, Institute of Educational Technology, Teaching and Consultancy Centre (report no. 28), mimeo.

Mendenhall, T. (1950) Lecturing – English and American, *Universities Quarterly*, 4(3): 262–5.

Menon, M.E. (1997) Higher education and the post-modern challenge, *Reflections on Higher Education*, 9: 103–13.

Meyerson, D. and Martin, J. (1987) Cultural change: an integration of three different views, *Journal of Management Studies*, 24(6): 623–47.

Middlehurst, R. (1993) *Leading Academics*. Buckingham: Open University Press.

Middlesex University (1996) *Long Term Strategic Plans for Middlesex University*. London: Middlesex University.

Middlesex University (1997) *Corporate Plan 1997–2001, Mission Statement* and *Vision Statement*. London: Middlesex University.

Middlesex University, Management Team (1997) The University's revised academic structure, mimeo. London: Middlesex University.

Moberly, W. (1949) *The Crisis in the University*. London: SCM Press.

Moore, D.M. and Hunt, T.C. (1980) The nature of resistance to the use of instructional media, *British Journal of Educational Technology*, 11(2): 141–6.

National Committee of Inquiry into Higher Education (NCIHE) (1997a) *Higher Education in the Learning Society* (Dearing Report). London: NCIHE.

National Committee of Inquiry into Higher Education (NCIHE) (1997b) *Higher Education in the Learning Society: Report of the Scottish Committee* (Garrick Report). London: NCIHE.

Nixon, J., Beattie, M., Challis, M. and Walker, M. (1998) What does it mean to be an academic? A colloquium, *Teaching in Higher Education*, 3(3): 277–98.

Nottingham, University of (1995) *Enterprise in Higher Education at the University of Nottingham: The First Five Years*. Nottingham: University of Nottingham.

Nottingham, University of (1998) *Teaching and Learning Strategy.* Nottingham: University of Nottingham.

Nottingham, University of (1999) Prospectus for supporting teaching and learning development and new learning technologies: draft for consultation, mimeo. Nottingham: University of Nottingham.

Nuffield Foundation Group for Research and Innovation in Higher Education (1973a) *Newsletter No. 1*: 9–17.

Nuffield Foundation Group for Research and Innovation in Higher Education (1973b) *Newsletter No. 2*: 16–30.

Nuffield Foundation Group for Research and Innovation in Higher Education (1974) *Newsletter No. 4*: 20–4.

Open Learning Foundation (1996) *Open Learning Case Studies* (series title of ten volumes of case studies). London: Open Learning Foundations.

Open University, The (1997) *Plans for Change: Lifelong Learning for a New Era.* Milton Keynes: The Open University.

Open University, The (1998) *Academic Board Committee Sub-structure Review: Fourth Report.* Milton Keynes: The Open University.

Open University, The, Faculty of Arts (1998) Unit Plan 1999–2003, mimeo. Milton Keynes: The Open University.

Open University, The, Faculty of Technology (1998) Unit Plan 1999–2004, mimeo. Milton Keynes: The Open University.

Open University, The (1999) Institutional learning and teaching strategy: discussion paper, mimeo. Milton Keynes: The Open University.

Open University, The, Senate (1999) The OU at thirty: strategies for 1999. A report by the Vice-Chancellor, mimeo. Milton Keynes: The Open University.

Ott, J.S. (1989) *The Organizational Culture Perspective.* Pacific Grove, CA: Brooks/Cole.

Partnership Trust (1996) Partnership Awards 1989–1995 mimeo. London: Partnership Trust.

Perkin, H.J. (1987) The academic profession in the United Kingdom, in B.R. Clark (ed.), *The Academic Profession: National, Disciplinary, and Institutional Settings.* Berkeley, CA: University of California Press.

Perry, W. (1994) interview, in The Open University, *Learn & Live: Celebrating Twenty Five Years of the Open University.* Milton Keynes: The Open University.

Peters, T. (1987) *Thriving on Chaos.* New York: Alfred A. Knopf.

Portsmouth, University of, Enterprise in Higher Education (1994) *National Project Directory.* Portsmouth: University of Portsmouth.

Robbins Report: c.f. Committee on Higher Education.

Riley, J. (1975) Course teams at The Open University (report for the Nuffield Foundation Group for Research and Innovation in Higher Education), typescript.

Rust, C. (ed.) (1990) *Changes of Course: Eight Case-Studies of Innovations in Higher Education Courses.* Birmingham: Standing Conference on Educational Development.

Rutherford, D., Fleming, W. and Mathias, H. (1985) Strategies for change in higher education: three political models, *Higher Education*, 14: 433–45.

Salford, University of (1995a) University of Salford Enterprise in Higher Education, annual report, mimeo. Salford: University of Salford.

Salford, University of (1995b) University of Salford Enterprise Unit, five year report, November 1990–October 1995, mimeo. Salford: University of Salford.

Salford, University of (1997) Criterion [sic] for promotion on the basis of teaching excellence, mimeo. Salford: University of Salford.

Salford, University of (1998) *The Strategic Framework*. Salford: University of Salford.

Schein, E.H. (1985) *Organizational Culture and Leadership*. San Francisco: Jossey-Bass.

Schuller, T. (1992) The exploding community? The university idea and the smashing of the academic atom, in I. McNay (ed.), *Visions of Post-Compulsory Education*. Buckingham: Open University Press.

Schumpeter, J.A. (1943, edition of 1976) *Capitalism, Socialism and Democracy*. London: Allen & Unwin.

Scottish Higher Education Funding Council (n.d.) Flexibility in Teaching and Learning Schemes 1 and 2, mimeo (listing with descriptions of funded projects). Edinburgh: Scottish HEFC.

Secretary of State for Education and Science (and Secretaries of State for Scotland, Wales and Northern Ireland) (1985) *The Development of Higher Education into the 1990s*, Cm 9524. London: HMSO.

Secretary of State for Education and Science (and Secretaries of State for Scotland, Northern Ireland and Wales) (1991) *Higher Education: A New Framework*, Cm 1541. London: HMSO.

Silver, H. (1999) Managing to innovate in higher education, *British Journal of Educational Studies*, 47(2): 145–56.

Silver, H. and Silver, P. (1997) *Students: Changing Roles, Changing Lives*. Buckingham: Open University Press.

Silver, H., Hannan, A. and English, S. (1998) *The Experiences of Innovators*. Exmouth: University of Plymouth; also available at http://www.fae.plym.ac.uk/itlhe.html

Skinner, B.F. (1959) *Cumulative Record*. London: Methuen.

Skinner, B.F. (1961, enlarged edition) *Cumulative Record*. London: Methuen.

Slowey, M. (ed.) (1995) *Implementing Change from Within Universities and Colleges: 10 Personal Accounts*. London: Kogan Page.

Sneddon, I. and Kremer, J. (eds) (1994) *An Enterprising Curriculum: Teaching Innovations in Higher Education*. London: HMSO.

Society for Research into Higher Education (SRHE) (1973) *Individualising Student Learning: the Role of the New Media*. London: SRHE.

Stenhouse, L. (1983) *Authority, Education and Emancipation*. London: Heinemann Educational.

Stoneman, P. (1983) *The Economic Analysis of Technological Change*. Oxford: Oxford University Press.

Tait, J. and Knight, P. (eds) (1996) *The Management of Independent Learning*. London: Kogan Page.

Taylor, P.G. (1998) Institutional change in uncertain times: *lone ranging* is not enough, *Studies in Higher Education*, 23(3): 269–79.

Thornley, L. and Gregory, R. (eds) (1994) *Using Group-Based Learning in Higher Education*. London: Kogan Page.

Thornton, J.W. and Brown, J.W. (eds) (1968) *New Media and College Teaching*. Washington, DC: National Education Association.

Times Higher Education Supplement (1996) Supplement, 'Research assessments 1996', 20 December.

Towle, A. (ed.) (1994) *Innovative Learning and Assessment*. London: King's Fund Centre.

Unwin, D. (ed.) (1969) *Media and Methods: Instructional Technology in Higher Education*. London: McGraw-Hill.

Unwin, D. (1985) The cyclical nature of educational technology, *PLET: Programmed Learning and Educational Technology*, 22(1): 65–7.

Van Maanen, J. and Barley, S.R. (1985) Cultural organization: fragments of a theory, in P.J. Frost, L. Moore, M. Louis, C. Lundberg and J. Martin (eds), *Organizational Culture*. Beverly Hills, CA: Sage.

Van Vught, F.A. (1989) Creating innovations in higher education, *European Journal of Education*, 24(3): 249–70.

Venables, P. (1978) *Higher Education Developments: The Technological Universities 1956–1976*. London: Faber and Faber.

Veysey, L.R. (1965) *The Emergence of the American University*. Chicago: University of Chicago Press.

Weick, K.E. (1976) Educational organizations as loosely coupled systems, *Administrative Science Quarterly*, 21(1): 1–19.

Weisgerber, R.A. (1968) *Instructional Process and Media Innovation*. Chicago: Rand McNally.

Whitty, G. (1985) *Sociology and School Knowledge: Curriculum Theory, Research and Politics*. London: Methuen.

Young, M.F.D. (ed.) (1971) *Knowledge and Control: New Directions for the Sociology of Education*. London: Collier Macmillan.

Young, M.F.D. (1998) *The Curriculum of the Future: From the 'New Sociology of Education' to a Critical Theory of Learning*. London: Falmer Press.

Index

The Society for Research into Higher Education

The Society for Research into Higher Education (SRHE) exists to stimulate and coordinate research into all aspects of higher education. It aims to improve the quality of higher education through the encouragement of debate and publication on issues of policy, on the organization and management of higher education institutions, and on the curriculum, teaching and learning methods.

The Society is entirely independent and receives no subsidies, although individual events often receive sponsorship from business or industry. The Society is financed through corporate and individual subscriptions and has members from many parts of the world.

Under the imprint *SRHE & Open University Press*, the Society is a specialist publisher of research, having over 80 titles in print. In addition to *SRHE News*, the Society's newsletter, the Society publishes three journals: *Studies in Higher Education* (three issues a year), *Higher Education Quarterly* and *Research into Higher Education Abstracts* (three issues a year).

The Society runs frequent conferences, consultations, seminars and other events. The annual conference in December is organized at and with a higher education institution. There are a growing number of networks which focus on particular areas of interest, including:

Access	Learning Environment
Assessment	Legal Education
Consultants	Managing Innovation
Curriculum Development	New Technology for Learning
Eastern European	Postgraduate Issues
Educational Development Research	Quantitative Studies
FE/HE	Student Development
Funding	Vocational Qualifications
Graduate Employment	

Benefits to members

Individual

- The opportunity to participate in the Society's networks
- Reduced rates for the annual conferences

- Free copies of *Research into Higher Education Abstracts*
- Reduced rates for *Studies in Higher Education*
- Reduced rates for *Higher Education Quarterly*
- Free copy of *Register of Members' Research Interests* – includes valuable reference material on research being pursued by the Society's members
- Free copy of occasional in-house publications, e.g. *The Thirtieth Anniversary Seminars Presented by the Vice-Presidents*
- Free copies of *SRHE News* which informs members of the Society's activities and provides a calendar of events, with additional material provided in regular mailings
- A 35 per cent discount on all SRHE/Open University Press books
- Access to HESA statistics for student members
- The opportunity for you to apply for the annual research grants
- Inclusion of your research in the *Register of Members' Research Interests*

Corporate

- Reduced rates for the annual conferences
- The opportunity for members of the Institution to attend SRHE's network events at reduced rates
- Free copies of *Research into Higher Education Abstracts*
- Free copies of *Studies in Higher Education*
- Free copies of *Register of Members' Research Interests* – includes valuable reference material on research being pursued by the Society's members
- Free copy of occasional in-house publications
- Free copies of *SRHE News*
- A 35 per cent discount on all SRHE/Open University Press books
- Access to HESA statistics for research for students of the Institution
- The opportunity for members of the Institution to submit applications for the Society's research grants
- The opportunity to work with the Society and co-host conferences
- The opportunity to include in the *Register of Members' Research Interests* your Institution's research into aspects of higher education

Membership details: SRHE, 3 Devonshire Street, London
W1N 2BA, UK. Tel: 020 7637 2766. Fax: 020 7637 2781.
email: srhe@mailbox.ulcc.ac.uk
World Wide Web: http://www.srhe.ac.uk./srhe/
Catalogue: SRHE & Open University Press, Celtic Court,
22 Ballmoor, Buckingham MK18 1XW. Tel: 01280 823388.
Fax: 01280 823233. email: enquiries@openup.co.uk
World Wide Web: www.openup.co.uk

ON BECOMING AN INNOVATIVE UNIVERSITY TEACHER
REFLECTION IN ACTION

John Cowan

This is one of the most interesting texts I have read for many years . . . It is authoritative and clearly written. It provides a rich set of examples of teaching, and a reflective discourse.

Professor George Brown

. . . succeeds in inspiring the reader by making the process of reflective learning interesting and thought provoking . . . has a narrative drive which makes it a book too good to put down.

Dr Mary Thorpe

What comes through very strongly and is an admirable feature is so much of the author's own personal experience, what it felt like to take risks and how his own practice developed as a result of taking risks, exploring uncharted territory . . . The book has the potential to become the reflective practitioner's 'bible'.

Dr Lorraine Stefani

This unusual, accessible and significant book begins each chapter by posing a question with which college and university teachers can be expected to identify; and then goes on to answer the question by presenting a series of examples; finally, each chapter closes with 'second thoughts', presenting a viewpoint somewhat distinct from that taken by John Cowan. This book will assist university teachers to plan and run innovative activities to enable their students to engage in effective reflective learning; it will help them adapt other teachers' work for use with their own students; and will give them a rationale for the place of reflective teaching and learning in higher education.

Contents

Introduction – What is meant in education by 'reflecting'? – What does reflection have to offer in education? – Is there a methodology you can and should follow? – What can you do to encourage students to reflect? – What is involved for students in analytical reflection? – What is involved in evaluative reflection? – How can you adapt ideas from my teaching, for yours? – How should you get started? – How can such innovations be evaluated? – Where should you read about other work in this field? – A Postscript: final reflections – References – Index – The Society for Research into Higher Education.

192pp   0 335 19993 3 (Paperback)   0 335 19994 1 (Hardback)

FACILITATING REFLECTIVE LEARNING IN HIGHER EDUCATION

Anne Brockbank and Ian McGill

A book that puts new forms of relationship and dialogue at the core of teaching and learning. It is likely to give courage to those who are daring to reflect differently on their teaching and learning practice, and to those who recognise the limitations of technology as some 'panacea solution' to challenges of mass higher education.

Professor Susan Weil

This book offers hope and the practical means for university and college teachers seeking a new experience of learning for their students and themselves. The book deals with learning which is real, genuine, relevant to learners now and for the future, and which is significant for their lives. Such learning embraces their relationships, work and careers, community, society and their world.

Anne Brockbank and Ian McGill provide direct support for teachers who wish to move from teaching toward facilitating learning, thereby transforming the relationship between teacher and learner and between learners. Information technology, whilst useful, is not a substitute for the learning advocated here; facilitation enables learners to use technology productively and complementarily as a part of the learning process.

This book enables teachers to acquire an understanding of facilitation and to enhance their ability to facilitate rather than teach in the traditional way. The authors emphasize the centrality of engaging in reflective dialogue with both colleagues and students. They explore the significance of emotion and action as well as cognition in learning. In addition they examine how teachers can best create the conditions for reflective learning.

This is a practical book for university and college teachers which will help them facilitate their students' reflective learning.

Contents

Part 1: Learning and reflection – Introduction to our themes – Learning: philosophies and models – What is learning? A review of learning theories – The requirements for reflection – Reflection and reflective practice – Part 2: Facilitating learning and reflective practice – Academic practice and learning – Developing reflective practice: the teacher using reflective dialogue with colleagues – Developing reflective practice: the student using reflective dialogue – Becoming a facilitator: facilitation as enabling reflective learning – Facilitation in practice: basic skills – Facilitation in practice: further skills – Part 3: Exemplars – Action learning – Academic supervision – Mentoring – Conclusion – Bibliography – Index – The Society for Research into Higher Education.

304pp   0 335 19685 3 (Paperback)   0 335 19686 1 (Hardback)

PROBLEM-BASED LEARNING IN HIGHER EDUCATION:
UNTOLD STORIES

Maggi Savin-Baden

Problem-based learning is contested and murky ground in higher education. In her study, Maggi Savin-Baden clears the thickets, offering a bold ambitious framework and, in the process, gives us a compelling argument for placing problem-based learning in the centre of higher education as an educational project. It is a story not to be missed.

Professor Ronald Barnett

This is a challenging and very worthwhile read for anyone concerned with the future of higher education, and issues of teaching and learning. The metaphor of 'untold stories' is powerfully explored at the level of staff and student experience of problem-based learning.

Professor Susan Weil

Problem-based learning is becoming increasingly popular in higher education because it is seen to take account of pedagogical and societal trends (such as flexibility, adaptability, problem-solving and critique) in ways which many traditional methods of learning do not. There is little known about what actually occurs *inside* problem-based curricula in terms of staff and student 'lived experience'. This book discloses ways in which learners and teachers manage complex and diverse learning in the context of their lives in a fragile and often incoherent world. These are the untold stories. The central argument of the book is that the potential and influence of problem-based learning is yet to be realized personally, pedagogically and professionally in the context of higher education. It explores both the theory and the practice of problem-based learning and considers the implications of implementing problem-based learning organizationally.

Contents
Part 1: A web of belief? – Part 2: Problem-based learning: an unarticulated subtext? – Part 3: Learning at the borders – Part 4: Problem-based learning reconsidered – Epilogue – Glossary – References – Index.

176pp   0 335 20337 X (Paperback)   0 335 20338 8 (Hardback)